SUPERCOHERENCE

THE RETURN TO LOVE

SUPERCOHERENCE
THE RETURN TO LOVE

THRITY ENGINEER

SUPER C PUBLISHING
UNITED KINGDOM

Super C Publishing
Supercoherence – The Return To Love
Copyright © Thrity Engineer 2015

Editor: Elizabeth Hutchins
Cover Design: Kermin Colaco
Interior Design: Benjamin Carrancho

Published in the United Kingdom by Super C Publishing

ISBN 978-1-910708-00-2

For Meher

Beloved daughter of my heart, soul companion and great associate

and

YOU

The infinite human full of possibility

'Do not undertake a project unless it is manifestly important and nearly impossible.'

Edwin Land, Inventor of the Polaroid camera

ACKNOWLEDGEMENTS

THOUGH THIS BOOK carries my name as the author, in truth I deserve only a tiny amount of credit. I know for sure that there is no way I could have written it without the input and wholehearted participation, support and enthusiasm of an extraordinary international team who took the Supercoherence frequencies, particularly the SRTLFs and made them their own.

My extraordinary agent Marianne Gunn O'Connor who started as a client and became not only a very dear friend but an enthusiastic advocate of this work. Though this book is self published, I consulted her every step of the way.

My greatest thanks go to the wonderful practitioners who took the Supercoherence system from a standing start and made it what it is today. In particular Lotta Naess from Sweden, Jane Cook and Angela McArthur from the UK, Catia Simionato from Brazil, Dilnaz Gilder from India and Judy Kao from Germany who have made huge contributions to this work and have provided most of the case studies which make up a large part of this book. Satoshi and Yuki Yoshizawa did a wonderful job of introducing the Supercoherence frequencies in Japan.

There are two other very special contributors who have also been indispensible for the growth of this system, for different reasons. One is the extraordinary Meenal Mehta, who has been the greatest and most enthusiastic advocate from day 1 in September 2009, when she attended the first ever seminar on Supercoherence. She has been tireless in promoting the

Supercoherence frequencies and I cannot thank her enough for the time, effort and love she has put into this work.

The second is Sandra Fiquet whose contribution to this work has been enormously important for two very different reasons. First she minds the Supercoherence websites and does all the web work in the most sincere and knowledgeable way. This system would not go out in the world without the websites. I am a duffer when it comes to the technical aspect of the web work, but I rest easy and sleep well because I know Sandra is there. The second and more valuable contribution Sandra has made to the Supercoherence system are the new protocols she has devised. I call Sandra the Protocol Queen. Other than that she is a great friend and a gifted practitioner.

I do not have the words to thank my friend Ursula Bauman. When I met her in October 2013 she made me an offer that both surprised and humbled me. She voluntarily took on the mammoth task of translating this book into German and getting the book out in Switzerland and Germany. It costs a lot of money to translate a book and publish it and I would not have taken on this task myself. Ursula did it for love of the Supercoherence System. It was her way of helping to get the system out into the world. On a personal level I can never thank her enough for her extraordinary generosity and her hard work.

In July I received an email from a client in Hongkong saying he wished to visit with me. James Wong came all the way from Hongkong to London for a flying 3 day visit. I was both touched and honoured. James is a successful self-made business man as well as very knowledgeable about subtle energy. A brilliant combination of qualities and capabilities. At the end of the visit he offered to translate the book into Chinese. Thank you James.

I am also deeply grateful to Flo Magdalena, the founder of Soul Support Systems, who uses the Supercoherence frequencies in her work and Vijaya Venkat, the dynamic and passionate founder of THAC (The Health Awareness Centre) in Mumbai, who has integrated the Supercoherence frequencies in her work. I have huge respect for the work of these extraordinary women.

My poet friend and client Sylvia Eagle, whose poems and songs grace this book deserves special acknowledgement.

I wanted a special image for the cover of the book. I drove myself slightly crazy looking at hundreds of images and then my daughter suggested I look at Katie Lee's website. The header image took my breath away and it was love at first sight. So I approached Katie and asked if I could license the image from her. Her great generosity and kindness touched my heart, for she not only gave me permission to use the image, but refused to take any money. That exquisite image was created by Martin Young of www.consciousnessdesigns.com.

I also thank Richard, Paul and Matt who actually make the Supercoherence frequencies. Again this work could not go out into the world without them. Each one of the frequencies is hand-made in a glass studio. It is a magical, complicated and time consuming process. The care and dedication with which they are made are truly impressive.

Above all it is with gratitude that I acknowledge the many clients in 26+ countries who use the Supercoherence frequencies. Though I have not had the pleasure of meeting many of you, you have a special place in my heart. This book could not have been written without you.

CONTENTS

Acknowledgements. ix

Foreword xv

Introduction. xvii

PART I: From Chaos to Coherence

Chapter 1: What Do We Know? 3

Chapter 2: Coherence and the Light-Energy-Information Age. 9

Chapter 3: Through the Portal of Miracles. 13

Chapter 4: The Conflicted Self 17

Chapter 5: The 'Star Trek' Technology 25

Chapter 6: VRIC Remote Imaging – Woo-woo, Wacky, Weird or
Impossibly Wonderful?. 35

PART II: From Meltdown to Miracle

Chapter 7: From Meltdown. 47

Chapter 8: ...to Miracle 53

PART III: Return to Love

Chapter 9: The Supercoherence Return to Love Frequencies (SRTLFs) 63

Chapter 10: The SRTLFs: The Acid Test 93

Chapter 11: SRTLFs in Practice. 103

Chapter 12: The Supercoherence Frequency Toolkit. 141

Chapter 13: Tales of Transformation 169

Chapter 14: Family Dynamics 213

Chapter 15: Clearing the Conception Pre-birth and Birth Imprint . 229

Chapter 16: Clearing the Ancestral Line Imprint. 237

Chapter 17: Death and the Multi-dimensional Universe 245

Chapter 18: The Supercoherence I AM Universal Frequency 255

Chapter 19: Love. 261

Chapter 20: The Nearly Impossible Project 265

An Offer and an Invitation. 271

Appendix I: How to Use the SRTLFs. .275

Appendix II: My Desert Island Book: Talking with Angels. 281

Notes and References 283

FOREWORD

AS HUMANITY LOOKS for solutions to end the seemingly eternal search for harmony in the world, we recognize that the harmony we seek comes first from within us. Practices like meditation, visualization, prayer, conscious living, and mindful choices assist us to focus and make choices for lasting inner peace.

However, the peace, acceptance, harmony and resonance we experience from these practices is conditional. Our good intentions are altered when we enter situations that challenge our wellbeing or that are perceived as unsafe. This reactive response reflects our innermost belief that we are separate from each other and that it is not possible to truly live from the heart, unconditionally. Our connection with ourselves and others falters, our life field is then incongruent, and we are no longer fully present. We begin the ride again—the search for lasting peace.

In Supercoherence, The Return to Love, Thrity Engineer simply and clearly explains how to balance our life field and experience coherence in even the most challenging and difficult instances, using light-energy-information tools called *SRTLFs* (Supercoherence Return To Love Frequencies).

The *SRTLFs* open and energetically balance our life field so that we find new freedom and a release from old patterns of reactivity without having to use our "normal" perceptual patterning. Imagine the sense of relief when our patterns shift, our energy opens and we can focus on being with others in a peaceful and harmonious way without the edicts of societal or religious pressure about how that has to happen.

The *SRTLFs* hold the zero point field, the creative and expansive "origin" from which we come. Thus when we hold them and work with them, they sustain our life fields in coherence so that we function optimally. In our most intimate relationships our patterns can then shift without psychologically processing the dualistic stories we have about our lives and each other. We are freed as if by magic—the zero point field offering us a rich and fertile experience of oneness and acceptance from which our lives can be lived comfortably and productively.

The *SRTLFs* are amazing and effective tools that return us to the matrix of creation where we respond organically from the perfection of the original union within our cells and DNA. Without the duality of beliefs, dogmas, conditions, or agendas, we are free to respond and create as photo sapiens, divine beings of light, and to live the promise of our heart's desire for unity and peace.

Flo Aeveia Magdalena - author of *I Remember Union: The Story of Mary Magdalena; Sunlight on Water: A Guide for Soul-full Living and Honoring Your Child's Spirit: Pre-birth Bonding and Communication.*

INTRODUCTION

'For those who can wonder, wonders appear.'

Talking with Angels

THE SHOCK CAME without any warning, suddenly, out of the blue. One moment my life was normal, happy, full of ambition, hopes and plans that seemed to promise a bright and prosperous future, and the next moment everything that I had planned had turned into a pile of dust and ashes. It seemed as though someone had taken the book that was my life, torn it to shreds and flung the fragments in my face. It was a violent event and I wanted to die.

This is the story of how that meltdown proved to be a miracle in disguise. My life went from being predictable, comfortable, safe and certain to a nightmare on wheels and then turned out to be an extraordinary adventure.

Many will find the ideas here challenging, even unbelievable. I understand that. If I had not lived this adventure I would find it unbelievable as well. Most of what I once believed and understood has been turned on its head and found to be very different than I thought. Direct experience is a great teacher and I have had to learn some lessons very quickly and as a result my belief systems have undergone an unexpected and radical shift. So my suggestion to you is not to dismiss what seems unbelievable or impossible without checking it out. I have found that looking at something new from the outside can never reveal its true nature. It is my hope that this book awakens in you the desire to experience this new system and be part of this adventure.

Because we are about to enter the portal of miracles.

Between 1978 and 1982 the proverbial genius tinkering in a garage 'accidentally' invented a real life 'Star Trek' technology and the rules of reality that we had lived by for thousands of years were bent out of shape.

He was an unknown American engineer named Patrick Richards and as a result of his landmark pioneering work and his determination to put this work out into the world, his life was destroyed. Meeting each rejection and disappointment with dogged determination and stoicism, he never gave up on what was his soul's purpose for incarnating in this lifetime. He left this world in 2008, at one level broken and disappointed, but he left a legacy, unmatched in my view, in known human history. In one sense he was a tragic figure, yet he was a shining soul and one of humanity's great benefactors.

Was he successful? The answer depends on what you call success. 'Pioneers get arrows in their backs', as the saying goes. Better to follow the well-trodden path once the pioneer has already been there and done the dirty work. That way we will be safe and certain of success. But have you noticed that yesterday's well-trodden path has turned into a slippery, dangerous quagmire?

'Never invent, always improve' is a 'smart' marketer's recipe for success. To him I say, if no one invented, what would there be to improve? If there had been no pioneers, would we still be living in caves?

A pioneer sees things differently from the crowd. Most of the major breakthroughs in the world have been made because of the unique and courageous foolishness of following one's vision, even when no one else understands. Thus the foolhardy genius with the ability to see differently and act upon it, even against great odds and opposition, is the hero/heroine that humanity has to thank, but very often does not.

Steve Jobs describes this way of being well:

'Here's to the crazy ones, the misfits, the rebels, the troublemakers, the round pegs in the square holes... the ones who see things differently – they're not fond of rules… You can quote them, disagree with them, glorify or vilify them, but the only thing you can't do is ignore them because they change things… they push the human race forward, and while some may see them as the crazy ones, we see genius, because the ones who are crazy enough to think that they can change the world are the ones who do.'

On the subject of pioneers, I recall meeting Patrick Richards for the first time in 1995. I had instantly recognized the extraordinary nature of the system he had created and was very surprised when he told me that it had not met with any acceptance from his scientific peers – in fact it had met with ridicule and rejection. Despite this, he had persisted in approaching more and more of his so-called peers, only to meet with the same unpleasing result. This had left him disappointed and disheartened.

I wondered why he had kept on approaching the same type of people. In those days I was more brash, blunt and outspoken than I am today. I said to him, 'You are a genius and a fool.'

Patrick was peppery and did not like the comment. He growled, 'What do you mean?'

I said, 'You have created the most extraordinary system there is, but what have you done with it? Why have you kept going back to the very people who rejected you? That is foolish – to keep doing the same thing and expect a different result.'

His response was, 'I wanted acceptance from my peers.'

I asked him, 'Did you get it?'

'No', was his honest answer.

I said, 'A pioneer has no peers, or he would not be a pioneer. His peers are those who have the eyes to recognize the new when they see it.'

It is also likely that they will come from a completely different field of expertise or from a different model of understanding. So in me, who was no scientist, Patrick had found a peer when he was least expecting it.

Patrick got it – he understood why he had been banging his head against a brick wall and that he could choose not to do it anymore.

I am writing about this incident to let you know that you do not have to understand the science behind this extraordinary system to participate in the magic. You can recognize it by the wonder you feel. I recognized it when Patrick described it on the phone to me the first time and the hair on the back of my neck and my arms stood on end. I knew then with absolute certainty that this was what my soul had been searching for over the span of many lifetimes. Had I been asked to explain it, there is no way I could have offered a 'reasoned' or 'reasonable' explanation. My linear mind and intellect had no idea what it was about, but my soul, my intuition and the wisdom of my body spoke in a language that was far more relevant.

Do you listen with your whole being or do you live only in your head? Would you recognize the new if it turned up in your life? Do you hear the call of your soul, your heart and spirit?

Being a pioneer is more important today than it has ever been in human history. Why? Have you noticed the rate of change recently?

With the earthquakes, tsunami and near nuclear meltdowns in Japan, plus all the turbulence in the Middle East, not to mention whole nation states declaring virtual bankruptcy and economies going down the toilet, the world is being turned upside down. Humanity seems to be teetering on the edge of an abyss.

In 2010 there were bombs in Mumbai when I visited and in the following month London, where I live, was in flames with the worst riots in many decades. I do not think I live in a dangerous city, but there is no real safety anywhere nowadays and it feels uncomfortable.

Are there any real options to break this cycle of chaos and violence? What direction are we moving in? Have you noticed that much of what worked the day before yesterday does not work today? Everyone around you is engulfed in cataclysmic change and no one is safe and secure. Which pioneer will you follow, which expert? If the rules of the game are turned upside down and no one really knows the answers, what do you intend to do? Do you have any strategies to handle what is coming? How will you survive this shift of the ages? What are the skills and tools you will need? Do you know? Or haven't you thought about it? Or do you think you will be safe doing what you have always done, hoping it will be OK?

Are you ready to see differently? Are you ready to act on that vision? Are you ready to be a pioneer? Are you ready to engage in your soul's journey?

If you are, this book is for you. To see the world through the eyes of a pioneer is to see through new eyes. In Zen they call it the beginner's mind. You cannot fit new ideas into old boxes, but be aware that your mind will try to fit this radical new information into an old box to 'understand' it. Why this is likely is because it is not comfortable with the unfamiliar. You have to beware of the stupidest phrase in any language, which is 'I know.' To know that you *don't* know is the beginning of wisdom. No one can be an expert on the new. What you will need instead is a sense of wonder and the eyes of a child – to feel the wow.

Who am I and why should you listen to me? I am an upstart, a maverick, a nonconformist with no formal academic qualifications. I simply had an extraordinary adventure and learned, through direct experience, some incredible new stuff which has transformed my life from disaster into miracle.

I do think the world needs a radical change, and yes, I intend to have a good crack at it – how about you?

However, a word of warning: if you are looking to follow a great expert with several letters after her name from a great university, I am not your woman.

Please understand this is simply an invitation to explore the truly new. I offer you no guarantees of any sort, except the pleasure and promise of discovery. The only guarantee in life is death – or eternal life, depending…

Also, I am not looking for followers or disciples. I seek no obedience or loyalty. But I do welcome associates, peers, fellow adventurers and explorers on this journey. Blind faith and absolute obedience without discernment will not help you today. Self-responsibility and the spirit of exploration, however, will take you far. They have brought me a long way.

When I first came across this real-life 'Star Trek' technology that was to change my life and my notion of reality forever, I was very ignorant. All I had in my toolkit was an appetite to explore the new, a sense of wonder and the ability to recognize when something was extraordinary. Most adults, I have to say, do not have this ability, or rather have lost it, due to too much education or simple ignorance. For me, it was enough to transform my life. When I first overheard a colleague at a conference talking to someone else about Patrick and his system, I knew that what she was saying was "impossible", but I was captivated. When I look back on that fateful moment, if I had not responded in the way that I did, my life would have been completely different and a great opportunity would have passed me by. Knowing what I know now, I can see what a close call it was. I passed the test by the skin of my teeth. If I had thought myself an expert, I would have dismissed the whole idea.

Do you recognize the extraordinary? Is your sense of wonder alive and well or do you already know it all? These are serious questions, so please answer them honestly.

If you wish to find out more and participate in this extraordinary adventure, it is time to put on your safety belt and wonder glasses and join me for a wild ride. Are you ready?

PART I

From Chaos to Coherence

CHAPTER 1
What Do We Know?

'It is in the admission of ignorance and the admission of uncertainty that there is a hope for the continuous motion of human beings in some direction that doesn't get confined, permanently blocked, as it has so many times before in various periods in the history of man.'

Richard Feynman, late Nobel Laureate in Physics

IN 2003 FOR 11 days the Hubble space telescope 'stared' at a blank piece of sky no larger than a grain of sand held at arm's length and what do you think it 'saw'? When the data were collected, to their amazement, the scientists found that this tiny 'blank' piece of sky contained 10,000 *galaxies*. Where there appeared to be nothing, there were billions of stars.

To take this a step further, particle physicists say that there is a mysterious force known as dark energy which seems to make up more than 70 per cent of the matter-energy content of the universe. The rest is mostly the equally mysterious dark matter. Ordinary matter – the stuff that galaxies, stars, planets and you and I are made of – is just about 2–5 per cent at best.

Coming closer to home, it is disconcerting to realize that we are aware of very little of our home planet. Seventy-five per cent of it lies underwater and it may surprise you (it certainly did me) to know that we have explored only 2–3 per cent of the deep oceans. The rest remains to be discovered and the highest mountains and deepest valleys lie not on land but under the sea.

Coming even closer to home, I will say that we know only a minute fraction of our human capabilities. This may sound absurd and nonsensical, but I believe it is the truth.

Notwithstanding all the extraordinary advances in science and technology that we have made, our ignorance of the universe we live in appears to be mindboggling.

So, what else aren't we seeing? What else don't we know? Would you agree that there is much to be discovered?

To know that you don't know is the beginning of both curiosity and wisdom.

And as fascinating and fantastic as the universe seems, with its billions of galaxies and stars, there is an even more fascinating universe that we have explored even less, and that is the universe within each of us. This unexplored terrain holds secrets and potential and incredible promise – there is great treasure hidden in the deep self.

There is so much for us to explore – possibilities that at this moment in human history we have no concept of. We will have to go forward in a spirit of not knowing, as explorers of the new, for the new is where the answers will lie. In a time of crisis such as now, the natural instinct is to fall back on the familiar, the old ways, but unfortunately these aren't working anymore and will only land us in deeper trouble. So we must step into the unknown, bravely, consciously and with the awareness that we may very well make mistakes. But we will also develop new skills, strengths and tools as a result of our foolishness and our courage.

Are you ready to embark on this exciting journey? Is your cosmic passport in order?

The Power of Subtle Energy

As I write, on 16 March 2011, there is a major energy problem in Fukushima, Japan and it is not because of a shortage of electricity. An energy that you cannot see, hear, smell, touch or taste is threatening the lives of thousands. That energy is atomic energy. We cannot see an atom, but we all know its destructive potential. Though it is invisible to us, its effects are clearly evident – and measurable.

There is, however, another force, equally invisible and far more potent, that cannot be measured by the instruments of twenty-first century science. This force can go through walls and Faraday cages and travel thousands of miles with no loss of power, faster than the speed of light. Just a few humans can access and harness it – with mind-bending results.

In mid 2010 a landmark book was published: *Life Force - The Scientific Basis*. The author, Dr Claude Swanson, is a physicist trained at MIT and Princeton, so his credentials are impeccable. Researched and written over many years, his book appears to be a labour of love, dedication and commitment. It is sorely needed at this time and in my opinion is what Dr. Swanson came to do this lifetime. The amount of work that has gone into it does not bear thinking about. I thank him from the bottom of my heart.

Dr. Swanson's book reveals in scientific terms that an intangible, invisible, unquantifiable yet extremely powerful force/energy not only exists but also breaks all the known laws of physics. It can explain phenomena such as remote viewing, distant healing, astral travelling and time travel. It has been shown through rigorous experimentation that it can destroy cancer cells in a lab several thousands of miles away. And, more unbelievably, it can even revive a dead shrimp on a dinner plate and cause boiled peanuts to sprout again. So, though you cannot see it or measure it directly, its effects are very real and can be measured.

Swanson affirms that all humans possess this potent energy. However, if you do not know this, you have no chance of accessing it.

This energy crosses the barriers of space and time and is not subject to the laws of the five-sensory reality. In China it is known as *chi* or *qi*, in India it is called *prana*, in English it is called scalar or torsion and Swanson simply calls it subtle energy. He also makes the telling point that mainstream Western science has pretty much ignored this potent force because it does not know how to factor it into its limited model. It is heartening to know, however, that breakthrough research into it is going on in other parts of the world. China and Russia are big players in this area.

What I love and admire about Claude Swanson, a true scientist in the best sense of the word, is that he has chosen to actually explore the subjects he is researching, such as the healer-medium John of God in Brazil and the crop circles in the UK, through direct experience. Looking at phenomena from the outside as an observer, reading research papers and having fixed opinions as a so-called expert cannot ever really reveal the true nature of the phenomena you are examining. It is the difference between writing about chocolate without tasting it and putting a piece in your mouth.

It is interesting to note that Swanson also writes about the technology developed by Patrick. This pleased me greatly when I read it. As there are so few of these devices on Earth I was surprised and delighted that he had come across the system and had chosen to explore and write about it, though the information was incomplete.

I am glad that I am part of an international family of explorers, even though I do not know the others personally. It does not feel good to be alone and isolated, as Patrick was, and as I have felt many times over the years I have been doing this work. Pioneering work can be highly rewarding and exhilarating, but also fearful and isolating.

To return to the unseen but real energy described by Dr. Swanson, we as humans are in effect conductors of this force, which in many senses is more powerful than atomic energy. The truly unfortunate thing is that in this day of doubt, scepticism and the domination of the left-brained linear mind, we remain ignorant of this most powerful resource and pay the price of that sad ignorance. In these critical times when we most need to harness all the incredible resources that lie sleeping in each one of us, we put our faith in experts and are ignorant of our true power. Imagine a starving beggar who does not know there is a banquet next door to him. He cannot see it and therefore his ignorance will kill him, but if he had explored further he could have had a feast. Do not be like that beggar. A feast awaits.

In the modern classic *The Alchemist* by Paolo Coelho, there is a cautionary tale for each one of us. The alchemist and his *protégé* are crossing the desert when they meet warrior tribesmen who challenge them and search them for hidden weapons. The alchemist is carrying the two greatest treasures of the master alchemists, the Elixir of Life and the egg that can turn lead into gold – two small innocuous looking objects of no apparent significance to one who does not know what they are or what they can do.

The warriors find these strange objects in the alchemist's bag and ask him what they are. To the shock and consternation of his *protégé*, he tells them exactly what they are and the power that lies within them. The *protégé* expects the worst, but the alchemist knows better. He knows he will not be believed, and he is right. The warriors simply laugh at him in disbelief and let them both go.

Would you have believed the alchemist if he had revealed the extraordinary nature of those treasures to you? Or would you have laughed and walked away?

CHAPTER 2
Coherence and the Light-Energy-Information Age

'All matter is frozen light.'

David Bohm

ALL OF US emit light. In fact, all life-forms emit light. The research of Fritz-Albert Popp, a German scientist, indicates that cells communicate through weak light signals, called UPEs (ultra-low photon emissions), and that light is the principal information carrier that tells each of our own 50 trillion cells what to do on a continuous basis. Light is a known carrier of information – one fibre optic cable thinner than a human hair can carry an incredible 210 million phone calls every second – and it now appears it is responsible for the orderly performance of the infinitely complex activities of the human body.

In October 2002 I was fortunate to hear Dr. Popp's lecture at the IAC conference in the UK. I was astounded when he mentioned that there were 100,000 chemical reactions in every cell each second. That these chemical reactions could only happen if the molecule which is reacting is excited by a photon (a quanta of light). He also reiterated what he had said many times before that man is essentially a being of light.

Popp has discovered that not only do cells emit light but, even more importantly, the coherence or incoherence of the light signals is related to the vitality and health of the life-form. Coherence, or order, means vitality and health, and incoherence, or chaos, means disease and disorder. All living systems constantly fluctuate between these two extreme and extremely different states.

The Power of Coherence

Light becomes coherent when the vibrations of light are polarized and in phase. 'Polarized' means uni-directional, and 'in phase' means the peaks and the troughs of the electromagnetic wave match exactly, with total precision. This characteristic of light was revealed when the laser was invented in 1960.

As William Tiller, Professor Emeritus at Stanford University, explains:

'The shift from incoherence to coherence can bring dramatic effects: a 60 watt light bulb whose light waves could be made as coherent as a laser would have the power to bore a hole through the sun – from 90 million miles away.'[1]

This means that the same amount of light, when it is differently organized, gives an exponentially different result, and the key to this exponential curve lies in one word: coherence.

So the question is: does your body-mind-energy system operate at the 60-watt light bulb level or the 60-watt laser level? What if a way could be found to enhance the coherence of the system – what would the results be and what would this human laser be capable of?

To expand on this important concept further, Dr Mae-Wan Ho, a scientist I admire hugely, says about coherence and quantum coherence:

'Imagine a *huge* jazz band of musicians making music, from very small instruments to the very large, playing very fast to very slow, with a musical range of 70 octaves. They are improvising from moment to moment, spontaneously and freely; and yet keeping in tune and in step with the whole. That is the ultimate quantum coherence.

One can have different degrees (order) of quantum coherence (see *The Rainbow and the Worm*). The fully quantum coherent state would be quantum coherence of *n* order, *n* being a very large number approaching infinity. This state is only reached rarely, perhaps once or twice in a lifetime for some of us, or maybe not at all. You get an inkling of it when you have an aesthetic experience, a very special aesthetic experience. Some people would call it a mystical experience.

You can have lower degrees of coherence; the work-a-day coherence that keeps life ticking over. If you have a fully quantum coherent system, you will never age and you will never die. But we do age and we do die. That's because of incoherence of varying degrees. In my book, I suggest that time is really the accumulation of incoherence.

When you accumulate incoherence, you age. So, I think a happy coherent person ages more slowly than someone full of angst and strife. It's fascinating to think about that.

It is like a symphony. And quantum coherence and Taoism are one, because coherent action is effortless action.

But I have no doubt that life is quantum coherent. Organisms are quantum jazz players, dancing life into being.'[2]

The Light-Energy-Information Age: Incomprehensible, Incredible, Real

We can see something of what is involved when we look at the light-energy-information age in which we live:

'In comparison with other communication systems, the telephone can carry 60,000 bits of information per second, FM radio carries 250,000 bits of information per second, television carries 6,000,000 bits per second and a laser beam can carry 100 billion bits of information per second... Just recently NTT Japan has developed a fibre optic cable that can transmit 14 trillion bits per second down a single strand of fibre. This means 2,600 CDs or 210 million phone calls every second. This capacity is tripling every 6 months.'[3]

It is said that new technical information is doubling every 72 hours. One week's worth of information in the *New York Times* is more than a person was likely to come across in a lifetime in the eighteenth century. The amount of new information generated in 2006 was estimated to be more than in the previous 5,000 years. In 2012, there are 88 billion searches on Google each month. In 2006 it was 2.7 billion. A person is likely to have had 10–18 jobs by the age of 38. On and on it goes – crazy, unbelievable, inexorable…[4]

This gives you an idea of why the rate of change is accelerating at the exponential and uncomfortable rate it is and why time seems to be speeding up. The rules of the game have changed drastically without much warning and we have to cope as best we are able. Many of us fall down – badly.

If you think about it for a moment, light travels at 186,000 miles per second and information travels even faster, they say. The internet, the tool of great knowledge, infinite choice and infinite confusion, is both a gift and a curse. It has bent the rules of time as we have known them for millennia, out of shape and there is no going back. This super-highway on which information is carried literally at the speed of light has put us out of synch with our bodies, which certainly do not operate at that speed. So we can have 100 e-mails arriving at the speed of light from all over the globe and piling up in our inbox, but our eyes, which have to read them, our brain, which has to make sense of them, and our hands, which have to type the response, unfortunately do not operate at the speed of light. The end result? Stress levels through the roof, with information overload, burnout and illness to follow.

To cope with this crazy rate of change we need personal coherence. In that sense coherence is a non-linear recognition of the intangible qualities of intelligence, harmony, symmetry and order coming together and creating an effective and pleasing result. We cannot really measure the quality of such coherence, but we can recognize it.

Personal coherence (or the lack of it) is dependent on the coherence of our light emissions – the two are inextricably linked. Until now we have operated pretty much at the meagre capacity of the light-bulb level. However, if we restore, or rather enhance, coherence in our energy system, we can access the exponential enhancement in function of the laser level.

But how do we do this?

CHAPTER 3
Through the Portal of Miracles

'The tiny point in the middle opens the gate of heaven.'

Talking with Angels

W E START WITH zero. The power, the magic, the mystery of zero.

Zero marks in the exam – not good. Zero money in the bank account – bad news. Zero cake on the plate – no treat. That is the reality of zero in this 3D physical reality of the five senses.

However, zero is a strange number. It is in effect no number, yet mathematics could not exist without it.

If you multiply zero by any other number, it swallows that number, for example 2 x 0 = 0.

If you add zero to a number, the number remains the same.

If you subtract zero from a number, it remains the same.

And I am told that dividing a number by zero is forbidden, as it is too problematic.

According to Wikipedia:

'…strange phenomena occur at zero. Absolute zero is the null point of any thermodynamic temperature scale. By international agreement, it is defined as 0K (0 degrees Kelvin) on the Kelvin scale and as –273.15°C on the Celsius scale. This equates to –459.67°F on the Fahrenheit scale. Scientists have achieved temperatures very close to absolute zero, where matter exhibits quantum effects such as superconductivity.

The electrical resistivity of a metallic conductor decreases gradually as the temperature is lowered. In a superconductor the resistance drops abruptly to zero when the material is cooled below its critical temperature. An electric current flowing in a loop of superconducting wire can persist indefinitely with no power source.

Because these materials have no electrical resistance, meaning electrons can travel through them freely, they can carry large amounts of electrical current for long periods of time without losing energy as heat. Superconducting loops of wire have been shown to carry electrical currents for several years with no measurable loss.'[5]

Zero input resulting in infinite output – it doesn't make sense, but it is real.

The Zero-Point Field – Realm of Miracles

> According to David Bohm, 'Space is not empty. It is full, a plenum as opposed to a vacuum, and is the ground for the existence of everything, including ourselves. The universe is not separate from this cosmic sea of energy.'[6]

Scientists today are beginning to understand the extreme power that resides in what is called zero-point energy and the zero-point field – an infinite all pervading sea of energy which is to be found even when there is no thermal energy at temperatures of absolute zero.

There are many names for this field of energy and it is recognized in many different traditions. In the Indian wisdom tradition it is recognized as a field of pure consciousness. The Russian physicist and author Vadim Zeland calls it the Space of Variations. In earlier days it was called the aether. It is also called the Vacuum.

The late Richard Feynman, Nobel laureate in physics, came up with the assessment that one cup of zero-point energy could boil all the oceans of the world. Others speculate that if they could harness this energy there would never be a shortage of energy on Earth and that it would enable us to travel to the stars.

In very literal terms at zero there is no friction, all resistance is eliminated and there is an eternal unrestricted free flow of energy. So, as humans, can we become superconductors of energy? And would that mean an endless supply of energy available to us for vitality and healing, the perfect formula for anti-ageing or rejuvenation? My answer would be yes, and yes, if we can access zero – and that's not all…

All things are possible at zero – all knowledge exists in the zero-point field and can be accessed simply by tuning into it, provided you know how. It does not matter whether that knowledge is of events millions of years in the past or in the future. The Indian wisdom tradition knows this and calls this realm the Akashic records.

It is in the Indian Hindu, Buddhist and the Tibetan wisdom traditions that the importance of zero is truly recognized. It is called *sunya* or *shunya*, and by accessing the zero state or *sunyata* one is considered to have become enlightened. To access the zero state is to access the state of bliss or oneness with the universe. It is what every meditator seeks – enlightenment and self-realization.

Zero is the perfect balance point – neither more nor less, but the middle – which the Chinese wisdom tradition calls the Tao or the middle way. That is the way of wisdom. So zero is the optimum point where everything works well together and is "in phase", or coherent, without friction, resistance or conflict.

Zero is also the alpha and the omega, the beginning and the end point, all-encompassing or better still, with no beginning and no end. It is that indefinable timeless instant when all creation began – the point of nothing-ness and everything-ness. In *Talking with Angels*, the angels teach the deep secret of creation and zero:
"Alpha–Omega… Omega–Alpha
The created human stands
between beginning and end.
The Creating Human stands
Between end and beginning.

Between beginning and end is TIME.
Between end and beginning is timelessness."[7]

Then they go on to explain that
"At the death of each instant
You can enter into eternity
Into the creating world."[8]

And that every instant is a gateway to infinite creation, and therefore open to possibilities that we do not know.

The most important part and the great secret and the mystery of ZERO is that

"The origin of everything, the birthplace of motion is between end and beginning."[9]

But throughout known human history we have not been granted simple, systematic and direct access to the mysterious, miraculous portal of zero. It is true that great yogis, qi gong masters, gifted energy healers and remote viewers can tap into this field to create the 'miracles' that they perform. However, years of meditation, prayer, reflection, contemplation and esoteric practices are necessary and huge effort is involved. This does not help mainstream humanity. We need something simpler and more accessible. We also need to know when we're there – we need objective parameters to let us know that we have reached the zero state.

What would it take for us to access zero? And what would be the effect of doing so? Could it end the millennial-old cycle of suffering – all the wars, the trafficking in humans and the cruelty – present on Earth today? Could it provide a way out of the mess that we have made for ourselves? Could it make all the difference?

What stands in our way?

CHAPTER 4
The Conflicted Self

'Ah, my poor brain is racked and crazed,
My spirit and senses amazed!'
Johann Wolfgang von Goethe (Faust, 1808)

THE BRAIN HAS two hemispheres or cortices, the right and the
left, which are completely separate from one another and they
both function very differently. They do however communicate
with each other through the corpus callosum. Both hemispheres process
sensory and other information but they do it very differently. In fact they
have different and opposite jobs. The left hemisphere thinks in words, and
is responsible for our logical, detailed, sequential and linear processing.
The right hemisphere thinks in pictures and operates in a non-sequential,
non-linear way and communicates through feelings and impulses. It thinks
in wholes and accesses a larger reality – the multidimensional reality of
which we are a part. To create balance and harmony between the two polar
opposites within ourselves is neither simple nor easy. They say the left brain
processes 11 bits of information per second and the right brain processes 11
million. The difference is astounding.

The two different halves of the brain often literally do not see eye to
eye and therefore do not operate harmoniously together. Very often they

give us conflicting messages and we find ourselves in the analysis-paralysis mode, with one foot on the accelerator and the other one on the brake. We experience this conflicted state when we say 'I am in two minds' about a decision. The linear left brain is calculating and fear-driven and acts on what has happened in the past, whereas the right brain is emotional, non-linear and expansive, because it is literally accessing a larger reality. Deep meditation and relaxation, energy healing, remote viewing and distance healing – all the so-called paranormal activities and extraordinary capabilities that we have – occur through accessing the right brain, the non-linear mind.

Intuition, that small soft voice, is also an expression of our right brain seeking to communicate with us through feelings and impulses, and yet very often the linear left brain will tell us it is silly or unreasonable and impossible. Herein lies the conflict which results in the "civil war between our two ears" which can create havoc in our lives. The non-linear mind is by far the greater and holds the keys to our future. The linear mind is a great implementation tool, but not the best decision-making tool, because then it has to factor in the larger reality, which is out of its remit. However it is important to understand that both aspects are important and necessary for our bodies and our lives to function well. These two polar opposite parts comprise a magnificent whole when they work harmoniously together. This happens when they are aligned and not in conflict.

Today we revere expertise and knowledge, but wisdom seems to be remarkably absent and takes a sorry second place. In my view this is the result of the chronic long-term imbalance between the right and the left brain and is responsible for the age old cycle of suffering. We have been left-brain dominant for a long time, with catastrophic consequences both for ourselves and for society.

As a result we access a tiny part of our vast and unlimited potential

The Blueprint

At one level, however, we are always pristine, pure, perfect and whole. We have awesome power, boundless love, infinite possibility and supreme intelligence – in fact, we *are* these things. We are extraordinary beyond any measure. This is the part of us that I call the blueprint.

The blueprint is the template of perfection, the divine, the creative principle or simply supreme intelligence. The feeling Intelligence that keeps the 50–100 trillion cells of your mysterious and miraculous body functioning and in order is no mean intelligence. It is the same intelligence that creates the galaxies and the universe. It cannot leave you; it is what you are. It is everything that is. It knows you as it knows itself and as you the personality can almost never know yourself. It holds the promise of success beyond your wildest imagining, if you could but harness the tiniest portion of its limitless power.

But we are in conflict with ourselves and so our lives do not reflect this blueprint. I remember telling a very troubled friend about the extreme perfection that existed within her, and her saying to me, 'Thrity, you are trying to brainwash me.'

My response was, 'You are already brainwashed.'

Imprint of the Past

Something else to take into consideration is that every single experience that we have had – and that includes the time when we were in our mother's womb – is registered, held and remembered at many levels of our being. In my view this past imprint also includes memories of past lives, though that idea may not be acceptable to some. This invisible and silent memory, accompanied by the emotional charge felt at the time of the initial experience, is held at the cellular level, in our psyche, in our subconscious and unconscious minds and, most important of all, in our energy field, the informational light matrix or energy 'body'. Any and all experiences are interpreted as pleasurable or painful, and that emotional information is registered and held in invisible secret code in the energy field.

This body of secret encoded information is our imprint, and is unique to us. It gives us our unique view and shapes our unique response to the world. At the conscious level we have forgotten a lot of those past experiences – indeed, if they were very painful, we may have suppressed them or they may have been repressed as the subconscious mind/energy system did not have the means to resolve them. However though we do not have ready access to this secret information at the conscious level, it is still present and has the power to influence and inform our responses and therefore our actions, which give us results we neither like nor want.

Our point of perception, from which we create our reality, is therefore neither clear nor neutral. It is coloured by subjective emotional information of the past. In effect, we cannot view the present moment except through the eyes of our past experience. This is the silent but potent creator of our less than perfect destiny.

Most of us will have experienced emotional traumas which are still discolouring our perception and our life. I consider that I had a happy childhood, for example, and I was certainly not subjected to any physical, emotional or sexual abuse. As a result I am not particularly fearful. However, my childhood was fairly traumatic in some ways. When my mother was pregnant with me she was caught in a burning tram and must have been terrified for her own life and that of her child. That terror would certainly have been felt by me. As a result, I was born two months premature.

Then, when I was around six years old, we were living in what is now Pakistan at the time of Partition, when India was divided into India and Pakistan. This triggered a storm of extreme brutality. All hell broke loose in the border areas and thousands were slaughtered on both sides of the divide. It was an extremely turbulent and traumatic time. My father, though working in Pakistan as a civil servant, opted to go back to Bombay (now Mumbai), which was in India. We had to take a train from Lahore to Karachi and then a ship to Bombay. I still have memories of people screaming and banging on the doors of the train compartment on that journey all those years back.

On another note, my dad was visibly unhappy in his job all his working life and suffered from depression and mild OCD (obsessive compulsive disorder). As a result I did not particularly relate to him and did not respect or love him in my teens. He retired early from his detested job at 54 (retirement age was 58 at that time) and became a changed man overnight. He blossomed, discarded his scruffy clothes and became fun to be with. Unfortunately this sweet period was to last just two and a half years. He died of a heart attack at 56, paying the price of all those years of stress and depression. This was devastating for my mother, and for me as well. I remember weeping inconsolably, wishing that I had loved him more and that things could have been different. Incidentally, he was slim, did not smoke or drink and had no vices to speak of. Stress and unhappiness are the killers.

I realize that most if not all of us have had to deal with the trauma of disease, death, deprivation, separation and other unhappiness in our family. Just in the last century we have had two world wars and several major economic depressions, with all the ensuing deprivation and pain. All these events will have left their mark on us.

Today there is a lot of evidence that unresolved emotional pain can result in physical pain and dysfunction. This can happen right away or many years down the line. Emotional energy, though invisible, packs a huge wallop. It is important not to underestimate its power.

The American insurance company Kaiser Permanente conducted a very important study called the ACE (adverse childhood experiences) study, which showed that adverse childhood experiences and traumas resulted in severe degenerative diseases many decades later, proving that time does not heal.[10]

The study took place over a period of several years and 17,421 adults participated. The study found that there was a powerful correlation between emotional experiences as a child and adult emotional and physical health. For example a 70-year-old diabetic who had high blood pressure and was morbidly obese as well as chronically depressed and had never married, admitted to having been raped by her elder brother when she was ten years old – six decades back. In effect, her life had been destroyed by this unresolved emotional pain.

The insightful author of the study pointed out that most doctors are comfortable looking at symptoms and prescribing medication but fail to address the deep emotional pain which may have led to the disease. Perhaps because they have not had the tools or the training to do so.

A further study by the same company showed that childhood trauma affected worker performance and health adversely. 9633 persons took part in that study. Again they found that childhood abuse and dysfunctional households negatively impacted worker performance with resulting job problems, financial problems and absenteeism.

Results: Strong graded relations were found between the ACE score and each measure of impaired worker performance, mediated by interpersonal relationship problems, emotional distress, somatic symptoms and substance abuse.

Conclusions

The long-term effects of adverse childhood experiences on the workforce impose major human and economic costs that are preventable.

Chronic back pain – cost to US business $28 billion per year; depression – reduced productivity and medical expenses $44 billion per year; and chemical dependency – $246 billion per year.'[11]

Though the study talks about the 'major human and economic costs that are preventable' it does not offer any means or methods of achieving this goal.

Other studies at Kings College London, Warwick Universiy in the UK and Duke University in the US also show that being bullied in childhood adversely affects mental and physical health many decades later.

So the whole of society pays a high price in financial and other terms for childhood trauma.

Another great pioneer in this field is Dr. Ryke Geerd Hamer, the founder of German New Medicine. He has proved beyond a shadow of a doubt that emotional trauma or shock will result in disease at the physical level and has come up with the insight that the disease is in fact the human system's attempt at self-healing.

The Disconnection

So, within us we have a perfect blueprint but also an imperfect imprint. The blueprint, the super-conscious Self, holds the seed of our salvation, while the imperfect imprint, the human personality, holds the seeds of our dysfunction, suffering and destruction, both emotionally and physically. Both levels of information are present all the time. Yet somewhere, sometime, somehow, it seems our human personality became disconnected from the super-conscious aspect of the Self. I call this disconnection of human energetic circuitry the greatest disaster that we have ever suffered.

I do not know how, why or when it happened, however, it is patently evident that it did happen. How else can one explain the glaring disparity in abilities that exist side by side in every one of us, where one aspect can silently, effortlessly and continuously keep 50-100 trillion cells that comprise the body-mind in orderly function in every millisecond, and the other create havoc doing all the incredibly stupid and painful things that humans seem to have done to themselves and others since times immemorial? At some point we became disconnected from ourselves, misaligned from zero.

As a result of this disconnection, the only reality that most of us know is that of our imprint. We do not truly know who we are. While we can long for and aspire to that which was once perhaps readily available to us, it is now almost impossible to attain.

Put in another way, at one level we are born drunk and in a state of imbalance. If we had been born sober, we would know what a drunken state was and could choose sobriety, but if drunkenness is the only state we know, then we cannot know what being sober feels like. So we are unknowingly creating our reality from a drunken state.

How can we get beyond this? How can we correct our inaccurate version of reality? This is easier said than done, as the emotional charge and unconscious belief "reality" that invariably accompanies it is hidden, silent and largely invisible. We have very little access to or awareness of it. And even when we do have an awareness, we do not necessarily have the keys to change those patterns/ beliefs. It seems that the door opens only one way – we cannot access our subconscious or unconscious realms, but they can and do access and influence our reactions and responses and so shape our destiny.

It is impossible to overestimate the power of the subconscious – you need to know that it is a million times more powerful than your conscious intent or your personality. It is a mountain of entangled conflicted energy held together with bonds that are stronger than super glue and cement mixed together. There is no easy way to bypass it or change the information that it contains. People spend years trying to come to terms with and resolve its lethal invisible baggage, only to find that non-nourishing and dysfunctional patterns of thinking and behaviour do not yield easily to being modified, despite the strenuous efforts and good intentions on all sides. This also gives you a clue as to why positive thinking and affirmations often have limited success.

This tug and tussle, push and pull, struggle and strain between the right and left hemispheres, between the conscious intent, subconscious/ unconscious imprint and the super-conscious blueprint results in the misalignment between the needs and desires of the personality and the soul and gives us results we neither like nor want, and makes our lives less than they can be.

The ancient Egyptians knew of this disparity between the two aspects and the need for them to work harmoniously and in balance. The pharaohs used two different rods, one in the right hand and the other in the left hand, to achieve a state of exquisite balance where neither side dominated. The scientist Valery Uvarov calls these rods the 'wands of Horus'. It seems the pharaohs knew the value of zero, the point of perfect balance.

The concept was also understood by the Buddhists and Taoists and outlined in the Upanishads (ancient philosophical texts of the Hindus). The western esoteric traditions also knew of the challenge of keeping the opposites balanced. The tarot card of the Chariot, a charioteer in control of two horses, one white and the other black, pulling in opposite directions, illustrates this point.

So these ancient wisdom traditions knew of the difference between these polar opposites and the need for them to work in harmony, and that the balance point between two opposites was in the middle, or at zero.

The system we are about to explore has some radical solutions to realign us with that zero point.

Does this sound 'nearly impossible'? Nearly, but not quite!

We are about to step into the magic.

CHAPTER 5
The 'Star Trek' Technology

'We have touched the Borderland where Matter and Force
seem to merge into one another, the shadowy realm between
the Known and Unknown... I venture to think that the greatest
scientific problems of the future will find their solution in
this Borderland, and even beyond; here, it seems to me,
lie Ultimate Realities, subtle, far-reaching, wonderful.'

Sir William Crookes, 1879

IN 1982 PATRICK Richards invented the Luminator and the greatest paradigm shift in human history occurred. From the three dimensional reality of the five senses that had confined and defined us for millennia, we plunged down the rabbit hole, or wormhole, into a parallel universe where the rules of 'Star Trek' and *Alice in Wonderland* applied.

Our understanding of who we are would never be the same again.

The Luminator: The Hubble of Inner Space

So, what is the Luminator? It is an enigmatic subtle energy device which needs no electronics or electricity to function. It creates a zero field or an altered magnetic field. In this field, suddenly, mysteriously, the rules that govern the space-time universe of the five senses are superseded. In effect the Luminator is the interface or meeting-point between two very different dimensions: the space-time dimension and the hitherto invisible 'quantum' dimension. The Luminator gives us access to realms that are beyond the reach of the most powerful electron microscope or the most state of the art space telescope.

Patrick did not intend to create this. He set out to invent a tool for efficient energy management and it turned out that it did a lot more than it was meant to do. Its hidden capabilities were discovered by 'accident' several years later.

VRIC Imaging – MRI of the Soul

In the special altered magnetic zero field created by the presence of the Luminator, an ordinary analogue Polaroid camera, with the flash masked, can take what some would call 'paranormal' pictures. This special imaging is called VRIC (visual reference of image coherence) imaging. It can only take place when the Luminator is present and does not work with digital cameras. It is a unique imaging system that gives us a view into a parallel universe.

VRIC imaging is not about the meridians or the chakras but another level that is further up the causal chain, a level that encompasses all the other energy systems. This is the command post from where the indivisible You controls and co-ordinates the impossibly complex quantum flux and flow of your 50 trillion cells, telling each one what to do, when to do it and how much of it to do, to keep your body-mind in optimal function.

VRIC imaging has a quality of extreme precision and cannot be faked, manipulated or 'Photoshopped'. It cannot lie. It is a binary system in the sense that the images are either clear or fuzzy, so there is no guesswork involved, unlike aura photography, Kirlian photography or the GDV imaging of Dr. Korotkov. The images are either clear and sharp or fuzzy and blurred, and that's it.

We understand the sharp image as 'coherent' and the fuzzy image as 'incoherent'. So VRIC imaging permits us to 'see' the coherence or incoherence of the light emission of the person (or other life-form) being imaged, in real time and real terms. That light emission contains all the information that the body-mind-soul of that person has ever experienced and is a bottom line parameter of their wholeness and function. This objective process allows us an unprecedented view of that person and permits us to enhance coherence for them with a quality of precision at this fundamental level of expression.

In my view the Luminator, coupled with VRIC imaging, is as significant, if not more so, than any other technology of the twentieth century. It offers both qualitative and quantitative information. It permits us to examine our inner landscape with a degree of clarity and precision unprecedented in human history. It also shows us in unequivocal terms that we are more than a physical body – that we are in fact beings of light-energy-information.

I came across the Luminator in 1995 in an extraordinary and magical way when I met the incredible genius who created it. From the moment that I heard about it, I was totally fascinated by it. Now, though I have worked with it since 1995, it still captivates me. It has repaid my devotion and commitment by teaching me secrets I never would have learned otherwise. This whole adventure that I have invited you to share could never have happened without the Luminator.

Today I feel that the Luminator has fulfilled one of the major jobs it came to do. And mostly we no longer use it in the way that we have done since 1995. Since 2009 we haven't been imaging each individual anymore, because – but I am getting ahead of myself. Suffice it to say that the Luminator and VRIC imaging are the root from which the Supercoherence system has sprung. I wish to acknowledge that and the immense debt of gratitude that I owe to Patrick Richards.

Reconnection and the Zero-Point Alignment

> 'When the doors of perception are cleansed,
> everything would appear to man as it is, infinite.'
>
> **William Blake**

With the Luminator and VRIC imaging, we have used two unique and specific methods over the past 15 plus years to assess a person's disconnection or mis-alignment from zero. Every single client has undergone this evaluation process and we have found that this disconnection has existed in nearly everyone we have assessed. It was shocking and disconcerting to find that it was present regardless of the client practising years of meditation, following spiritual practices or personal development methods or healing modalities. At some level, the disconnection had remained untouched and was still creating chaos. This hidden drama was taking place outside the boundaries of the five-sensory reality – and even of the 'sixth sense' – with grave consequences.

It is a case of you don't know what you don't know. And what you don't know *can* hurt you in ways you cannot comprehend or quantify, and keep you from fulfilling your destiny. As a result we are limited to functioning at the level of a light bulb instead of accessing the magnificent possibilities of the laser level.

Until the Luminator and VRIC imaging came along we did not have a clue about this state of affairs, so had no means of rectifying it. But now we had some insight. So what did we do?

Assess the Disconnection

(Please look at the striking VRIC images in the plate section - Plates 2, "2a, 2b, 2c. All the imaging has been done in the field of the Luminator using VRIC imaging.)

The person being imaged has two plastic bottles placed on the floor at least 6–8 inches away from their feet, one at a time. They *do not know* what the bottles contain and do not touch or handle them in any way. One contains the energy signature of the female frequency in a carrier cream and the other contains the energy signature of the male frequency in a carrier cream. These energy signatures cannot be detected or measured by other scientific tools.

Two photos are taken – one with the male frequency bottle at the person's feet and the other with the female frequency bottle.

This simple seemingly innocuous yet profound process is very revealing. Most people's image fragments badly – becomes fuzzy and incoherent – even though they do not know what is in the bottle in front of them and they have no physical contact with the bottles. This fragmentation is happening without our awareness, knowledge, concurrence or conscious volition. So we can see the picture is revealing hidden information and it exists at the field/frequency level.

So, what does it mean?

If the female frequency fragments your field and you are a woman, that is bad news. It means that you cannot hold your frequency as a female. Your energy field is your primary filter and will shape your response before you can think. So if your field is incoherent with a female frequency, this can result in less than ideal relationships with other women – or men. In effect you can only relate to other women, or men, through the incoherent reality perceived by your field – and you do not even know it. Every area of your life can be adversely impacted as a result.

If you are a man and the male frequency fragments your field, the same insights apply.

To give an example of how this can work in practice: the field of a young man who had a very dominating father fragmented badly when the male energy bottle was placed at his feet. In his life, he was totally unable to hold his ground as far as his father was concerned. His father did not listen to or respect him and he was unable to do anything about it. He was 34 years old at the time. When this disconnection was rectified, he became a changed man in the space of one month and for the first time in his life stood his ground with his father and told him off in no uncertain terms. And his father listened and took note of what his son said.

So what happens if you are a man and the female frequency causes fragmentation in your field, or if you are a woman and the male frequency causes fragmentation in your field? This, I am sorry to say, is equally bad news. This means that your relationships with the opposite sex have a good chance of being less than you would like them to be.

I remember vividly a rather dramatic example of this. The subject was a lovely gentle woman in her early forties. She had a good professional background, but had not had a successful relationship with a man. When I put the male energy signature bottle at her feet, we were both shocked at the image that appeared. This lovely woman's face looked as though it had been burnt and severely scarred, even though nothing like that had happened in her life – this time around at least. It showed her the serious hidden unconscious challenge that was preventing her from having a good relationship with a man.

This hidden information can create havoc in all our important relationships, including the most important one: our relationship with ourselves. It can prevent us from seeing clearly and living and loving fully. Our sense of self can be damaged and it can become difficult, if not impossible, to truly become that which we – at one level – always are.

Assessing for Zero-Point Alignment – See Plates 3 and 3a

Perception is deception. When Patrick Richards first said that to me, I thought, 'What on earth does he mean?' It sounded outrageous and absurd. But the zero-point alignment assessment process showed me the truth of this seemingly crazy statement.

The zero-point alignment process – the process of uniting the two polarities in the infinite complexity that is a person – is at one level a simple one. Yet again the person undergoing the assessment process is imaged in the zero field of the Luminator using VRIC imaging. But this time they are imaged first with the left eye closed and the right eye open and then with the right eye closed and the left eye open. According to our experience, the right eye connects to the left 'brain' and left eye connects to the right 'brain'. Remember, the right side of the brain accesses the intuitive, non-linear, non-sequential, non-analytical, emotional aspect of a person and the left side the analytical, critical, logical, sequential, rational aspect. In this system we also consider the right eye and the entire right side of the body represents the father or the male aspect and the left eye and the entire left side of the body represents the mother and the female aspect. This is true for both males and females, and is not dependent on whether people are right or left-handed. We find that if a person has had a challenging relationship with either the father or the mother, that side of the body will often suffer physical challenges.

In most people the imaging reveals incoherence when one or the other eye is closed. In effect that means that there is a state of imbalance between right and left brain processing. It indicates that one side is dominant.

In a strange way this is not beneficial for the dominant side but is detrimental to both sides. Since the eye is our physical organ of perception, if that perception is out of balance, we are creating our reality from that imbalanced standpoint, without being consciously aware that we are doing so. The sad fact is that we have been doing it unknowingly for who knows how long, with the result that our lives are out of balance at many different levels.

I have to clarify something here: the zero-point alignment process is and is not about synchronizing the activity of the two brain hemispheres. It is and is not about learning to access alpha and theta brain states for relaxation or meditation or super learning. On the one hand, it probably does that; however, it goes much further up the causal chain. This process is beyond the brain, in the sense that the brain is subject to it and not the other way around. It takes place at field level and the field is prior to the brain. As research scientist Val Hunt says, the brain is a dandy computer – it is a processor and not the source of the information.

Rectify the Zero-Point Alignment

What we really want to see in the imaging is that you are coherent and at zero with both the male and the female frequency and with each eye open. When perception is at zero, what you will see will be clear and neutral and therefore true. And the actions that you take and the results that you get will be the best they can be. You have started a coherent 'chain reaction' in your life. In effect, your life becomes a different life. Your energy field and you as an individual can hold your resonance with both males and females. Your fundamental relationship with yourself has been repaired and restored and this will transform all other relationships. Because of this new-found ability, relationships have the possibility of becoming authentic and comfortable, no matter how fractured or unsatisfactory they have been before.

In effect we are strengthening you by recalibrating your field to zero at a fundamental level of perception and being. You can never feel 'less than' again. You can hold your own without the need to use fear, force and control, or use emotional manipulation, or become a victim. The unconscious need will simply not be there.

Experiencing the Zero-Point Alignment

I remember vividly my first experience of the zero-point alignment balancing process. It was 1996, early days, the Luminator had arrived only a few months back, it was fun to image with it and we were trying all sorts of experiments. My son, who used to help me at that time, suggested I try the process for myself. I readily agreed.

At that time I was going through huge emotional turmoil of a personal nature. I would call it gut-wrenching. I could not think clearly and felt engulfed by forces that I had very little control over. I had not felt this way in years and it was disconcerting. There did not appear to be an easy resolution to the situation.

My son did the VRIC imaging for me. I was imaged first with the right eye closed and the left eye open and then with the left eye closed and the right eye open. One of the images was incoherent. I was then re-imaged holding the female frequency in my right hand (male side) and the image cleared. I duly applied a dab of the female frequency cream under my right eyebrow and that was that. I thought no more about it.

It took me a couple of days to notice that I felt completely calm, and had indeed been calm for the whole two days. The huge emotional turmoil had completely dissipated. I was no longer obsessed with the thoughts and emotions that had been troubling me. I remember thinking, 'Am I mad? How can I feel so dramatically different when nothing has changed?' The outer circumstances had not changed at all. However, my gut and my solar plexus area, which had borne the brunt of my turbulent emotions, felt quiet and empty. Thinking about this strange effect left me curious and puzzled.

It was only later that the penny dropped and I realized what had happened and why.

More importantly, I could see the situation with far greater clarity than just a couple of days previously.

The emotional turmoil did not return. I learned, or rather my energy body learned, a far more effective and comfortable way of dealing with events.

On a more curious note, several months later I realized that the very fine hair on my right upper lip had completely disappeared. It has never grown again.

A more interesting observation has been that I have become less self-critical and more forgiving of others since that time. The old anger which would well up out of nowhere seems to have disappeared.

These radical and welcome changes involved no effort on my part, for which I am grateful. They all came from putting a dab of cream with light-energy-information under an eyebrow – changing the trajectory of a life with the power of zero.

In my view what we are doing here is re-educating the energy field imprinted with our past suffering, our fears and the resulting distorted perception, by making it remember the frequency of super-intelligence, clarity, neutrality and truth from which it has been disconnected. When the perfect balance point is restored through the process, a new reality is perceived and shaped at every level.

It is difficult to describe in words, but a close analogy would be that of a tuning fork. We are tuning our field so that it resonates with the frequency of perfection, of wholeness, super-consciousness or super-intelligence, the 'lost chord'. As the field remembers this frequency, it is reconnected to the Source and remembers its real, natural, pristine state. Fear leaves and is replaced by clarity, peace, strength and the limitless understanding of love. We have come home to ourselves and can find it easy, effortless and enjoyable to follow the way of the mindful heart and the heart-full mind and cannot easily separate the two ever again. We are in the perfect place, which is everywhere and nowhere.

One could also use the disconnected circuit analogy. The process is reconnecting the disconnected energetic circuitry so that the flow of super-intelligence is restored to the personality. In my view it is impossible to exaggerate the importance of this reconnection.

Furthermore, there is no effort involved. This is a simple, easy, powerful, effective and universal process, and extremely elegant. Anyone can take advantage of it to realize their own wonder and greatness, regardless of whether or not they meditate, pray or use esoteric practices. It is a simple matter and nobody needs to be left out in the cold of ignorance and suffering.

Until the Luminator came along, this was just not possible. Though the significance of zero had been clearly understood in the past, we had never had direct systematic access to it. But now the master key had been found that would open the portal of miracles.

But the story was not over and there were many other events to unfold...

CHAPTER 6

VRIC Remote Imaging – Woo-woo, Wacky, Weird or Impossibly Wonderful?

'There are two excesses: to exclude reason, to admit nothing but reason. The supreme achievement of reason is to realize that there is a limit to reason. Reason's last step is the recognition that there are an infinite number of things which are beyond it. It is merely feeble, if it does not go as far as to realize that.'

Blaise Pascal, 1623–1662

Beyond the Brain and Beyond Reason

ONE OF THE most extraordinary and shocking capabilities of the Luminator and VRIC imaging is that they bypass space-time in real terms. Your first instinct may be to say that is impossible, mine was. And it *is* impossible in terms of how we understand the laws of reality as they operate in this physical dimension. But the laws of reality are not as fixed as they seem. And a new set of amazing possibilities emerges as a result of that new understanding…

You may have heard of distant healing and remote viewing. Essentially, in both of these processes the laws of space-time are bypassed. The distant healer or the remote viewer can 'see' and influence people and things that are physically many miles away from them. VRIC remote imaging is similar in that the person who is being imaged is not physically present.

I realized the system was capable of this in 1996, when Patrick and I did an experiment with astounding results. Since then I have done remote imaging for many years in London. I did not write about it in the first book because I felt it was too shocking for people to get their heads around and I was afraid it would discredit an amazing system because of its radical implications. I confess that when I first experienced it, I myself could not believe what was happening before my eyes.

How do we do remote imaging? It can only be done when the Luminator is present. We use a photo of the person who is to be imaged and then take a VRIC image of the photo. We then take various VRIC images with the different frequencies placed next the photo. The photo will appear fuzzy or incoherent when photographed with the 'wrong' frequencies placed in front of it and become sharp, clear and coherent when the 'correct' frequencies are placed in front of it. In short we conduct an assessment exactly as if the person were physically present, though they may be physically in another country, unconscious in a hospital or 'dead' in another dimension – remember there is no space-time in the field of the Luminator. We are in effect in hyperspace, the space of no space and the time of no time, or in the zero-point field, which is also supposed to be beyond space-time. Sounds absurd, but it is true. We have crossed over into an elegant parallel universe where reality operates by completely different rules.

This is a case study that was done in 2002.
Walter P

Interview with Phiroza Paris on 16-2-2002
Assessment on January 8th 2002

Phiroza is a dear friend of mine of many years standing. She is warm, capable and caring. She also has a fiery temper and is like most humans very sensitive. She had been married to Walter – her second marriage – since 1980.

Walter was a quiet, thoughtful, soft spoken, yet strong-willed 79 year old Scotsman, very well read – over 3000 books in his library with subjects ranging from science, history and religion to philosophy, politics and more, indicating a far reaching and fine intellect. Walter's health had been progressively failing for a while and the process had accelerated in the last several months. He had lost mobility, was unable to walk beyond a slow shuffle and his short term memory had been failing.

Thrity: Give me an idea, a bit of background about Walter, what was happening.

Phiroza: 'Walter went into hospital in October. He was in hospital on 24th October (2001) to have an operation. He hadn't been moving very well and his memory was failing, the neurologist thought that perhaps he had slight fluid on the brain – "hydroencephalopathy" or something and they thought putting a shunt into his brain would help to drain the fluid and help his movement (mobility), memory and stuff. He had the operation on the 25th October and the operation was fine, no infection or anything. He healed up in four or five days and that is the time I said (to the hospital staff) "Please start making him move, because his movement is not good and if you don't get him mobile soon he is going to really have difficulty walking'.

Walter was tall and his upper body was broad and strong, but the legs have been very frail and unable to sustain the weight of the upper body. His walk was a slow shuffle before he went to hospital. But he had actually walked into the hospital. Phiroza'a concerns were very real, that he would lose the little mobility that he had if his legs were not mobilised.

Phiroza: They said "Sorry, but we don't give too much physiotherapy in this department on this ward, because most of it is for people who have had operations, might catch chest infections and things. When he goes to elderly patients he can get physiotherapy there. This went on for days and days and days, by the third week I was really panicking, all they were doing was hoisting him from the bed into a chair and back into the bed. He was getting more and more depressed, because he couldn't move at all. I emailed the consultant and they found him a bed in elderly patients the next day. He went down and from there to a third ward eventually and he was really not at all happy. He was still in a wheelchair, although the ward is quite a nice place, the one he is in now. He had a couple of falls, because his memory is quite poor, he does not remember that he can't get up, stand up and walk. So he had a couple of minor falls, then just before Christmas he had quite a serious fall, hurt his back quite badly, he was in a lot of pain. As the month progressed to the end of December, beginning of January, he caught an infection of the kidneys, because he has only one kidney after an operation in April 2000 and following that he got a chest infection. Now you had asked me sometime at the end of December to give you some photographs of Walter if you could do anything to help him.'

I thought I would do a remote imaging VRIC assessment for Walter. I told Phiroza, that I was not sure that I could achieve anything useful, but I was prepared to have a go. I told her to bring me a large A4 size photo of Walter. In remote VRIC Imaging we take photos of the photograph to assess the state of coherence of the person in the photograph. Phiroza got me the photo a few days later, as there was nothing terribly urgent (I did not know that he was very ill) in that Walter was being looked after in the hospital and I was busy, I left it for a few days. Then one evening (Jan 8th), I just knew I had to do the imaging right then. It was about 8.30 and the impulse became an imperative. So I took a base line photo of Walter's photo and it was very incoherent (fuzzy). As I looked at the photograph I had a very uncomfortable feeling that he was in crisis. I just knew that. I tried to establish coherence for Walter using the zero point alignment process by placing the male frequency to the right and the female frequency to the left of the photo. There was no way, the VRIC image remained incoherent, if anything it became worse. At this point I picked up the phone and called Phiroza. I had not spoken to her for a few days. I felt there was a huge crisis going on and I felt Walter might be getting ready to leave his body. I phoned her, didn't initially tell her, just asked her about Walter. I knew she visited him every evening.

Phiroza: Yes I remember you ringing and that evening I had come back from the hospital, he was very ill. He had high fever, he was in pain, with his back, with his kidney, they were giving him antibiotics and I had been putting cold compresses on his forehead and I was very worried about him. He was depressed and unhappy. He told me "I just want to die". When you rang up and I said he is very ill you said "Yes I know" and I was really shocked. You said you had just done the imaging process and it showed clearly that he was really unwell. You told me to prepare myself about – (his leaving) and had I thought about what would happen if Walter leaves."

I told Phiroza in clear but guarded terms, that he might be getting ready to leave and that every soul had the absolute prerogative to leave peacefully when it was appropriate and that if she wanted to help him, she should pray for him and send him light and healing. I asked her if she had done her emotional preparation for that. Phiroza had a tendency to get very impatient with Walter, treating him as though he was absolutely normal, when he was actually very unwell and was totally incapable of being what Phiroza wanted him to be. This was in part because of her desire to have him well again and a non-acceptance of the painful reality that was the truth. I asked her to visualize him as well, peaceful and happy. We know through VRIC imaging and through many other studies that prayers and healing intentions are potent healing forces and actually reach the target of their intention. It would also benefit Phiroza in that it would ease her mind, keeping it focused on healing which was positive and not just worry, which would be of no benefit to her or her husband.

On the other hand after putting down the phone I still felt disturbed that I had not established coherence for Walter. As I stayed with my discomfort, another thought, another option came to mind. I knew after six and a half years that you can always establish coherence, so my task was not complete. So I decided to carry it further. I used the Biolumanetics techniques and chose 3 Lumanetic frequencies out of a possible total of 160 frequencies. I imaged him again with the three Lumanetic frequency vials on his photo and sure enough, the photograph cleared and became sharp and coherent. I was enormously relieved to see that.

So I phoned Phiroza immediately – it was about thirty minutes after my first call – to tell her the good news.

Phiroza: 'When your phone call came I thought it was the hospital ringing me up and I was really on edge and I was really relieved with the news.'

I also asked Phiroza to let me know if anything changed. I did not know whether anything would change in a noticeable way at the physical level. I knew something had changed in the photograph/s, but there would have to be an outward indication of that energetic change. I wanted some feedback and told Phiroza to keep track and let me know if anything did change.

The next evening, I phoned Phiroza to check.

Phiroza: 'I was not seeing him till ten o'clock the next morning. I went to see him in the morning and he was much, much better. He was looking happier, his temperature was down, he looked much more cheerful and I was very relieved he was not in any pain, the pain had gone and in fact he said to me 'Today I feel much better than I have felt for ages'. Those were his actual words.

Since then he has been progressing quite well. He is much more peaceful, he continues to read.'

That assessment was a turning point for Walter and he never looked back. From great distress and unhappiness in the space of a few hours his life had been turned around to peace, understanding and acceptance. Changing the trajectory of a life with the power of zero.

From total crisis to comfort overnight. Why and how was this possible?

From Phiroza's conversations, I could sense Walter's emotional pain, because he wanted to go home, and he couldn't go home, so there was a lot of unhappiness. Every day he would say to Phiroza when she visited him, 'When am I coming home?' This would upset her as she knew he probably would never be able to go home again and she would get slightly angry and remind him that she had told him just the previous day that he could come home when he was mobile. This happened every day, as he had forgotten by the next day what had been said. He also accused her of not wanting him home, that his wife was deserting him in his hour of need. This used to distress Phiroza enormously, and make her feel guilty. At some level there was a deep unfulfilled need and a non-acceptance of the reality that was his life. He could not help himself, nor could he do anything different. The interesting thing is that after the VRIC assessment Walter found that quiet place in himself and the struggle was over. At one level in the external reality, it would seem he had lost his sense of time – but in a sense in that way he had also lost the sense of the length of his suffering. When Phiroza told him he had been in hospital for four months – he was surprised – he thought he had been there for only a fortnight. So is it a good place or a bad place? In my view, it is a very good place – whether he does or does not know the date is irrelevant. He enjoyed his food, reading his books, which was what he had enjoyed all his life, he recognized his wife and was happy to see her and chat with her intelligently. He had found contentment – which is what life for him is about. He was in the eternal present and could stay in the moment without the worries, the trials and the pain of his failing body. It may not suit us – but it certainly suited Walter. His emotional pain had been resolved – his body and soul had found peace. All of this was accomplished by putting three vials containing water (with information) on his photograph – many miles from where his body happened to be - chosen by his super-conscious Self. Yes I selected the vials – but Walter's super-conscious Self had the final say. I was the facilitator, but Walter was the prime mover. Walter was out of the cycle of suffering and this was a blessing for his devoted wife as well. Phiroza has visibly relaxed and found it possible to be more tender and less impatient in his presence and was much more accepting of his condition, but more importantly of herself. Emotional alchemy of the most mysterious, yet utterly beautiful and effective kind – through the power of subtle energy.

Walter died peacefully in a nursing home on the 1ˢᵗ January 2004.

The concepts of omnipresence and omniscience acquired a new meaning. Space and time, which seem so real, and *are* real at one level, were suddenly shown to be not so immutable and I was shown another, equally real level of the eternal reality where space and time were transcended and were patently as 'unreal' at that level as the concepts of eternity and immortality seem to be at the physical level of the five senses.

We have also been able use remote imaging to make important decisions. I remember when my youngest uncle on my mother's side was in hospital in Mumbai. He had been ill with diabetes for a long time and had developed gangrene in his foot due to lack of circulation. The doctors wanted to amputate it, but the risk was that he would not survive the operation, given the state he was in. My other uncle, who looked after him, was distraught about making the wrong decision.

Two images were taken. I placed a folded note saying 'Beneficial to amputate' in front of my uncle's photo and took a VRIC image of the photo. Then I placed a note saying 'Non-beneficial to amputate' in front of the photo and took another VRIC image of it. The notes had been folded and shuffled first to prevent any bias from the person doing the imaging. It was the prerogative of my uncle's soul to make that decision.

The answer was surprising, but unequivocal – it was non-beneficial to amputate. We couldn't understand why this was so, but we did not need to know the reason why. We phoned my uncle in Mumbai and gave him the result.

The next day my diabetic uncle passed away and he did not have to suffer the further trauma of the amputation. The decision shown by the imaging is always the right one, because with VRIC remote imaging you are bypassing the brain and the personality totally and are speaking directly with the super-conscious Self – the soul – in a direct, impeccable way.

On a lighter note, one evening I received a phone call from my daughter. She was in Ikea and liked a red sofa suite and a black suite, but could not decide which one she should have. Would I please do some remote imaging right away and let her know the outcome?

Two VRIC images were taken of her photo, one with a folded note saying 'Beneficial to buy red suite' and the other with a folded note saying 'Beneficial to buy black suite.' It must be noted the suites were not just different colours, but of a different design.

The imaging was clear and unequivocal, as always. The red suite was the one that made her image coherent, so that was the one she bought.

It later turned out that had she chosen the black one there would have been a real problem, as the sofa could have not been maneuvered through her narrow hallway. In fact it simply would not have been possible to get it into the house, which would have been a complete disaster!

Ask yourself how a photo can read a message on a folded note and give an answer by turning clear or fuzzy. It begs the questions of who we really are and what our capabilities as humans might be.

VRIC Remote Imaging shows us with uncompromising clarity in the most irrefutable, incontrovertible and unequivocal terms that we are not our physical body, that we are something other. And that we have the power and the means to reach across the universe instantly, in fact we are present wherever we need to be and that information, intention and intelligence are the prime creators and movers of reality. You and I are the super-conscious

Ones having a physical experience. VRIC remote imaging makes it possible for the "ordinary" human to realize and move from the mundane mechanical view of themselves to the understanding of their true magnificence and activate and actualize that in the reality of their life.

Remote imaging is a process which sends the imagination soaring with possibilities.

PART II

From Meltdown to Miracle

CHAPTER 7
From Meltdown...

'Outside everything crumbles...'
Talking with Angels

O N ONE LEVEL, 2008 was a cataclysmic year. As you may remember, the world went into meltdown, with banks and stock markets crashing and extreme turmoil in the financial world. My own life also went into meltdown.

At that point I had been working with the Luminator and VRIC imaging for 13 years. It was my lifework and I was totally committed to it. I was now looking forward to getting this beautiful work out into the world with the publication of my first book, *Supercoherence - The 7ᵗʰ Sense*, in May. I felt the thrill and delight of holding the first copy in my hand. I had waited many years for this to happen, so it was a major life event. The elation, however, was short-lived.

A huge bombshell was about to be dropped and I was totally unprepared. Up until then we totally relied on VRIC imaging, which could only be done with Polaroid instant analogue film. Digital cameras did not produce the VRIC effect, so the film was an essential, indispensable, irreplaceable part of the system. While we all knew that the days of Polaroid instant film were numbered, I was constantly reassured by my good friend Andy from Chiswick Camera, who had supplied the film for many years, that Polaroid sold loads of film and it was unlikely that they would discontinue a product for which there was considerable demand.

However, just as the book came out, a client and friend phoned me.

'Thrity, do you know Polaroid have just announced they are stopping the manufacture of Polaroid film? What are you going to do?'

I went into shock. It felt like a blow to the solar plexus. What *was* I going to do?

Suddenly the way forward, which had been so clear, was as clear as mud. It was ironic, exquisite timing. I felt as though my world had ended, as though 13 years of my life had become meaningless and futile. Not a fun place to be.

There was more to come.

I had very much wanted the book to be published for my great associate Patrick Richards, the genius inventor of the mighty Luminator, as a token of the gratitude I felt towards him. Being a sensitive man, he had suffered a lot from the rejection of his work and he was looking forward to the book coming out.

As soon as it was out, I sent him the second copy (the first copy went to my mother) and I waited. Two weeks went by and there was no response from him. I wondered whether he had not liked the book for some reason and did not wish to tell me – or *was* this his way of telling me, as no response is also a response? Very tentatively, I picked up the phone and called him, not knowing what to expect.

When he answered, I asked him if he had had a chance to read the book. I was totally unprepared for what he was about to tell me: his younger son had been killed in a tragic accident. The raw pain in his voice was heartbreaking. I was devastated. He could not truly enjoy what he had waited many years for.

Furthermore, Patrick had not been well for several years. Decades of struggle coupled with emotional pain had taken their toll. I knew he would not survive this deep shock.

And so it was. He died in September. Though I knew it was inevitable, it was a major blow.

Though my work with Biolumanetics and VRIC imaging had shown me beyond the shadow of a doubt that the soul does not die and can be communicated with, when Patrick died, a part of me was deeply saddened. I had lost a great associate, mentor and friend. I missed our chats and now there was no one I could ask if I had a query about Biolumanetics. I felt alone and responsible for getting the work out into the world – and it was not a good feeling. Another door closing.

As for Patrick, I have always wondered why this great soul and bene-factor of humanity chose such a hard life and why at one level his great work did not meet with the recognition and rewards that it so richly mer-ited in his lifetime.

The turmoil and turbulence were not over for me. A lot more was about to be heaped on a plate that I thought was already pretty full.

Within the space of four months, two of my mother's younger sisters died totally unexpectedly and my darling mother was distraught. She was the eldest and she wondered why they had gone before her. It was hard to hear the distress in her voice.

Several of my darling clients also lost near and dear ones at this time. I love my clients – many of them become dear friends – and I was beginning to feel the cumulative effect of all this emotional pain. The joy that had come with the book had faded.

I was reeling. All the plans that I had made to have teleconferences and to promote the work were suddenly out of reach. I simply could not find the motivation and I had to let go of the urgency and simply learn to cope with the pain that surrounded me. I felt numb.

All the old doors were being shut in my face. I just did not know how to move forward. The universe was showing me something, but I did not seem to be getting the message.

At one point I went into a real tailspin and crashed. This is an excerpt of what I wrote during my darkest days:

'Yesterday I felt as if my world was ending. Distraught, desperate, hopeless and with no future, unsupported, sad and helpless… I don't want to carry on, I have had enough. Any choice that I have considered has just made me feel unhappy… Where do I go and to whom do I turn to for con-solation? Tears are rolling uncontrollably down my cheeks as I write this… Where has all the lightness gone? Everything feels grim and hard…'

How could I cope with all the turbulence? What could I do to restore some semblance of equilibrium and get some relief from the pain?

Fortunately, I do not smoke, drink or do drugs. There are too many negative trade-offs which make those activities unappealing. Instead I used music and had a colour dome session, which helped. I also slept a lot and did not answer the phone. But most powerful and effective of all was simply holding a particular zero-point alignment frequency in the left hand.

I know that this system, or the cosmic joker, always uses me as the experimenter and the experiment when it wants to teach me something new. Because of this, I know what works as a result of direct experience, so I can say hand on heart to someone in a similar situation that it will help. Now I was being shown what it was to be in crisis and what could relieve it. Holding a particular zero-point alignment frequency in the left hand, I realized, would help anyone in turmoil. It would bring a measure of equilibrium when everything was being turned upside down. And it worked instantly. This was useful information.

I also knew I was being pushed to the next level. Friends and enthusiastic clients told me things were moving in ways that I had not foreseen. The word was spreading and I knew this was only the beginning of the beginning, but parts of me were in fear. Part of me felt like a fake and a fool, and totally inadequate to the task, which appeared impossibly huge and difficult. I had to give myself a good talking-to – in fact angels did this for me. I had misplaced my desert island book, *Talking with Angels*, and missed it a lot, and then suddenly, when I was desperately in need, I found it again. Reading it every morning helped me to find my true perspective again and reminded me that I was on the right track and that I should not take myself too seriously.

I had already suffered one meltdown in my life, in 1989-90. Then, when I had lost my marriage and all my money in the space of two cataclysmic months, I had wanted to kill myself. There was one major difference between that meltdown and this one. Then, I would say, I was largely unconscious or asleep and did not understand the true implications of the crisis. Since that time, my understanding and my belief systems had undergone a radical transformation. So this time around, despite all the darkness that seemed to be enveloping my life, I was not asleep and understood that this was my soul's journey and the universe did not mean me harm or hurt, but was always benign. I knew that no matter how terrible things appeared to be and how bad a part of me felt, there was a gift waiting for me, a gift which would reveal itself at the appropriate time. So, though I could not function at the speed I wished to and felt quite numb with the pain of all the losses, I knew for certain that this would pass.

I also knew that the universe only ever moves you in the direction of a higher order. I knew this from personal experience and not from blind faith.

And I knew one more thing with absolute certainty and total commitment: that I was not giving up on my work. No matter what happened I would carry on. Giving up was simply not an option. Call it stupidity, stubbornness, bloody-mindedness, persistence or whatever, that was it. A way forward would reveal itself.

And I was right, a miracle was about to unfold. A miracle that was greater than anything I could have planned or hoped for.

CHAPTER 8
...to Miracle

'But inside the new is born.'

Talking with Angels

S INCE THE BEGINNING of my involvement with this work, my intent had been to get the benefits of this extraordinary system out into the world. That is what I had planned all along and the book had been written with that intent in mind. Yet with the way the system was before 2008 it would have been very difficult, if not impossible, to achieve this. Before then we were working with a vast toolkit of 160-220 frequencies, plus topical creams and frequency pads, every session was unique and it took a lot of imaging to create coherence for the client. In realistic terms, though I did not realize it at the time, if I was to fulfill my original intent, I needed a universal process which was effective, safe and powerful.

Could there be a universal frequency which would create coherence for all? It seemed an unlikely prospect. After all, each one of us is unique and has our own individual requirements. In fact, to tell you the truth, I had never really thought in terms of a universal frequency, it had simply never occurred to me that it was necessary or even possible.

Nevertheless, the zero-point alignment assessment process (ZPA) which I had tested for years and used with every single client was extremely effective at neutralizing trauma in the energy field only 90 per cent of the time. I wanted 100 per cent.

Also, the ZPA process still needed the imaging, and the film was not going to be available. But I was about to get some help.

The Return of the Sweet Mother

There is a reality which exists at the frequency level beyond space and time. Call it an invisible all encompassing cosmic grid, a web, a matrix, a field where love is all that exists. There is no judgement there, only understanding and acceptance of all that is. It is essentially a place of tenderness which in human terms we best understand as the sweet mother.

In 2001 a friend had given me a special photo. The explanation which accompanied it said:

'This photo of Mary was taken in the early 1970s at the shrine of San Damiano in Northern Italy. She appeared to this pilgrim and asked him to take a photo. He pointed his Polaroid camera at the sky and took a photo. When the photo came out, this was the image on it.'

From my teenage years to my early fifties I was an atheist, and if someone had given me that photo and explanation then, my response would have been that of a total sceptic. I would quite simply have dismissed it as superstitious nonsense. However, since 1995 my experience with VRIC imaging had taught me in absolute terms that there was a level of reality that was truly beyond the five senses, a level that was real, powerful and totally miraculous. So in one way I knew I was blind and had been made to see through the eyes of my little Polaroid camera.

Seeing thousands of VRIC images and being exposed daily to the extraordinary nature of reality had reduced my ignorance and scepticism, so I did not debunk the image and accepted it for the sweet gift that it was. In a funny kind of way I found the story fascinating and credible precisely because the image had appeared from this invisible and impeccable dimension. The fact that it was not man-made was a plus point as far as I was concerned.

Also, looking at the image, I was touched. There was a soft strength there, coupled with serenity and sweetness. I was looking at the archetypal sweet mother. I now call her the Divine Mother, an archetype which is universal and exists in every wisdom tradition. This was what I call a high frequency image – love is high frequency stuff – and it was the face of unconditional love.

I decided to test the effect of the image on clients who had special issues with their mother. There was one case in particular which was very poignant and which I have written about in my first book. He was a young man who had been adopted and did not know his biological father. After seeing him once, his biological mother had refused to meet him again. In a rather shocking way he had found out that he was the child of a rape. He was extremely distraught as a result. At the time I used the Divine Mother photo along with the photos of his two mothers and did an energetic alignment using Biolumanetics frequencies to neutralize the trauma. Four days later he phoned me to say, 'I have hit the ceiling!' That was his way of saying he was on top of the world. Extreme trauma and deep emotional pain had been transformed into joy and freedom within a matter of days using the Divine Mother image and the relevant Biolumanetics frequencies. It was a case that touched me deeply and stayed with me through the years.

So, since 2001 I had been using the photo occasionally for clients with special mother issues and had obtained excellent results. However, for some reason, or no reason, I did not use it with everyone. There were many other effective methods and processes, and this was simply one of them.

That was the way it was until the sky fell in on my world and Polaroid decided to stop making film and it seemed that all of Patrick's work and my work of many years would count for nothing.

Then the thought, the idea, came from nowhere, it just came. I would not call it a brainwave; I would prefer to call it the soul's nudge. The idea was strikingly simple and had been staring me in the face for many years, but I had not seen it.

It started with a 'What if…?' What if I combined the zero-point alignment, the most powerful and universal process in Biolumanetics, and the photo of the Divine Mother? We had never done this before, as there had been no need. After all, we had many processes and many frequencies available for establishing coherence for our clients. Now, however, the need was different. It was time for another experiment.

I am glad I am a tester, an explorer and an experimenter, Patrick taught me the necessity and the fun of testing and experimenting. And I love the precision and impeccability of VRIC imaging as a tool for testing. So I got going...

The Experiment

The burning questions that I wanted answers to were: would the zero-point alignment frequencies in combination with the Divine Mother image work for everyone? Would it make a difference, would we increase the effectiveness of the ZPA process beyond 90 per cent? Could the process be standardized? If it could, and only if could, then the Polaroid film and imaging would be redundant.

Before I start to explain what happened, I wish to make a very clear point: I do not wish to have this process tied to any particular religion, even though the photo is claimed to be of Mother Mary. While the fundamental essence of religions is a search for the sacred, in real terms over the last many hundreds if not thousands of years human religious practice has been the cause of more suffering than almost anything else. I definitely do not wish this extraordinary process to be defined as a religious practice or tied to any religion. Please remember it is about zero point and the zero-point frequencies, which are simply frequencies, with no religious affiliation of any kind.

For me, if there is a universal religion, it is love, with no barriers, boundaries or definitions. That affects how I look at this extraordinary picture. When I look at it, what do I see? I see the distilled and pure essence of softness, sweetness and incredible strength. What do you see? You will have to go past your conditioning, which can be deeply rooted, to truly see what is happening before your eyes.

The first stage in my experiment was to invite my female clients to participate. Hindus, Muslims, Catholics, Jews, Protestants, Zoroastrians and total non-believers all took part. All of them already had experience of the zero-point alignment frequencies. Would there be a difference just adding the photo of the Divine Mother? That was the question.

It was also quite a broad question, because the female frequency has been devalued, denigrated and debased here on Earth for the last several thousand years. This is pretty much a universal phenomenon and is prevalent in every single culture and tradition even today. A lot of the chaos that we see in the world is a direct result of this acute and long-term imbalance. This is not a feminist diatribe, simply a statement of fact. Nor do I mean to accuse or blame either gender, as you and I have experienced being the other gender in other lifetimes. We have all knowingly or unknowingly participated in perpetuating the cycle of suffering.

This imbalance is also often reflected in our relationships with our biological mothers. Many of these relationships are far from ideal. All of us want to love and be loved, totally and unconditionally, especially by our mothers, but the truth is that mothers are simply human and are themselves part of the same cycle of suffering and so less than perfect in the way they show their love or even in the way they can love. Mothers are supposed to be all-loving, all-giving, always there when needed, and are not supposed to want or need much for themselves, but is this a realistic expectation, especially in our current world?

What I was seeking to do with the experiment was to create an energetic alignment with the high frequency of the Divine Mother and the human mother (biological or adoptive) and the daughter. We know that the highest, strongest, most coherent frequency will prevail, and so the idea was that the female frequency would be restored and brought into balance.

So I did the alignment-clearing using VRIC imaging with the zero-point alignment frequencies and the Divine Mother photo for my female clients and their respective mothers. The process worked beautifully and I was really pleased. *(See plate 4)*

The next step was to expand the remit of the process. So we aligned and cleared the relationships with the father using the Divine Mother image and the zero-point alignment frequencies. Excellent results again.

After that we were getting more confident, so we tried aligning and clearing the whole family using the same method. Family images can create huge chaos, as we have seen over the years, and we were delighted that the process worked even under these challenging conditions. This was very impressive.

The next step was to bring in some male subjects. The process worked for them as well.

It also proved effective whether the person was a believer or non-believer or even a self-professed atheist. It did not matter.

By this time I was sure that the process was pretty near 100 per cent effective. The way forward was clear.

But I was in for a rude shock – and another gift which took me to the next step.

The Next Step

I had three new clients, all women in their fifties and sixties. All of them had done a huge amount of personal development work and one had followed a strong spiritual practice over many decades. All were lovely women, yet when I went through the process which by now we had tested successfully for several months, it did not do the job. The trauma and the charge of certain life events would not clear using the Divine Mother image and the zero-point alignment frequencies.

The first time it happened, I was stunned. For one thing, it was so unexpected. Also, the difficulty with this imaging system is that there is no time to think about a problem. One cannot go away and mull it over and come back the next day, or even a few hours later, with the right answer – the client is in front of you and everything is happening in real time and has to be resolved there and then. However, the beauty of the process is that one knows immediately whether the choice made is the right one or not – there is no scope for error.

As I stood there nonplussed, not knowing what to do next, another stroke of inspiration came and I got the idea of using two other frequencies which would soften and strengthen the zero-point alignment process. I tested them with the imaging and the trauma cleared.

Though I didn't fully realize it at the time, I had found a way – or, rather, a way had been found for me – to fulfill my original intent, my big dream, my 'nearly impossible' project of breaking the cycle of suffering that we have endured for the past few thousand years.

The universe had to close the door on me to make me realize that I had to go a new way, otherwise I would not be able to send the system out into the world on the large scale that was necessary. The seeming crisis with the Polaroid film shutting down was actually a gift in disguise. I was always being gifted and guided, but I had got myself into a real flap. I can laugh now, though it was not funny then.

Today I know that grace is always present. I hope I can remember that all the time.

PART III
Return to Love

CHAPTER 9

The Supercoherence Return to Love Frequencies (SRTLFs)

'Someday, after mastering the winds, the waves, the tides and gravity, we shall harness for God the energies of love, and then, for a second time in the history of the world, man will have discovered fire'.

—Pierre Teilhard de Chardin

S O NOW I was using the zero-point alignment process with the photo of the Divine Mother and two particular frequencies. These new frequencies were a combination of the zero-point frequencies and two other frequencies. I called them the Supercoherence Return to Love Frequencies (SRTLFs), because they reconfigured, recalibrated and realigned the human energy system, with a quality of precision, to supercoherence, coherence plus something more, a parameter of super function. They aligned the human energy system with the frequency of unconditional love as symbolized by the Divine Mother image, essentially, they returned the human energy system to love. All trauma, all suffering, dissolves at the speed of light when the human energy system is realigned with love in its purest form.

At this point I thought we were 100 per cent certain of getting 100 per cent result 100 per cent of the time. But I was still only 99.9 per cent of the way there, as I was to discover a while later.

A lovely young woman, well educated, highly qualified but unhappy, came for an assessment. Again I had a shock: I went through all the steps and she held the Divine Mother image with the SRTLFs, but we could not achieve a clear coherent photo with a particular challenge.

Again there was an inspiration from my seventh sense. I asked her to make a verbal statement while holding the SRTLFs and the Divine Mother image. We had used the statement or affirmation method over many years and had seen the power of a simple statement to create coherence. That statement was 'I love and accept myself exactly as I am.'

That was it. Her image became coherent.

And the rest, as they say, is history. The circle had finally closed. Love and self-acceptance at this deep level are the golden keys to happiness and function.

Caroline m → self esteem

Instruments of Grace

The Supercoherence Return to Love Frequencies are instruments of grace – the grace of the divine, granted to us so that we may understand our true nature: that we are all-encompassing love. They are primarily a consciousness technology and a tool for transformation. They are also a twenty-first century tool for efficient life-force energy management.

They are now presented in the form of light-energy-information encodings encased in glass using a specialized proprietary technique. A simple way to understand them is to compare them to a CD or DVD, which are also encodings of light and information. With a CD, if you cannot see the title, you cannot know the music it has recorded on it until you play it on a CD player. Is it a Beethoven sonata or the Beatles? Whatever it is, it is encoded information. We are surrounded by coded information; it is another form of language.

The primary purpose of the SRTLFs is to restore supercoherence in our bio-light field. Supercoherence, our seventh sense, operates outside the boundaries of the rational mind, the intuition, emotions and five-sensory reality. It is the realm of total knowledge and super-function that exists at all times in every one of us. It is the part of us, the master controller, that coordinates the activities of our 50 trillion cells, informing each one what to do in every second of our waking and sleeping existence, keeping our miraculous bodymind in optimal function.

The SRTLFs are calibrated to the zero field of the Luminator and the high frequency of the Divine Mother, which we know dissolves incoherent emotional information from the human energy field. I call them instruments of grace because there is no effort and struggle involved in using them to restore ourselves to supercoherence, regardless of past pain and trauma. They restore the source code of intelligence and love simply for the asking.

The term 'source code' originally comes from the world of computers. In the context of this book the phrase kept popping into my head and would not go away, so I decided to look into the origin of the term. I went to the great god Google to find out and it turns out that the source code is software:

'A computer is a machine which essentially consists of a lot of on/off switches.

In order to make these switches do something useful, [the programmer of the software has] to plan out which switches to turn on and in what order. This is where the ones (as in the numeral 1) and zeros (bits) come in. This binary language of ones and zeros is called "machine code" because they tell the machine which switches to turn on or off.

As software got more complicated, this machine code got longer and longer. Today's software programs are constructed of billions of bits!

To make really complicated software, it is much more effective for the programmer to write the program in a high-level language. The code which is written in this high level language is called the "source code". Then another program (a compiler) translates this source code into machine code of 1s and 0s.'[12]

The 'machine code' for computers bears a striking resemblance to the genetic code for humans. As I understand it, the human genetic code is not the source code – there is another code further up the chain which informs each gene when to turn itself on or off. This source code is programmed by the creative super-intelligence. It runs our body-mind-soul system and our life.

Ask yourself what sort of program would be needed to run a complex non-linear system of 50 trillion cells? How many billion trillion bits would be needed to instruct each cell what to do to keep a person fully functioning? How complex is a human in comparison with the most sophisticated and advanced software program?

So at one level our source code would seem to stretch into infinity and be unknowable. However, the new revelation is that the central key to decode the human source code is love and grace through the portal of zero. This is all that is needed. No begging or bargaining for forgiveness, no prayers or entreaties, no sacrifice – simply the flow of grace. Grace does not have to be earned, cannot be demanded; it is simply present and available at all times. The SRTLFs open that closed door in our being and allow its exquisite presence to be felt in the magic that unfolds.

Tools of Transition

In my understanding the SRTLFs are tools of transition. On a global level, we are facing a major transition and exponential rates of change, and reconnection to love and clarity is of vital importance. I don't think we will need the SRTLFs 100 years from now. As more and more of us become coherent in this precise way and humanity enters the golden age of the possible universal human, they will not be necessary anymore. But for now and for the foreseeable future I see the SRTLFs as vital tools for accessing clear perception and restoring optimal function to ensure both survival and success.

I believe the main reason for the SRTLFs being on the Earth plane is to break the cycle of human suffering. However, on an everyday level they are being used in many different ways and for many other reasons.

As I mentioned before, they are a tool for efficient life-force energy management. They contain non-Hertzian frequencies that bring us into optimal balance and align us with the zero-point field and other frequencies that connect us with the heart centre. They do not contain any chemical substances or anything that is measurable by traditional scientific instruments or methodologies.

The SRTLFs are immutable. They are not affected by heat, X-rays, radiation or a person's energy field – they will hold their own frequency regardless of what is or is not in the energy field of the user. They can be used by many different people without the need for cleansing or reprogramming, unlike crystals.

Getting Started

The pink (drop) and green (round) Supercoherence Return to Love frequencies form a pair and must be used at the same time. They are side sensitive, which means that they need to be held or carried in the correct hand or pocket. The pink SRTLF is to be held or carried on the left side and the green SRTLF is to be held or carried on the right side.

As an **everyday practice** you can hold or carry the SRTLFs (green on the right, pink on the left) every morning for 20 minutes. In the evening, at the end of the day, use them reversed (pink on the right, green on the left) for about ten minutes. You may increase the time gradually over a period of weeks.

It is beneficial to use them every day because as we live in times of great and unrelenting change, stress levels are reaching breaking point for a lot of us. Illness, burnout or constant anxiety can be the result as we seek to cope with the demands that life makes on us. As the stress levels have no easy way of discharging or lessening, they take their toll, resulting in a slow, cumulative, insidious loss of function. How do you feel at the end of a long day at the office, after a commute, when you come home and face the demands of your family? How do you feel at the end of the week, at the end of the month? How do you unwind? It's not so easy. Using television or alcohol as an anaesthetic is common, but these are simply coping mechanisms which will not give the result you would like. In contrast, using the SRTLFs reversed for ten minutes can take away your tiredness and give you access to calm, clear energy and vitality to enjoy the rest of the day. You will feel the cares of the day simply melt away as your system unwinds and hits zero.

There are huge benefits in following this simple effortless practice. When your energy system accesses zero in this way, stress is not allowed to build up. This is one way to keep well, as your system has a chance to repair itself every day. There are enough studies that tell us that long-term stress is a killer. The unfortunate thing is if you do not pay attention to your stress levels on an ongoing basis and do not know how to neutralize them, they will keep mounting slowly – or not so slowly – and suddenly, when the system can take no more, it tips into the chaos of dysfunction, disease or depression.

The following case study by Supercoherence practitioner Jane Cook illustrates what can happen with the build-up of daily stress:

DH, a 44-year-old man, runs his own business. Although it is steadily expanding, there is a lot of pressure and work to do. He began having headaches and pain behind the eyes, which led to lack of sleep and tension in his neck. He thought of acupuncture, but my friend told him to call me and see if my new method could help. He came when he had the headache. We turned on some relaxing music and I gave him the SRTLFs. I left him alone. After 30 minutes he came out saying he felt great, all the pain had gone and he actually felt he had more energy. He has come weekly now for five weeks. In that time he has not suffered the headaches or the pain behind the eyes or the neck pain and is coping with the workload and having his three children at home through the summer holidays – an extra strain. We are trying once-a-fortnight visits now, as he is reluctant to give them up completely.

Of course he would do better if he got himself a set of SRTLFs and used them every day.

Using the SRTLFs daily also allows us to use our life-force energy efficiently, as our energy system learns to remain coherent and operate close to zero, the point of optimal function. Because it is coherent, we are more aware and will feel discomfort more quickly and therefore be able to address it before it starts to build up to unmanageable proportions.

Clearing the Imprint of the Past

One of the first things to use the SRTLFs for is to clear the imprint of your past. The process is powerful and works for everyone. (See Plate 1)

Clearing your Family Relationships

Take out your family photos. It is important to have separate ones of your father and mother, of your brothers and sisters and of yourself as a baby.

You should also have one of your parents together. It is good if you also have a single photo of your whole family when you were a child or a teenager. This is a good starting-point.

If you do not have your parents' photographs, you may write their full names on a piece of a paper and use them instead. If you do not know who your parents were, please write a note which says "my biological mother this lifetime" or "my biological father this lifetime" (*See Plate 9*)

Please do this process even if a parent or other family member has passed on.

Even though you may have other relationships which may be challenging right now, it is better to clear the family timeline as far back as possible. You can clear your energetic relationship with anyone using this process, but do the family first.

All steps should be done on both sides – the right side/hand and then the left side/hand.

We have found through testing with VRIC imaging that holding the Divine Mother photograph along with the SRTLFs softens, strengthens and enhances the effectiveness of this process.

- Hold the green SRTLF in your right hand and the pink SRTLF in your left hand.
- Take each photo of your family members in turn and hold it, along with the photo of the Divine Mother and the SRTLFs, for five to ten minutes on either side. After this please hold the photo in both hands while still holding the SRTLFs and the Divine Mother image. The final step after this is to make the affirmation "I love and accept myself exactly as I am and I love and accept (name of the person whose photo you are working with) exactly as s/he is.
- Repeat this process with the photos of everyone in your family. Do the same with the photo of the whole family.

Clearing Other Relationships

If there is someone with whom you have had a particularly difficult relationship, make a special effort to get their photo. Alternately you can write their name on a note. *(Look at Plate 9)*

- Hold it first in one hand for ten minutes and then in the other hand for ten minutes and finally hold bringing both hands together. The final step after this is to make the affirmation "I love and accept myself exactly as I am and I love and accept (name of the person whose photo you are working with) exactly as s/he is.

You may choose to work with someone you have or have had issues with or people you love and want to connect with or send loving energy, thoughts or attention to. It does not matter whether the person is physically close by or not, or even if they have passed on, the process still works. It will give you freedom from the present or past pain and this will be of immense benefit to you giving you renewed energy and hope. *(See Plate 9)*

You can enhance the results by your conscious participation in the following ways:

Affirmations

Whilst holding the pink SRTLF in your left hand and the green SRTLF in your right hand, you can make any affirmation that you choose. It is best to say it out loud (although not necessarily loudly!) and repeat it a few times.

Some suggestions:

- 'I feel calm/strong/centred/joyful/hopeful, etc.'
- The statement we have tested the most and found extremely effective is: 'I love and accept myself exactly as I am.'
- Also, 'I love and accept [the person you are having the challenge with] exactly as s/he is.' (If you can't bring yourself to say 'love', simply say 'accept' and hold the frequencies until the feeling changes, as it will.)
- Another important affirmation, especially when things are going 'wrong' (courtesy of James Wong) is to simply say your name followed by "All is well".

- You may also use any other affirmation that is right for you at the time,
- Just make sure you are holding the SRTLFs.

Calming Emotional Distress *(See Plates 8, 8a, 8b)*

Hold the SRTLFs in your hands (rather than just carrying them) and make a statement, for example 'I feel calm/relaxed/centred' or 'Even though I feel fearful/anxious/upset, etc., I still totally and completely accept myself.'

In particularly stressful circumstances, you may choose to reverse the SRTLFs (i.e. hold the green one in the left hand and the pink one in the right hand) until you feel calmer and more stable. After that, please put them back in the usual configuration, i.e. pink on the left and green on the right.

In case of extreme distress or emotional crisis, use only the green SRTLF in the left hand until you feel more settled.

Verification with VRIC Imaging

When you hold the frequencies or carry them on your person, your bio-light field or light matrix recognizes the information instantly and becomes coherent, neutralizing stress and trauma. This happens at the speed of light. So the job is already done and you do not need to do any-thing else. You may feel nothing, but the job is still done.

We know this because of the many tests that have been carried out using VRIC imaging. VRIC imaging actually gives us an idea of the incomprehensible speed with which the charge around trauma is nullified using the Supercoherence frequencies. We see that if a client simply holds them, along with a photo that formerly made that client incoherent (as shown in a fuzzy VRIC photo), they become coherent (as shown in a clear VRIC photo) in no time *(see plate section 8,8a and 8b)*. This is amazing to witness, as the trauma may have been there for many years, or even many lifetimes. With clients over the years I had found it disturbing that despite years of therapy, healing, meditation and spiritual practices, the imag-ing revealed that the charge around painful emotional events remained present, potent and unresolved. Now there was a way to break free from the invisible prison.

Using the SRTLFs Remotely: The Supercoherence Return to Love Blessing, Soul to Soul Communication

One of the ways we recommend you use the SRTLFs is put them on the photos of people you want to help, to heal, to bless. You can also put them on your own photo. This sounds pretty far out and 'impossible', as there is seemingly no connection between the two persons involved. And what can something as innocuous as putting two little pieces of glass on a photo possibly do? This is the hardest thing for the linear mind to comprehend. My suggestion would be to simply experiment with the SRTLFs and observe the results. You do not have to understand the mechanism of how it works, just as you do not have to know exactly how your computer or your car works, or for that matter how your body works. Just have a go and then decide.

Again, we know this works through loads of experiments with the SRTLFs and VRIC remote imaging, which clearly demonstrate the phenomenon. Often, but not always, this method works better than actually holding the SRTLFs physically. The results are staggering.

This is an extremely useful procedure, because there are many times when a relationship becomes troubled and fractures and it is hard to approach the person concerned. You know that if you do talk to them, they may not understand your pain or your point of view. The discussion can degenerate into an argument and the whole exercise becomes counterproductive. Using the SRTLFs remotely on a photo of your antagonist can break the logjam and clear misunderstanding.

The way I understand it is that the process totally bypasses the personality and speaks directly to the soul. That is why it is so effective. The personality may have flaws and troubles and may not be amenable to discussing and listening, but at the level of the soul there is no resistance. The soul is always pristine and always seeking the best for itself and everyone else. In essence we are speaking in as direct a manner as possible to the supercoherent Self.

The process can also be used when the person(s) you wish to help/

heal/bless is in another country or in another dimension – remember the rules that govern space-time do not apply here.

SRTLF Effects

One of the main effects that people experience when using the SRTLFs is a feeling of calm. Emotional turmoil and extreme trauma are dissipated for no apparent reason. The trauma can be recent or of many years' standing; it makes no difference. The outer circumstances may remain the same, but it is impossible to connect with the painful feelings around the event anymore.

For example, a client who had unexpectedly lost her beloved daughter and was understandably distraught told me that when she held the frequencies, the load of grief and sadness suddenly disappeared and she felt she was going mad, as she could not understand how the painful emotions had gone so unexpectedly.

A lady in her fifties who had had an extremely challenging to non-existent relationship with her mother since childhood described how she was 'freed' from the pain after doing the process once. This was a seasoned practitioner who had done a lot of work and used many modalities but had not gained freedom from her suffering.

As I understand it from my observations, as soon as a person holds the SRTLFs and the image of the Divine Mother, their energy field is reconfigured, recalibrated and reset to zero. It is like pressing a master reset button – the system reverts to its source code at the speed of light. As a result the emotional energy that was locked in the painful event is freed up, made coherent and redirected, and the old information is deleted from the person's 'hard drive'.

As the emotional energy is released and redirected, there is a positive triple whammy. First, the fear and emotional pain around the trauma are gone; secondly, the unconscious non-nourishing belief systems that held that trauma in place are replaced by peace and hope; and finally, most importantly, you gain access to your creativity and joy again. You are free from your invisible prison and can taste the sweetness of freedom – your life is truly yours.

Tools of Wholeness – Whole Life Healing

So, what will it do for you? What results can you expect? Will the SRTLFs cure your backache, your cough, your... whatever?

You are an infinitely complex configuration of energy – soul, mind, body, emotions and spirit. All these different aspects are interconnected and in a constant never-ending state of flux and flow. Each aspect continuously interacts with all the other aspects, exchanging information and creating change at every level all the time. And your whole is much greater than the sum of your constituent parts – that is the model of understanding that underpins the Supercoherence system. So there are no 'typical' results and no statistics.

Two important words to remember are 'non-linear' and 'multi-factorial', in the sense that there is no one so-called root cause which, if identified, will fix a problem, there are always multiple complex factors in the creation of any circumstance, whether it be physical illness or some other challenge. The universe does not work in a linear way, however much we would like it to do so. So in this system we do not aim to 'cure' 'disease', nor do we offer any 'treatment'. This is *not* a therapy, though it can and is used by therapists. That language belongs to an older, different and more limited paradigm. Please understand that clearly when you engage with this system.

What I know through the imaging and the experiments is what the SRTLFs do for everyone – they restore the energy system to its original source code, to the intelligence of love in its total and purest form. They return you to love. That is the Supercoherence master alignment. How that manifests will be different for each person. Each of us is a soul on a journey, and that journey is unique.

So you can understand why I say that the Supercoherence system does not address symptoms directly or specifically and therefore does not promise or guarantee 'cures' and should not be considered a 'treatment' or a therapy. You may consider it an activation or an initiation, a rite of passage to being a Universal human. It is a new way of seeing and being.

However, while I cannot say what specifically will change for you when you use the SRTLFs, know for sure that changes will occur, sometimes immediately and sometimes a while later and that they will always be in the direction of order or coherence. They may be unbelievable, unpredictable, incomprehensible, sometimes seemingly uncomfortable and sometimes incredible. What happens will depend on what your soul considers you need and not what you think should happen or what you want to happen. Your soul and personality may have very different agendas and needs, and can often be in conflict. When this happens, the soul's agenda will always prevail. However, the good news is that as your system becomes more coherent or aligned, the needs, wants and desires of the personality and the soul will no longer be conflicted and fragmented and pulling in different directions, so your dreams and wishes can come true as the magic of supercoherence unfolds in your life. Treat it as an exploration and an adventure and the results may very well surprise and delight you.

**Plate 1 Clearing the Past Imprint that Time has not Healed –
With the Supercoherence Return to Love Frequencies (SRTLFs)**

Holding photo of self at 9 years old - Incoherent

Holding photo of self at 9 years + SRTLFs and the Divine Mother image
- Coherent

Plate 2 - The Disconnection and the Supercoherence Return to Love Frequencies (SRTLFs)
Lethal Hidden Information Fragments the Field and Your Life
What You Can't See and Don't Know Can Hurt You – or Heal You

Male Frequency in the field - Incoherent

Male Frequency in the field and holding SRTLFs Coherent- Challenge Cleared

Plate 2a -The Disconnection and the Supercoherence Return to Love Frequencies (SRTLFs)
The Master Reset Connection to the Source Code of the Infinite Human
Breaking the Millennial Cycle of Human Suffering

Female Frequency in the field - Incoherent

Female Frequency in the field - Holding SRTLFs - Coherent - Challenge Cleared

Plate 2b
The Disconnection and the Supercoherence Return to Love Frequencies (SRTLFs)
Lethal Hidden Information Fragments the Field and Your Life
What You Can't See and Don't Know Can Hurt You – or Heal You

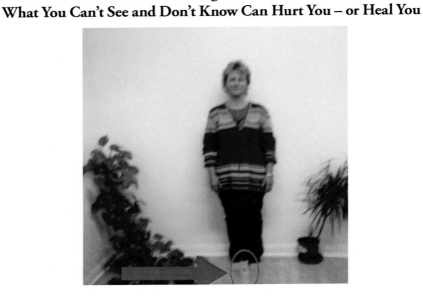

Female Frequency in the field - Very Incoherent

Female Frequency in the field holding SRTLFs - Coherent - Challenge Cleared

Plate 2c - The Disconnection

Male Frequency in the field - Very Incoherent

Male Frequency in the field holding SRTLFs - Coherent - Challenge
Cleared

Plate 3
The Zero Point Alignment with the Supercoherence Return to Love Frequencies (SRTLFs)
Entering the Mysterious Miraculous Portal of Zero
Direct Systematic Access to the Zero Point Field of All Possibilities - and Beyond

Left Eye Closed

Right Eye Closed - holding SRTLFs
- Coherent

Right Eye Closed - Incoherent

Plate 3a
The Zero Point Alignment with the Supercoherence Return to Love Frequencies (SRTLFs)
Restoring Coherence to the Central Point of Perception
Conflict to Clarity – Uniting the Divided Self

Left Eye Closed - Incoherent

Right Eye Closed

Left Eye Closed + holding SRTLFs
- Coherent

Plate 4
Healing the Feminine Line with the Supercoherence Return to Love Frequencies (SRTLFs)

Holding Mother's photo - Incoherent

Holding Mother's photo + SRTLFs and Divine Mother image - Coherent

Plate 5
Letting Go of Past Emotional Pain of Failed Marriage and Divorce with the Supercoherence Return to Love Frequencies (SRTLFs) Hurt and Anger Dissolved and Replaced with Forgiveness and Kindness
– No Effort Involved

With daughters and photo of estranged ex-husband - Incoherent

With daughters and photo of ex-husband + mother holding SRTLFs - Coherent "It's magic" she said.

Plate 6
The Suffering of the Parents Picked Up by the Children Neutralised with the Supercoherence Return to Love Frequencies (SRTLFs)

Holding photo of estranged parents - Incoherent

With photo of parents + SRTLFs + Divine Mother image - Coherent

Plate 7
Chaos of Family Dynamics Neutralised with the Supercoherence Return To Love Frequencies (SRTLFs)

With Family, ex-Wife and Girlfriend - Incoherent

Family, ex-Wife and Girlfriend + Divine Mother and SRTLFs - Coherent

Plate 8
From Crisis to Coherence at the Speed of Light
with the Supercoherence Return to Love Frequencies (SRTLFs)
Part 1 of 3

Holding Father's photo - Incoherent

She was pregnant with her first child. Her beloved father had been diagnosed with terminal cancer and her mother was in huge distress. Altogether a very distressing situation and she was feeling and bearing the brunt of it. She was also worried about the effect of all this emotional pain and worry on her unborn child. She lives in London and her parents lived elsewhere in Europe. She has always been a very loving and caring daughter. The images showed her in clear and exact terms the effect of what she was experiencing and what would restore peace and acceptance."

With Father's photo +SRTLFs + Divine Mother image + verbal statement "I love and accept my Father exactly as he is and I love and accept myself exactly as I am" - Coherent

Plate 8a
Emotional Turmoil to Tranquillity
with the Supercoherence Return to Love Frequencies (SRTLFs)
Fear Worry and Sadness to Peace Acceptance and
Understanding
Part 2 of 3

Holding Mother's photo - Incoherent

With mother's photo +SRTLFs and Divine Mother image + verbal
Statement "My Mother is strong and capable of looking after herself"
- Coherent

PLATE 8b
Fear Worry and Sadness to Peace Acceptance and Understanding
with the Supercoherence Return to Love Frequencies (SRTLFs)
Part 3 of 3

Holding photo of parents - Incoherent

Holding photo of parents with SRTLF + Divine Mother image
- Coherent

PLATE 9
What's In A Name?
A Name contains the Coded Energy Signature of the Person
Total Knowledge-Information of that Being

Holding boyfriend's name in left hand - Incoherent

Holding boyfriend's name in left hand + SRTLF + Divine Mother image
- Coherent

PLATE 10
Supercoherence Panic to Calm Frequency
Fear and Panic to Calm, Clarity and Confidence
Holding Your Nerve and Holding Your Ground

Holding legal papers - "I feel panicky" - Incoherent

Holding same legal papers + Supercoherence Panic to Calm Frequency
- Coherent

CHAPTER 10

The SRTLFs: The Acid Test

'The proof of the pudding is in the eating.'

Proverb

T HE TIME FOR experiments was over. Now it was time for the acid test. Would the SRTLFs work in the real world without the Luminator and VRIC imaging that we had relied on since October 1995? Would these two little frequency carriers fulfill the promise they had shown in the imaging? Would they restore the human energy system to its central point of super-function, to the central and fundamental understanding that its true nature was love beyond reason, beyond right or wrong? Did we have a real opportunity to break the millennial old cycle of suffering?

We had seen during the imaging over the past months that the SRTLFs and the photo of the Divine Mother neutralized trauma in the human energy field at the speed of light. How would this manifest in the laboratory of life? It was crunch time.

The SRTLFs were first introduced to the world on 18 September 2009 at a small select seminar of 70 persons. The seminar was only open to my Biolumanetics clients and readers of my first book. People came from France, Ireland, Holland, Sweden and the UK. I was delighted and honoured. The seminar was successful, and out of the 70 persons present 67 acquired one or more sets of the SRTLFs.

I was very pleased. In one sense I had fulfilled a major life task that my soul had taken on, which was to send this system out into the world. I was not needed in the same way as before. I was to some extent redundant. The system would survive without my physical presence. It was now free to fly and do what it was meant to do. Anyone anywhere could access the state of supercoherence just by holding two magical little pieces of glass for a few minutes. It was not limited anymore.

The SRTLFs have now gone out largely through word of mouth in an organic way, which is what I wanted. I truly believe in the concept of 'no force' except the elegant forces of desire, gentleness and intelligence.

Since the system went out into the world in September 2009 there are SRTLF users and enthusiasts in Sweden, Ireland, India, Japan, Germany, Italy, Malaysia, Singapore, Hong Kong, South Africa, Australia, New Zealand, Brazil, Spain, France, Ghana, Indonesia, Costa Rica, Latvia, Estonia, Taiwan, the US and of course the UK. The seeds of the Supercoherence system have been planted and will continue to grow and flower and spread their silent beneficent message.

Feedback for the SRTLFs

These case studies illustrate what happens when you use these new tools. There are more examples in the following chapters. You will notice that each is unique yet the thread of grace runs through all of them. There are many dramatic examples of long-damaged relationships healing with no effort; old hurts and traumas being neutralized; long-standing, deeply engrained and unyielding patterns of impatience, anger, intolerance and distrust being reversed and replaced with serenity, tolerance, gentleness and loving kindness. And all this happens simply by holding two little magic pieces of glass for a few minutes each day on an ongoing basis.

There have been many reports of beneficial physical changes as well, some of them extremely dramatic. I have purposely not included those case studies for obvious reasons.

All these miracles have happened as a result of re-establishing coherence – or rather supercoherence – in the human energy system.

LU (Sweden)

I don't know if I can call my relationship with my sister an almost impossible project, but it has certainly felt that way... When growing up we had a hard time with each other, so I wasn't surprised when it ended totally after our mother died. I put the SRTLFs on her photo twice and since then... she has phoned me, she has invited me for dinner and she even phoned and congratulated me on my birthday, which hasn't happened in four years. Actually we didn't speak in those years at all. Now even my father's son from a previous marriage seems to want to keep in touch. Amazing!

SW (Sweden)

Here is a story about me and my daughter. After telling me everything I did wrong during her upbringing, she didn't speak to me at all for about six months. In that time she gave birth to a little daughter, whom I was not allowed to see.

A while ago I used the frequencies with the intention of having a 'loving and mature' relationship with my daughter.

A couple of weeks ago she called me and asked me over for lunch and now I have been to her house twice and have been served a very good lunch and had a good time with both my daughter and little granddaughter, who is now nine weeks old. And now everything is fine between us.

WP

I have at last finished clearing all previous imprints, first from myself then from my family. It has taken a while as I have a large extended family. I am now feeling good despite starting divorce proceedings due to my husband's adultery. Six weeks ago, at the bottom of the abyss, I would not have believed I could progress so far in such a short space of time. It is truly miraculous! I feel stronger and more confident, balanced, grounded, am walking taller, my head and my heart are no longer in conflict, good things are beginning to happen and my needs are being met on many levels. Friends and family are amazed at how well I am doing and how well I look. If you follow the right steps, this healing system really works!

Julie P.

Last year was a tough year for us financially and emotionally. We came very close to having to rent out our lovely home in order to survive.

My husband, Mike, wrote down a wish list for his ideal job:

To work mainly from home.

To work with an ethical product.

To have the opportunity to use my light aircraft licence to commute and attend meetings.

To earn the same or more than in my previous job.

To work with good people

To have the opportunity to sometimes work abroad.

To enjoy it.

We both held the wish list with the SRTLFs and placed them on the job description. I am happy to say that he now has that job and it meets his requests.

I lost both of my horses through illness and old age and spent two years without a horse, partly due to finances and mainly because the death of one of my horses was so traumatic that I never wanted to go through that again. I told friends and family I would never have another horse.

I started to hold the SRTLFs and photos of my horses – all sorts of photos, some of me competing and some of me just with them. I now have a beautiful horse and have two rescue ponies – a complete turnaround.

A 20-year-old Overcomes Major Tragedy

Six months back the daughter of this woman committed suicide, and her older grandson, who was 20 at the time, found the body. As a result of this trauma and tragedy, he completely shut down – he would not communicate with anybody, would not sleep at night and basically became unreachable. He was deeply disturbed, justifiably so.

The grandmother was at her wits' end and not really sure how to proceed. She got a set of SRTLFs and I suggested that she put them and the Divine Mother image on the young man's photo. I was not sure, given the way he was, that he would be amenable to holding them. His grandmother later told me that he did hold them once. I also told her to put them on the photo of her departed daughter, which she did not do.

Within seven days of having the SRTLFs and Divine Mother image put on his photo, there was a remarkable turnaround in the young man. He woke up, literally and figuratively, and decided he was going on holiday with his friends. The wonder of it was that he phoned home every day from that holiday and said, 'How is everybody? I am missing home.'

This was a radical shift from not communicating with anyone, and all in the space of a few days. Just by having two little magical pieces of glass placed on a photograph and holding them once, there was a complete flip. In this sweet, gentle and extremely loving way, this young man's suffering was lifted and his life put on a different trajectory where hope, function and even fun were possible again. It was a very beautiful act of grace.

Roshni

I met Roshni through a very dear old friend in India. She came from a wealthy industrialist family and had a son and a daughter and several grand-children. She appeared very well adjusted and was soft-spoken and gentle. I was surprised when she told me that she wanted an assessment.

I asked her what she wanted out of the process. She told me that her relationship with her son was extremely difficult. For whatever reason, he was always rude and angry with her and the atmosphere in the house was not good. They lived together, as often happens in India with the joint fam-ily system, and she said she was doing everything to help him in a busi-ness he had started, but no matter what she did, she got no thanks, only unpleasantness. What she most wanted was her relationship with her son to be a loving one.

Roshni had a strong spiritual practice, had a guru whom she had fol-lowed faithfully for many years, did meditation, *puja* (religious rituals) and prayers, and of course consulted astrologers. None of this had made the slightest difference to her relationship with her son.

I asked her to send me individual photos of her family members and a large photo of herself and I did a remote VRIC imaging session for her in London.

The first imaging session revealed that the greatest challenge was not with her son but with her husband. There was a challenge with her son as well, but this time around it was the lesser one. We neutralized the challenge using the zero-point alignment process and the Divine Mother image. I also sent her the frequencies with instructions on how to use them.

We kept in touch by phone. After the session there was a huge explosion in the family. Her husband, who had been suffering silently, burst out with the possibility of the two families not living together anymore. However something strange happened. Some days after this event her son came to her and said, 'Mum, you and I are different and I accept that you can be different.' That was a huge breakthrough. Things improved.

Then there was a blip. Her daughter, who lived in the US, came for a visit and the relationship with her son went wonky again. She told me this and asked what she should do. I did another assessment and sure enough this time the energetic challenge revealed by the imaging was with her son.

This time I recommended that she put the frequencies along with the Divine Mother photo on his photograph.

Some while later, something miraculous happened: she was going out to a party with her husband and son, and her son commented, 'Mother, you are wearing a beautiful sari!' She was taken aback, as he had not paid her a compliment in a very long time. They went to the party and later her son dropped his parents back at home and returned to the party on his own. On the way he phoned his father on his mobile: 'Please tell Mother I don't hate her, I love her!'

Since that time the anger has disappeared, the relationship has healed and a year later it seems to be holding up well. I know this because the mutual friend who introduced me to Roshni reported that when he went to visit the family he could not believe the changed atmosphere in the house. Where there had been a lot of unspoken anger now there was happiness and harmony.

All this from putting two little frequency tools containing light-energy-information on a photo, combined with the wish to love and be loved. Magic, mystery, miracle!

Remote Family Healing and the SRTLFs

Krysia is a very sweet and loving soul. She lives in London with her husband but comes from Poland. Her parents and brother live there. She does not have a particularly friendly relationship with her brother. At a gathering of the SRTLF users in April 2010, I asked her about it. English is not her first language, but she has a good go and has come a long way in her proficiency, so I have not corrected her English here in the interest of authenticity:

'He has problem with alcohol and he is aggressive because of this. And I put these frequencies [SRTLFs] three weeks ago and I don't have his current photo and I put on a piece of paper on which I wrote his name and surname. And when I spoke to my father and I asked what happened during the Easter because every Easter, Christmas, there is problem. He comes to visit them or not and they would quarrel and he left. And this time my father said he came and he stayed with them for five hours, no arguments.'

A word of caution: You cannot use the SRTLFs to manipulate people for your benefit or to influence them to change their 'bad' habits. Use them simply as a blessing and leave the outcome in bigger hands. You will get the best results that way.

So try it on photographs – it works magic. Sounds a bit crazy, but we are talking of a different model of the universe and you will be surprised how it works.

The Divine Mother Image Controversy

The Divine Mother image is an integral part of the Supercoherence system. However, there has been a very mixed response to the image. Many people love it and are very happy to use it with the SRTLFs, while others find it extremely challenging and flatly refuse to use it. Those who are anti-religion and see the image as a religious symbol dismiss it entirely and simply refuse to hold it. Also, people who are orthodox followers of other religions sometimes do not wish to use the image. I was advised by many not to include it in the kit.

People have questioned why it is necessary to use the image at all. And why *this* image? Why not the image of Tara, the Tibetan goddess of compassion, or Kwan Yin, the goddess of compassion in the Chinese wisdom tradition, or Saraswati, the Indian goddess of wisdom, or Laxmi, the goddess of wealth, and so on and on and on. An accusation has been that I have not tested the Supercoherence process with the images of other goddesses and therefore it is unscientific and not worthy in some way.

This is my answer to these objections: I follow no religious practice and have not done so since my teens. I have not had any 'holy' pictures in my wallet or on the walls of my home and did not intend to ever have any. Today I have the Divine Mother picture in my living room not because it is holy (in my current understanding the whole universe is holy), but because I have tested the effects this picture has through VRIC imaging and recognize it as a high frequency photo. In simple terms, I feel good when I see the face and connect with it. I give the woman no name except the Divine Mother and for me she is simply the embodiment of the sacred feminine principle which is present in each one of us.

Why did I not test the process with the other goddess images? Simply because I did not feel the need to do it. My only reason for doing the experiment with the Divine Mother image in the first place was to determine what this particular image would do when combined with the zero-point alignment frequencies. That was all. When I found that along with the SRTLFs it cleared all trauma from the field of everyone who went through the testing process, including non-believers and atheists, that was enough. It did the job it was meant to better than I could ever have foreseen, so why would I want to go on testing the process with other goddess images? It was far more important to get the information out than go on endlessly testing, when the job had already been done.

What we also found through the VRIC imaging was that when the SRTLFs did not clear the charge around an event or a person, simply adding the image of the Divine Mother (either holding it or putting it on a photo) did the job.

So this is my suggestion to you: if you have a problem using the image, just look at the woman without giving her a name and sense what feelings she evokes in you. Do you see the gentleness, the sweetness, the serenity and the strength or do you not? What do you feel?

There is one other experiment I would recommend. I have done this myself and it works for me every time. When you are upset with someone, just sit and hold the SRTLFs and the image for a few minutes and monitor your response. Do not analyze the challenging situation or try to resolve it consciously, just let the grace of the process unfold for you. You will find your upset simply dissipates with no effort and for no reason and you are free to function again without the emotions that disturbed you just a few minutes before. Peace, clarity, understanding and acceptance will be available to you again. If you wish, try using only the SRTLFs first and then add the image and see if you feel the difference. Do this simply as an experiment. Put aside whatever preconceptions you have for a while and see if the process works for you.

If you absolutely cannot bear to use the image, then do not use it, but know that you will miss out on the full benefit of the process. In this instance, it is truly a case of the whole being greater than the sum of the parts.

CHAPTER 11
SRTLFs in Practice

'Today we are faced with the pre-eminent fact that, if civilization is to survive, we must cultivate the science of human relationships.'

Franklin D. Roosevelt

ALL THE CASE studies, except mine, in this chapter come from practitioners of the Supercoherence program. Not a single one had access to the Luminator or VRIC imaging: the results were achieved solely with the use of the SRTLFs. Note that the SRTLFs are universal in their application and are effective regardless of the different cultures, traditions, education or belief systems of the users.

These case studies illustrate the practical results that can be obtained by using the Supercoherence frequency tools. For me personally, the big picture, the 'nearly impossible project' of breaking the millennial old human cycle of suffering by restoring happiness, love and function, is the primary purpose for this system on Earth. Everything else is incidental. However, I also understand that practical results in the 'real' world also lessen suffering on Earth. This is in line with the primary purpose of the system.

SUPERCOHERENCE – THE RETURN TO LOVE

SRTLFs: Clearing Toxic Relationships

Some of us find ourselves in relationships that are non-nourishing to the point of being toxic. Even though we may know this to be the case, for whatever unconscious reason we find ourselves unable to get out of the clutches of this self-imposed suffering. Looking from the outside, it is easy to say, 'Nonsense. They can end it if they wish to. Nobody has tied their hands or put a chain around them.' But in my view there is more to this scenario than meets the eye. Sometimes there are unresolved karmic ties or a fatal attraction that keeps us magnetized to some quality in the person who will end up destroying us. There seems to be a quality of helplessness that prevents us ending something that is patently not in our best interest.

The SRTLFs will sever those unfortunate ties mercilessly and fast, because as our system is reset to zero, old imprints of unresolved suffering are neutralized. Our system's super intelligence is restored or reconnected, and the old unintelligent dynamic becomes impossible to hold in place. We will not find that person attractive anymore and the invisible chains that bind us will simply fall away, leaving us free to find our heart's true desire.

Jenny H.

I had been in a very difficult relationship for eight years. I loved my partner very much, but he constantly upset me and was very selfish! I later found out that he probably suffered from narcissistic personality disorder. I had not heard of this condition before and when I read about it, I immediately realized why I had had such a tough time with this man!

During this stormy relationship, I had monthly sessions with Thrity. This was when she was still using the imaging. She said to me that I really needed to separate from this man and get on with my life. I knew deep down that she was right, but the reality was I still could not give him up. I loved him too much. I felt so strong when I left after each appointment and found I was able to cope a lot better with the situation, but I could not end the relationship!

I was one of the first people to use the SRTLFs. They were wonderful and soon I made the decision to end the relationship that was wrecking my life! I'm not saying it was easy – I still felt all the pain associated with a relationship break-up, but somehow this time (I had tried before, but failed) I found the strength to make it final and have a fresh start in life. I used my SRTLFs morning and night and I found that it was possible to cope with the emotions while using the frequencies.

I think I would still be floundering in that destructive relationship now if I hadn't been fortunate enough to have my beloved frequencies. They feel like my trusted friends; I never go away without them. I do have days now when I may not use them at all, but they are always there for me to pick up if I have any emotions that are hard to cope with.

JG

I was first introduced to the Supercoherence Return to Love process by Dr. Tony Coope during a consultation in September 2010. I was suffering with endometriosis, which was the symptom of a hormone imbalance that I believed was connected to the ME that I had been diagnosed with in 2003. In the seven years since that diagnosis I had undertaken various holistic therapies. For the most part my health was very good, but the problem of the monthly pain was still there.

Tony explained to me how a number of his female patients who had suffered with endometriosis had also experienced a highly emotional event connected to their femininity either during puberty or at some point in their earlier years. I was fortunate enough not to have experienced any-thing as traumatic as a rape or sexual assault, but I had been involved in a fairly abusive relationship with a previous boyfriend which had left me with some definite negative emotions connected to my femininity. It was at this point that Tony mentioned the Supercoherence Return to Love process. We did not consider it an immediate option, but the thought of being able to remove all negative feelings towards a previous relationship (or indeed a current one) stayed with me and after a few weeks I decided to ask Tony more about it.

The first thing that I did when I received the kit was to dig out some old family photos and some photos of myself with Nick, the boyfriend I had had the particularly difficult relationship with. I followed the instruc-tions provided and held the Divine Mother photo in one hand, a photo of some members of my family in the other hand and the stones [SRTLFs] in the appropriate hands. I followed the instructions and held the photos and the stones in this way for several minutes. During this time I found myself thinking back to how I had felt at the moment that each of these photos had been taken. That in itself was a very cathartic process. I have never really been the type of person who looks back over the past. I don't believe in having regrets and most of my time is spent looking forward and planning for the next thing.

Immediately after the first session I did not feel any great change. In fact I felt quite sick when I looked at the photo of myself with Nick. It had brought up a whole host of memories and emotions that I did not really want to feel or accept, but this in itself made me feel sure that continuing with the process was the right thing to do. From that point on I held the Divine Mother photo and the photo of me and Nick in opposite hands and the crystals [SRTLFs] in the relevant hands for 20 minutes each evening while I watched television. I no longer looked at the photos or even thought about them, I just carried out the process as part of my evening routine. During these 20 minutes I often felt the stones becoming very hot and my hands and arms starting to tingle, but Tony had mentioned to me that this might happen, so I was not at all concerned and just accepted it as part of the healing.

I must admit that for a week or so I did not give much conscious thought to whether the process was having a positive effect or not, until one morning I woke up after having the most amazing dream. In my dream my ex-boyfriend apologized to me for having treated me in the way that he had done. This may not sound like a particularly amazing dream to most people, but for me it was a definite sign that things were starting to shift in the right direction. In the past I had suffered on a fairly regular basis with bad dreams associated with my ex-boyfriend, so this dream meant a lot to me.

I continued with the Supercoherence Return to Love routine every evening for another week or so. Then one morning when I was putting the photos in my bedside drawer, I took a second to look at the photo of me with Nick. It was at that moment that I realized that all of the feelings that I had originally felt when I had looked at the photo had totally gone. I could not actually find an emotion to attach to the image of Nick – it was as though someone had wiped away the bad feelings and had just left a nice clean neutral space. When I had first dug the photo out of my loft and looked at it, I had felt very angry – angry and disgusted that I had allowed someone to treat me that way and ashamed that it had taken me almost two years to pluck up the courage to leave him. Now when I looked at the image of myself over ten years previously, I saw a girl who was very lonely, someone clinging onto a bad relationship because she felt sure that it was better than being alone.

The Supercoherence Return to Love stones had done the job. I must admit that to this day I do not really understand the science behind the process, but all I do know is that it totally, 100 per cent worked for me. My life has changed for the better and I no longer carry around the guilt and shame that I used to. I no longer feel disgusted by the experience I had and I do not feel any hatred towards Nick. The slate has been wiped clean and I am now able to move on with my life.

I cannot be sure of the effect that the process has had on the endometriosis, as I am still receiving other treatments. What I can, however, say is that if you feel that you have unfinished business with a particular individual and you would like to be able to move on but have not yet found a way of doing so, try the process. After all, how difficult is it to hold a couple of SRTLFs and to dig out a few old photos?!

A Relationship That Needed to End

In this case the relationship was not toxic but needed to end. It involved a woman I know very well. Very capable, very kind, caring, helpful and totally reliable, she is altogether a lovely person. She has a high-powered job but is unmarried. At the time she was in her late forties. She met a man on a matchmaking site. A sweet relationship developed via e-mail and later by phone and she found herself head over heels in love. The problem was that he was divorced and lived on another continent. And, once he got to know her better, he told her he wasn't interested in getting married – to anyone – but liked her a lot as a friend.

By this time she was crazy about him. At some point I cautioned her that this relationship was going nowhere and she should let go of it. But she was waiting for the daily e-mail from him and sending him a report of her life every day as well. I could not see a happy ending for this relationship, but she could not let go of it. She travelled thousands of miles to visit him and he was welcoming and kind and gave her a good time, but nothing more. It was obvious that she was fonder of him than he was of her. However, she kept insisting that she was OK with this state of affairs and content with the knowledge that he would not marry her.

This went on for a fair while – it was well over a year, or even two – then out of the blue there was a bombshell. She phoned me one night, distraught and weeping. He had sent her a terse e-mail saying he had fallen in love with someone else and was getting married and could not keep up their relationship. She was devastated, as it was so unexpected.

I love her dearly and the first thing I said to her was, 'The universe has done you a big favour. You could not let go of this relationship which was not good for you, but now the job has been done for you.' This may sound unsympathetic and unkind, but it stopped the out of control weeping and gave her a different perspective. She did not like what I said, but knew I was right because she knew there is no way she would have terminated the relationship. She just could not bear the thought of it. Yet it was not going anywhere and there was no space in her life for anyone else.

I did an assessment for her and fixed her broken heart with the SRTLFs and some handwritten notes.

The result was, in her words: 'Now I can only think of the good times. I don't have any ill will… I have come to that stage where I don't feel any anger, hurt or animosity at all. I just feel that we had a part to play in each other's lives and we have done our bit for each other and we have both moved on.'

In her big-hearted way she celebrated the day of his wedding to someone else by preparing some special dishes that we have on birthdays and weddings. The grief was gone and replaced with peace, acceptance and understanding.

She does not obsess about him anymore and now her life works better than it ever did. What seemed like an unmitigated disaster was a blessing in disguise. It is a coherent universe.

SRTLFs: Parents and 'Difficult' Teenagers

The relationship between parents and teenagers is often fraught with conflict and misunderstanding and the generation gap can be wide. While love is always present, like is often more difficult. Teenagers can be 'rebellious', 'disobedient' and worse, and parents can be 'controlling' and 'impossible' in other ways. Anger, irritation, frustration and mutual distrust can be the unpleasant result. I know this all too well, as I was a very difficult teenager all those decades back. My poor parents had a hard time with me and I with them.

How to break this logjam of misunderstanding?

Dilnaz Gilder: TS

TS is 46 years old. She is a warm, sensitive person with a strong sense of right and wrong. She is in a marriage in which the partners are poles apart. In most such cases, each would have gone their own way a long time ago. However, early on in their married life this couple decided to stick it out together, regardless of their differences. Given the circumstances, TS misses genuine love and togetherness, and life is a compromise.

One day, she borrowed a pair of SRTLFs as she wanted to try them out. The very next day I received a text message saying they were not working and she didn't feel any different. I immediately called her and the first thing she said was that she was feeling happy – no, not happy, but calm. So I asked her to listen to what she had just said, considering that none of the external factors around her had changed. She thought about that and decided to continue using the SRTLFs for a while longer.

She and her husband had always been at loggerheads over the upbringing of their son. In fact, it was one of the main bones of contention in their marriage. She felt her husband was too lenient and indulgent with the boy. In turn, the son felt his mother was too strict.

One evening TS and her husband got home from work and for the first time in several years they ate dinner and watched a movie together at home while their son went out with his friends. At around 11.30 p.m. they received a call from him asking if he could bring some friends over for a drink. Since these were all 14–15-year-old girls and boys, TS of course did not approve, but passed the phone on to her husband to decide on the matter. Surprisingly, the father told his son not to bring his friends home as it was too late at night. When the call ended, TS complimented her husband for handling the issue very well and he said he did not know what made him say no to his son on this particular occasion. As expected, the son returned home not in the best of moods. However, his father sat him down right away and gave him a long talk about what was permitted and what was not at his age. This was also something TS had not expected and it came as a pleasant surprise to her.

When her son was ready for bed, TS went to say goodnight to him. He asked her to stay in the room, so she did, and then quite out of the blue he started talking to her about his friends, where they went and what they did! Needless to say, she was amazed at this outpouring of information from her teenage son, which went on till 4 a.m! Although she went bleary-eyed to work the next day, she felt extremely grateful for this experience.

So, in many ways, it was a breakthrough for all of them.

Later TS started using her SRTLFs on her son whenever he was unwell. He started calling them 'his frequencies' and now feels upset if she even as much as lends them to any of her family members! One amazing thing she has discovered is that each time she uses them on him, once he feels a little better he starts confiding in her and sharing things he never would have told her otherwise. She loves it!

Lotta Naess: UW

UW, a 50-year-old woman, is married and has three children: a daughter of 19 followed by 16-year-old twin boys. The problem was with one of the boys, OW: he was unmanageable from her point of view. He was emotionally closed with the family and was punishing them, and himself, in different ways by being 'unreasonable'. He refused to go to parties and did not participate in family activities. He didn't say goodnight when going to bed; he was aggressive and was only doing things for his own benefit.

He had always got along well with his sister, but now she was distancing herself from him. His twin brother was sick and tired of him, as he had always been pushed around by him.

OW had no problems at school or in other social activities. But at home and when it came to taking the initiative to do things with his friends in his spare time, he didn't function well.

UW was having daily conflicts with OW. He was angry and she would get angry and it would always end up with arguing and shouting. This was unsustainable and she was willing to do anything to solve this huge problem.

I suggested that she start to clear her past with her closest family and then with other people with whom she had had emotional challenges. And that she put the SRTLFs on the family members' names or photos when not using them herself.

Two days later UW called me. She was so optimistic! The very first evening OW had said goodnight when he went to bed, and that was a big thing, since he had not done that for a long time. Then he had accepted her help with his homework. That had only been possible on his terms before. He had also confessed to a 'white lie' when he was late to a lesson in school. When it was time to go to bed that night he had even allowed her to touch him on his back and say goodnight.

I urged her to go to his bedroom and thank him for that day, wish him a good night's sleep and say 'I love you.' UW followed my advice. It wasn't easy for her, but she did it.

When I saw her three months later I found that she had had some huge insights about herself.

First she had felt very sad and cried a lot. She had not even been able to remember when she had last cried. Then suddenly she had realized that her love for her son OW was buried deep down inside her, out of reach. She was terrified! How could it have gone so wrong?

Then by chance, a week after she had wished her son goodnight and told him she loved him, they had been at home alone on the Friday night and she had surprised herself by suggesting that they watch a movie together.

The evening had become extraordinary. They had sat beside each other on the sofa, watched a movie and shared a huge bowl of popcorn. All by themselves.

UW said to me, 'This was a big thing! We didn't even argue about what kind of movie we should see or about who should go out to the kitchen and get the refill of popcorn. And when we were sitting there beside each other I had a glimpse of a feeling deep inside. First I didn't realize what it was, but then I am sure it was love!'

SRTLFs: Mothers and Daughters-in-Law

This case concerns a professional guy, solid, down to earth, very well read and intelligent. When I am in India, I visit him at his office for a catch-up and a chat. He is interested in the work I do. He has the SRTLFs and uses them to keep his system coherent. We were discussing their various uses one day, including putting them on photos, when he confessed, 'You know, Thrity, if anybody else had told me this I would have thought it complete superstition, but because it's you and I trust you, I believe you. Could you do something for the relationship between my wife and my daughter-in-law?'

He explained that there was no overt animosity, but no closeness or warmth either, and there was a definite invisible but impassable barrier between the two of them. This had been the case for ten years.

My suggestion was to put the SRTLFs on their photos. He did this in his office and put them in a drawer. He said, 'I can't let them know what I am doing, at home.'

He asked how he would know they SRTLFs were working. I told him to look out for anything atypical happening, anything unexpected.

A few days later there was a phone call: 'My daughter-in-law has phoned twice in the last few days. That just doesn't happen!'

The next phone call came a while later. This time it was dramatic. He explained that on his daughter-in-law's birthday she had cordially invited his wife to lunch at her house and the two had got along like a house on fire. He said they had never got on like that in the previous ten years. The invisible barrier had come down.

He said, 'Shall I still keep the SRTLFs on the photograph?'

I replied, 'Yes, you can if you want to.'

Since then the relationship between the two women has become much more cordial. A year later I heard it was still in good order and the beneficial changes were holding.

SRTLFs: Addictions

As far as addictions go, my views are unusual. I believe they serve some purpose for the addict and are not easy to let go of – as most of us find when we are trying to give up a 'bad' habit, be it smoking, excessive alcohol, coffee or soda, chocolate, sex or drugs. Simple will-power is nowhere near as effective as we would like it to be. The Kaiser Permanente ACE (adverse childhood experiences) study referred to earlier bears this out. The addiction is at some level meeting a deeper hidden, unconscious, emotional need.

So in general I do not try and force the issue with clients about giving up their addictions. What, however, I do know is that when the system becomes coherent, the needs of the person change and for 'no reason' the 'bad' habit gives them up. It does not do this in a predictable time frame, however. Sometimes it can be dramatic and immediate; sometimes it can happen a few months down the line.

Leif (Sweden)

Last Sunday I decided to stop drinking coffee, because it didn't taste good anymore. I knew that I was going to get a heavy headache, so I had the SRTLFs in my pocket, reversed, the whole day, and the next day my head was fine. Wonderful!

Dawn H

My youngest son, 26, held the SRTLFs for a couple of minutes with the photo of the Divine Mother, not knowing what they could do. A few days later he said he had the desire to stop smoking for the first time in ten years. Then he said the desire to stop came a couple of hours after holding the frequencies, and that very evening he stopped, so he feels they must have done something.

Two months later, he is still off cigarettes.

A word of warning from Supercoherence practitioner Jane Cook

'As a user of this system and person who has had a tendency towards drinking too much alcohol, I have noticed that as my system becomes more balanced and coherent, the drink affects me differently. I now have to be very careful, because in the past I could drink two or three glasses of wine on an evening out and not be badly affected, whereas now even just one glass can make me appear drunk and I do not feel that great or in control. So beware, drinkers, these frequencies can help you give up because you have to!'

SRTLFs: Motion Sickness

The little girl was five years old. She was bright, confident, healthy and extrovert, but she got car sick and threw up even on a drive of two miles or less. I remembered my daughter used to get car sick when she was little, so I could sympathize.

Her mother was in a dilemma of no small proportions. The little girl had been invited to a family wedding by her father, whom she had not seen for over 18 months, and he lived a five to six-hour drive away. The mother had not been invited. She did not mind this, but was worried about her daughter. When she explained that the child got car sick, the father did not believe her. There had been a lot of mistrust on both sides for a long while.

The little girl agreed to go, but as the time of the journey drew nearer, she got clingy and insecure. She had not been separated from her mother for a very long time. The principal of the nursery school called the mother, told her that this confident little girl had become noticeably insecure and asked if there was a reason for it. When the mother explained, the principal advised her to accompany her child and stay at a guesthouse to be there for her. What should she do?

My advice to her was very different. Challenging situations are always opportunities for growth and it was important that the mother learned to let go and trust that the father, even though he had not been an ideal father, would look after his little girl. It wouldn't be easy to do, given the history between them, but I also reminded her that this would give her a bit of precious me time – which she had not had since her daughter was born. As any single parent knows, the demands of even a beloved and wanted child can be unrelenting and exhausting. This mother knew the feeling of being exhausted very well and could relate to what I said.

But how was the car sickness problem to be resolved? She simply could not bear the thought of her little one going through that hell for so many hours.

I told her that there was a solution, if she was prepared to try an experiment. She was to put two particular Supercoherence frequencies on her daughter's photo and leave them there for the duration of the trip. That was all.

There was also a warning, however. I told her, 'Do you realize that if the little one doesn't get sick, in the eyes of the father you will be a liar or a drama queen?'

She was happy to be called a liar as long as her child did not suffer. The typical sweet mother.

The drive up took six hours and the child was not car sick once. She phoned her mother as soon as she reached her destination and was bright and bubbly.

The drive back was over five hours, with the same incredible result – no car sickness whatsoever. In fact the girl phoned her mum from the car on the way back and when the mother asked her what she was doing, she said she was munching through a bag of chips.

She came back after two drives each over five hours, in the space of a weekend, her happy, bouncy and confident little self, to the great relief of her mother.

The mother *was* a liar as far as her ex-partner was concerned, but it did not matter.

On a more important note, the process of letting go and trusting more had begun for the mother. There was a glimpse of freedom for both mother and beloved daughter – through the grace of the frequency universe.

Three months later the little girl was on holiday with her mother and they were on a bus ride. The mother had forgotten to take the Supercoherence frequencies on holiday. The little girl complained of not feeling well in her tummy and her mother was panicky that she would throw up but she did not. That was a huge relief. So the work that had been done with the Supercoherence frequencies was still holding with no further input.

Four months later the girl went on another trip involving a five-six hour drive each way – with no sickness.

Jane Cook: DH

My friend DH, 55, has suffered from car sickness right from childhood. The only time she is fine in a car is when she is driving herself. She lives in Brisbane, Australia, now with her son and an elderly partner whom she has to drive about a lot. When she heard of the SRTLFs she wanted to have a go. We did the family clearing and then we tackled the car sickness. We put a note saying 'I love and accept travelling in a car as a passenger with no sickness' on her name as well as the SRTLFs for an hour a day for about two weeks. Since then she has been out with her son for some test drives and can hardly believe it, but so far she has not felt or been sick at all, sitting both in the front and the back seat of the car, and has even tried reading a magazine to try and make herself feel sick (she has never been able read a magazine in a car) and still no sickness!

SRTLFs: Fear of Flying, Fear of Spiders

Fear of flying and fear of spiders are very common. Age does not grant freedom from these fears. They come from a place beyond our conscious control and evoke reactions which are very physical, from profuse sweating to absolute unreasoning terror which can paralyse us. I do not suffer from fear of flying, but I did suffer from fear of spiders until it was neutralized when the Luminator and VRIC imaging came into my life.

Fear of Flying

Farah B: Mehru

My friend Mehru was travelling with me from Mumbai to Chennai and back. As we were taking off, I noticed her clinging to her seat for dear life and sweating profusely. I immediately got her to hold the green SRTLF in her left hand and she automatically sat back within a few minutes and was more comfortable. I did this for her on the return trip as well and it was much easier to have her sit next to me. Something changed in her and I know it was due to the SRTLFs. Mehru never looked back after that.

Catia Simionato from Brazil

I started wearing the SRTLFs maybe 18 months ago. I received them at the airport when I was going to travel. I had been very afraid of flying all my life, with symptoms of hands shaking and heart beating faster at check-in. During a flight I wouldn't be able to eat or sleep – I wouldn't be able to do anything but walk, feeling very nervous.

When I received the Supercoherence frequencies, I did not know much about them. I put them in my pockets and after five minutes I went to the check-in queue. Some minutes later I noticed I wasn't shaking and I wasn't afraid, and that was very surprising. When I got on the plane I still didn't feel afraid and I could sleep and eat. It was a very easy flight. I know it was because of the SRTLFs, because I hadn't done anything else. Since then I have never been afraid of flying.

Fear of Spiders

Jane Cook: SM

SM, 38, was a lovely man with a real flair for his work of landscape gardening. He had been doing very well and was happy, but he had one major drawback: a terrible fear of spiders. He could not come to see me as he lived in another part of the country, so I asked for photos of himself and his family. He had none of the family, but he gave me all their names and I did the family clearing (using the photos and the SRTLFs). He just reported that he felt fine.

Then I did the clearing with him and a note – 'I love and accept spiders exactly as they are' – with the SRTLFs.

Only five days later he called, very excited – he had been able to work alongside spiders in the garden and had been able to remove one from the bath in the house he had been working at, something he would have always got someone else to do in the past.

It is important to note that the whole process was done remotely using photos and the SRTLFs – the person was not physically present.

Lotta Naess: VN

VN, aged 19, had been terrified of spiders for many years. Since he lived with his family in a 100-year-old house, he met a spider on and off, for example in the basement. According to him, they were always *huge*, almost the size of a mouse! His fear became worse every time he met one.

One day he came running up the stairs from the basement, waving his arms and screaming like a three-year-old child: 'Mum! A spider, a spider! It is in the laundry room! Take it away!'

She did. But afterwards she suggested that he should clear his fear of spiders.

He was very negative about the process and questioned how it would work, but she was tired of all this childish behaviour about spiders – after all, he was 19 and this had been going on for years – so she was persistent about the clearing and after a while he agreed to do it, but as an experiment only.

He did it, but with the attitude that it wasn't going to work.

A few weeks later he came into the garden as his mother was sitting in a chair drinking coffee. When he stood beside her he noticed something.

'Oh, there is a spider on the armrest,' he said. Without thinking about it, he casually swiped it away with his hand and it fell onto the grass.

His mother said, 'What did you just do? You are afraid of spiders.'

VN's shocked response was: 'Yes, I am! No, I am not! Anymore! Did you see I touched it?! It works! Really, it works!'

His fear of spiders was gone, just like that.

That clearing was done by writing a note with the word 'spiders' on it. The note was held in first one hand, then the other, with the SRTLFs and the image of the Divine Mother. He also said out loud, 'I love and accept myself exactly as I am' and then 'I love and accept spiders exactly as they are' while holding the note with the SRTLFs.

A variation that would also have worked would have been to write

'I love and accept spiders exactly as they are' on the note without making a verbal statement.

SRTLFs: Nightmares

Lotta Naess: JP

JP, 48, had suffered from terrible nightmares for many years. He was a refugee from a country with a military dictatorship, where he had been imprisoned because of his political opinions and had suffered mental and physical torture. This was at least 20 years back but he was still ruled by nightmares.

His daughter came to see me about the problem. The family was sick and tired of her father screaming, shouting and yelling, scaring the whole family to death night after night. Sometimes this happened seven days a week. They really felt sorry for him, but also helpless because they couldn't do anything to help him. Maybe the SRTLFs could?

I asked his daughter to put the SRTLFs on his photo to begin with. Since he was not open at all to this kind of healing, she felt that she had better wait and see before she started to clear his past.

She called me two days later: the nightmares had stopped instantly when she had put the SRTLFs on the photo.

That was four months ago and as far as I know JP is still free from the nightmares and the family sleeps well at night – all of them.

SRTLFs in Extreme Crisis

SRTLFs and the Earthquake and Tsunami in Japan

The earthquake and tsunami in Japan happened a couple of days ago and the devastation has left me feeling numb, helpless and sad. Last night Satoshi, my Japanese client and friend, phoned me from Tokyo. I had been concerned about him. He had been in his office on the twenty-fourth floor when the earthquake struck. He told me that he had not felt fear or panic and had been calm. He said in the past he would have been panic-stricken and this time around his response was surprisingly different. He uses the SRTLFs every day.

Today Eiichi, another SRTLFs user, e-mailed me from Sapporo in Japan:

'My wife and I are safe… We also felt a big one last Friday and many aftershocks bigger than M5 [magnitude 5 on the Richter scale].

Thanks to the SRTLFs we are calm – we were holding them to calm ourselves down.'

Coherent Choices and Decision-Making in a Crisis

There is a part of you that is always clear, calm and coherent and knows at all times and in all circumstances what is best for you. Using the SRTLFs helps you to recognize and connect with this part of yourself and to access it at will. The view from zero point is always clear and neutral. It is vital to learn to access this part of the self, to regularly practise using your intuition and, as importantly, to check carefully whether what you have 'intuited' is true in the 'real' world. It is desperately easy to fool yourself. As the late Nobel laureate in physics, Richard Feynman says, 'The first principle is that you must not fool yourself and you are the easiest person to fool.'

Clear true perception with discernment is the prize, the goal and the process that will lead to survival and success in this age of extreme turmoil and uncertainty. Training and practice help in increasing this skill, as with any other skill.

This is a skill all of us have to master – you cannot wait for a crisis to learn it. In a crisis, of course, it proves its worth.

I had been wondering how Satoshi was getting on, as I had not heard from him for several days and the nuclear situation in Japan was critical. I was going to e-mail him when he phoned. He wanted my opinion about the nuclear situation and whether he should leave Tokyo for Singapore and carry on working from there. He said he did not feel afraid and he did not get the feeling he should leave Tokyo, even though he knew the media would probably not be telling the truth and would be downplaying the situation. It was interesting that he was evaluating a very serious situation from a totally calm perspective.

SRTLFs and Learning Difficulties

Lotta Naess: JN

JN is our youngest son. He is 13 years old. He has always been special to me in many ways, not just because he is my son and I love him, but also because he is my big challenge.

When he was a baby he wouldn't sleep longer than 40 minutes at a time before waking up yelling. He started to talk very late, at the age of four and a half. Due to that it was difficult to understand him and I had to do a lot of guessing his intentions. Of course it is not easy not being understood, so he was often frustrated, irritated and angry.

His first teachers told me that school would not be easy for him. His class was a mess because there were a few children who were emotionally disturbed and needed a lot of extra support and there was not enough money for an extra teacher, so one teacher had to handle all 26 pupils alone. It didn't make the school situation easier for JN.

We were told that he was very easily interrupted and had difficulty concentrating and remaining focused. It was also hard for him to sit still for long periods and he often had to stretch his legs and run and leap around the schoolyard. As time went by we also discovered that his memory wasn't good.

I pushed through a computerized training program for him, but he wasn't happy about it. He really disliked going to a separate room to do the computer training. All he wanted was to be like everybody else.

The training program helped a little, but JN had to catch up at home with the work that he hadn't done at school during the day. And I had to help him, because he didn't want to do it at all.

This situation made it hard for him to be with his friends, because schoolwork took up such a lot of time. Besides he didn't seem to find anyone to get together with. None of his schoolmates called him and he didn't dare to call them and suggest meeting up in case they turned him down. He often felt misunderstood by other children and I related it to his late language development.

Over the years we tried a number of alternative therapies to help him and the turning point came in December 2009. We had been to a school meeting with his teacher, who made it very clear to us that his marks in the main subjects like Swedish, mathematics and English were not acceptable and he would have to work extra hard on them. For a moment I lost all motivation to go on. How could it be possible for him to study even more? He was already doing so much schoolwork at home!

I had received my SRTLFs and decided to try them. When I told JN that they would help him with his schoolwork, he wanted to try them immediately. He started to carry them in his jeans pockets while doing his homework.

After a week I noticed that he could sit still for longer than ten minutes. That was worthwhile progress! He also seemed to be able to concentrate better.

After a month he remembered his English vocabulary and had a full score in his weekly test. Maths was still hard, but because he could focus much better he could get tasks done more easily than before. In Swedish he was writing page after page about historical battles and old kings.

I noticed that his language had suddenly developed. He was using the right tenses, which he had found very difficult before.

Something was really happening to him!

It was as though something had fallen into place. He turned

into a happy boy with new self-confidence. He started to take responsibility for his homework. Friends started to call him and he made arrangements by himself to see new friends he had got to know in different classes at school. New friends from other schools in town were also showing up. This was amazing!

Suddenly he was always busy and he seemed to handle both his schoolwork and being with his friends. He kept on using the SRTLFs, but he often told me that he didn't need the Divine Mother photo. He didn't use the SRTLFs regularly in the morning and evening, but he told me when he needed them. I guess his field informed him when to use them for a while.

'The frequencies have changed my life,' he said. 'Now I am a popular guy, you know! And I can understand what I am reading in my books. It isn't always easy, but I'm not the worst pupil in my class anymore. That feels good!'

At the end of term meeting, his teacher started by congratulating him on his test results. His marks were good, very good and excellent! There was no need for extra support now. His teacher also said he had very good social skills and was very well liked by all his schoolmates.

I feel that JN is really listening to what I have to say nowadays and he also has a lot of things to tell me. He is calmer and more centred. It is wonderful to hear him argue for something he thinks is right – before he would either be crying with anger or shouting at me when things didn't go his way. There are minimum conflicts between us, and also between him and his two brothers.

In the autumn he starts a new school and we will all follow his progress with interest. He continues to use the SRTLFs when he feels he needs them.

Jane Cook: HMG

HMG, aged eight, came to me for help with severe learning difficulties. He was far behind in his reading, writing and maths.

He was a good and happy little boy, but from a fragmented and disturbed family.

We only just started last Friday and already there have been signs of change. The educational psychologist had been unable to visit his school to see him for over six months and his dad and his partner had been getting desperate. Even whilst we were still in the middle of the family clearing, the partner phoned up and said, 'Your aligning thing is working! The EP is arriving for a special visit for only one child on Friday! We can't believe it!'

Apparently H had also said that he would love to learn and do better at school, so was going to start reading after tea every day. His sister had come top with her homework – that had *never* happened before either – and the family clearing was not yet completed!

Two days later a phone call came from the school asking for the parents and guardians to attend a meeting. All three of H's teachers stayed on after school on a Friday for this 'because they thought H. was worth it'. They have now begun setting him special homework and individual reading programmes and are suddenly offering him masses of help and encouragement at school. H. is enjoying all this attention, whereas previously he would not have been bothered! Also, he has been enjoying doing some cooking *and* reading the recipes!

These are huge breakthroughs and have all happened since the family clearing began.

SRTLFs: Self-Harm

MB and Son

My son, 20, had had a tendency to self-harm since he was 13. He usually did it when things got out of control or when he got very angry or depressed.

We had a tough year last year and there were lots of times when he self-harmed. Then, when we were going through one very difficult phase, I bought the frequencies [the SRTLFS], told him a little bit about them and just asked him to put them in his jeans pockets. He did put them in his pockets, and whereas normally we would have had a few episodes of him cutting himself with a knife and things like that during that difficult phase, none of that actually happened.

He said he couldn't understand it – he prepared himself to self-harm because of the emotion that he was feeling, but then it just didn't seem the right thing to do, so he didn't do it.

He has a Chinese sword that we bought for him in San Francisco. It is a beautiful sword and he would keep it very sharp and use it to harm himself, but now he says he does not want it anymore and it is now in storage. Pretty big deal! He still gets angry and upset, but he is not harming himself. He swears by the frequencies now.

Note: MB was in a very abusive marriage when her son was little. She experienced a lot of physical violence and divorced her husband, the father of her son. Her son subsequently told her how much it had upset him that he had not been able to protect her.

FH and Granddaughter

FH, from Australia, originally bought the SRTLFs because she was concerned about her 14-year-old granddaughter, LD, physically harming herself. It had been going on for two years. She cut her arms with knives, razor blades and other sharp instruments and once had to be treated because the blade was rusty and the wound became infected.

There were two significant events at the time LD started self-harming: her mother broke up with a man she had been in a relationship with for the previous ten years, and her sister, who was aged 23 at the time, left home to live with a couple of friends. Her mother worked shifts from 3 p.m. to 11 p.m., so there was no real support for the young girl when she needed it, as she had just commenced high school. She had always had poor concentration and been lower than average academically, and she may have felt abandoned. The self-harm was superficial, as though it was a cry for help or attention.

The self-harm ceased within a month of FH commencing using the SRTLFs on LD's photo on a daily basis. Then she used them to ask that LD's anger and aggression be taken away from her, and that also happened fairly quickly. The girl's mother, TD, was absolutely amazed at the results. She actually told FH about the improvements before she knew she was using the SRTLFs.

Now LD has also cut her ties with (so-called) friends who were not a good influence and has been seeing a counsellor at her school for 12 months or so.

TD has recommenced her relationship and her partner is a positive influence on her daughter. He has bowel cancer and LD centres on how he is feeling.

FH is continuing to use the SRTLFs remotely for her granddaughter's benefit.

SRTLFs and Meditation

Many SRTLFs users practice meditation. They often report that using the SRTLFs allows them to meditate more deeply than before. If you think about it, the purpose of meditation is to go to zero and get the benefits that are available from that state. As mentioned before, the Indian and Tibetan wisdom traditions, which have been around for several thousand years, recognize the importance of accessing zero, or *shunya*, as the goal of meditation.

The benefits of meditation are well documented. Regular practice is considered essential to reap these benefits. Using the SRTLFs is a short cut to accessing zero – your energy system recognizes it instantly and you can access the benefits of that state without doing any formal meditation. It is the lazy person's meditation – you get the benefits without the effort! However if you are a meditator and use the SRTLFs, you will experience an exponential enhancement in your results.

MM

M is an active, bright, intelligent 78-year-old. She is very disciplined – is up every day really early to do her yoga, her *pranayam* (special yogic breathing exercises) and meditation, and has done so for many decades. She manages a large household and is full of energy. Since October–November 2009 she has been using the SRTLFs, holding them in her hands for 20 minutes while she does her meditation.

I met her in early January 2010 and asked her what changes, if any, she had noticed in herself. She told me that she had always been very impatient with herself and with those who worked for her. She did not like this trait in herself, but had not succeeded in changing the pattern despite her best intentions and the years of daily meditation. However, since the SRTLFs came into her life she had noticed a huge difference in her response, especially towards those who worked for her.

Modifying long-standing non-nourishing patterns is neither simple nor easy. But here the pattern of a lifetime, which would not yield despite the person's best efforts, has been modified with ease and grace in the space of a couple of months. MM is much happier, feels much calmer, and things that bothered her before do not have that power over her anymore.

Mr. M.

Mr. M. from Japan's response on holding the SRTLFs for the first time was: 'Now you do not have to explain about these. Because only in a few minutes, my body is in the same condition as when I exercise with yogic breathing for half an hour.'

Using the SRTLFs during a Ten-Day Vipassana Meditation Course

A client reports:

I had previously taken two ten-day silent Vipassana courses and one three-day course, as well as serving as a volunteer on a ten-day course. On my third ten-day course I decided to wear the SRTLFs, as in principle both methods have the same goal in mind.

First, I noticed that I entered the meditation much more deeply without any additional effort on my part. In a Vipassana course one meditates for 11 hours a day, so usually the experience involves a lot of resistance, but using the SRTLFs I noticed that I experienced far less mental agitation, and a deeper awareness came to lead me through the course from a very early point. I was also able, using the Vipassana technique, which is essentially a process of scanning the body and physical experience with one's awareness, to enter my internal experience as never before. It was revealing and mind-blowing.

Secondly, a large part of the resistance experienced during a ten-day course is that of physical discomfort – knee and back pains legitimize the struggle, feet and legs become numb, searing pain arises in various parts of the body. In my previous experiences, by about halfway through the course I could move beyond this pain whilst meditating, although upon leaving the meditation (for a break) I would re-enter a world of numbness and pain, my legs needing a few minutes to come to life enough to support my body to walk out of the meditation hall. Additionally, I would be very spaced out. I took this to be a normal part of the process. Also, when I began speaking after ten days and left the meditation centre to re-enter the outside world, I would experience a real shock to my highly sensitized system and struggle to reintegrate myself into what seemed like a harsh environment.

Using the SRTLFs, I moved effortlessly into and out of meditation. The day after I arrived I began to experience intense physical pain in the form of sciatica in both legs, as well as pain in another nerve in both legs, pain along the sides of my legs, in my lower back and hips and in my upper back and head. It was almost constant, and agonizing. Like most people who know how to help themselves but forget, I didn't think to use the Supercoherence Panic to Calm frequency until after the course had begun. I had tried it with friends suffering from severe and chronic lower back pain before, yet without the efficacy I had expected. Again, using the Supercoherence Panic to Calm frequency on my lower back, I didn't seem to benefit from an obvious reduction in the pain. However I subsequently thought to use it on my foot, with a rough understanding of the position of the lower back used by reflexologists. Within moments the 'sciatica' had disappeared. Moving the frequency around even slightly could affect the pain relief. At times its position did not seem to bear an obvious relationship to my hips or lower back, but because the effects were felt in such a short space of time I could move it around until I found just the right place without fear of the pain affecting my calm experimentation.

After that, I experienced almost no pain for the duration of the ten days, no numbness and no delay in getting my legs to pick me up (after meditating sometimes for two hours without moving position), and when I began speaking on the tenth day, rather than feeling jittery and overwhelmed by the sensory stimulation, I felt calm, congenial and well-integrated. This experience stayed with me as I left the centre.

It's worth pointing out here that I usually use two sitting positions during a ten-day Vipassana course and at least three cushions. Using the SRTLFs, I was able to reduce this to one sitting position and no cushions at all. This may not seem significant, but remember, the course requires 11 hours sitting a day for ten days, on the floor!

SM (Malaysia): Cindy

I gave the SRTLFs to a friend of mine during a seminar where guided meditations were part of the programme. This friend, Cindy, always falls asleep the minute the music begins playing.

She is quite unable to keep awake. This time I gave the SRTLFs to her to hold during the meditation time. She was ecstatic, as she was able to stay awake and enter into the theme of the meditation, including visualizing in colour. This was the first time she had been able to enter so deeply into the meditative state.

SM (Malaysia): Bereaved Friend

A friend of mine's only brother killed himself two months ago. She had been distraught and had been asking herself over and over if she had missed some sign that could have alerted her. She had even lost control and become hysterical with her husband.

When she came to see me, I handed her the SRTLFs and told her to just hold them. Though she had prepared herself for a light social call, she talked for three hours, relating how she really felt – the challenges and the distress. I sometimes interrupted her to ask how she was feeling. She remarked that she was surprised that she could laugh again. She felt lighter and left in a better frame of mind. The effect on her was truly remarkable.

SRTLFs and Animals

Cats

These case studies are from Supercoherence practitioner Sandra Fiquet.

Snowy the Cat and the SRTLFs

Snowy is a bit of a heavy-pawed cat, especially when he jumps off things. Twice in the past he hasn't landed quite right, has injured his front left paw and has been treated with anti-inflammatory drops.

The third time it happened, an inner voice said, 'Why don't you try the SRTLFs?'

I was in two minds about it, as a part of me said to still use the anti-inflammatory. The inner voice came up again saying, 'You know the SRTLFs would really be better for him than medication.' And I thought, 'Yes, I'll use the SRTLFs instead and see how it goes.'

I put the SRTLFs on Snowy's photograph with the picture of the Divine Mother first thing in the morning.

By the second day, his paw had improved a tiny bit, but I wasn't sure if it was because he had been walking around less or not.

By the evening of the third day, Snowy was running and jumping about as if he'd never been injured.

The anti-inflammatory had taken a week to work on both previous occasions, but the SRTLFs with the Divine Mother photograph put Snowy back on all his paws in three days.

Snowy the Cat and the Disappearing Lump

In the autumn of 2010 we were stroking Snowy when we noticed that he had a sizeable lump on his right side. It was about the size of a golf ball and quite firm, but he didn't seem to be in pain with it. In fact he didn't seem to be at all bothered about it.

Snowy has a rare condition which means his blood does not coagulate well. So various possibilities went through our worried non-medical heads. Maybe he had some very minor internal bleeding and the blood had somehow accumulated and eventually coagulated into this ball. Maybe he had some kind of cyst. Maybe he had a nasty tumour: we had been going through some very stressful times for a good while and it is said that pets tend to pick up the negative energies from their owners (I don't really like the word 'owner' but can't think of a better one).

So I put the SRTLFs on Snowy's photograph with the Divine Mother.

At the end of the first week, the lump had started to shrink considerably.

At the end of the second week, the lump was even smaller.

At the end of the third week, the lump had completely gone.

I kept the SRTLFs and the Divine Mother on Snowy's photograph for another week for good measure, but the lump couldn't be felt at all at the end of the third week.

Dogs

Jane Cook: S.

S., a seven-year-old bitch, wears the SRTLFs every day in oven gloves attached to her like a saddle bag, first on one side and then on the other. At the beginning she wore them for ten minutes at a time night and morning and we have gradually increased this by a few minutes each day. At night we put the SRTLFs on her photograph. She has liked them from the beginning and comes wagging her tail for them when she sees the oven gloves coming out.

She has been very ill for some time and at one point was given only weeks to live. Slowly she is getting some of her old energy back. It is slow progress, but it is progress – she is eating better and keeping more of her food down.

S. lives with two other bitches – her sister and the sister's daughter. When we did the clearing of the family for her, just as we do for ourselves, things moved onto another level, with all the dogs getting on even better than before. We then did clearing with the owner and her dogs, and that all went very well.

We now have a functional family of dogs and owner. S. is still using the SRTLFs daily, along with the photo of the Divine Mother. She is continuing to show signs of improvement in all areas of her life.

Jane Cook: Judy

Judy is from a working collie background and was a typical outward-going, energetic, sometimes naughty puppy, but at the end of May 2010 her owners noticed that she wasn't keeping up with their other dogs when running and soon 'switched off' completely from her training. She had no desire to play or chase and just wanted to lie down or curl up in the corner of the room.

Judy then spent a great deal of time at the vets', but after many tests and X-rays, they were none the wiser as to what was causing the problem. She appeared to be depressed.

We started with the oven gloves containing the SRTLFs, ten minutes in the morning and ten minutes in the evening. We began to notice they were slipping onto the hindquarters area each time.

After a few treatments Judy seemed to relax and enjoy having the therapy, wagging her tail on arrival for her Supercoherence session. Her owners started to notice a few behavioural changes, such as her wanting to come up on the sofa in the evenings and then instigating 'play time' with the other dogs, neither of which she had done for months.

In the meantime the vets referred Judy to a specialist for further tests. Again, all the tests were negative, but this time the vets said that she showed some pain reactions in her hindquarters. The MRI scan showed that she had a degenerated disc in the lumbar region and also that her hips were fairly weak and 'popped out of place' when under anaesthetic. The advice given was to put her on high doses of Metacam and rest her.

I was amazed that in each session the SRTLFs had come to rest above the place where the MRI scan had showed the weakness was.

Judy's owners remembered that when they had first had her she had got too excited and fallen off a chair, landing on a solid fire surround, and had yelped and run away with her tail between her legs. The following day she had seemed fine and had been so for some months afterwards. It was only now that they started to consider that this incident could have been the cause of her problems.

It was obvious that Judy needed help. Her owners decided to allow the medication and take some swimming sessions for Judy once a week in a controlled pool with a vet at hand. Judy still came for her SRTLF sessions.

Now, after eight weeks, the combination of treatments has produced a fantastic result. Judy has got her youth back. She runs flat out with the other dogs, has her 'naughtiness' back, instigates play with the others and now runs with a very flat, straight back, with no sign of her previous trouble. She does not use any painkillers and friends cannot believe the difference in her. She is enjoying life again and has restarted her training.

Kaz H: Dex

I even use the SRTLFs on my dog, Dex. He is a dear friend to me, but old and arthritic. He seem more chilled out and contented now and I don't think I'm imagining it. He actually seems to look forward to having the scarf tied around his neck with the SRTLFs and photo of the Divine Mother attached. As soon as I pick up the scarf, his tail wags and he 'smiles'.

Lotta Naess: Two Coherent Dogs

One of my clients has two dogs, beautiful grand poodles. One is black and female – she is named Berta – and the other is white and male – his name is Bosse.

Since my client, SF, has integrated the SRTLFs into her daily life, the frequencies are always around their home. She always keeps them in the little green and pink bags. She often holds them when she goes to bed in the evening. She drops them in her sleep but always finds them easily in the morning, under the pillow or blanket when making the bed.

One day when SF was making her bed she couldn't find the green SRTLF. She looked everywhere – under the mattress, under the bed, between the sheets – and finally she found it on the floor, but no green bag!

Two days later, when she was out walking, the green bag turned up, coming out the 'natural way' from Berta!

And it happened again. This time SF's daughter, EF, couldn't find her pink SRTLF. They looked all over the house, but it was gone. At last EF found it in Berta's basket, hidden under a blanket. Berta had taken it down two flights of stairs and hidden it very well. The pink bag was gone and only the tiny handle on the zipper was left.

SF tried to be more careful about where she kept the SRTLFs, but one morning she caught Berta standing on the bed trying to get both bags. SF looked at her severely. The dog looked back and it was as if she said, 'I know they are yours, but I want them anyway!'

When Berta was born SF received a photo of her from the breeder and put the SRTLFs on it and wished all the best for the little puppy. When it was time to pick her up and bring her home, the breeder told SF that Berta was the calmest and most stable of all the puppies in the litter. She even wondered whether she was ill. She wasn't – only very calm and coherent, obviously.

SF says:

'Every morning Berta comes up to my husband's bedside. She stretches her neck out as far as she can and he puts the SRTLFs around her neck, one on each side. She sits completely still for as long as necessary. After a while she stands up and walks away.

If my husband doesn't do it, she walks into our daughter's room and does the same thing. It can also happen occasionally during the day. Apparently she wants a reset.

We started to call on Bosse to see if he wanted to do the same. He is not as keen on it as Berta, but he does it almost every day. Berta has always shown more interest in the SRTLFs than Bosse. Maybe it is because we worked with them on her photo when she was a puppy. We didn't have the SRTLFs when we got Bosse.'

SF travels around showing Berta and Bosse at different dog shows:

'Before we do the walk round and show them to the judges, I always "reset" them, and the person who leads the walk round keeps the SRTLFs in their pockets while doing the showing.

Since I am not showing the dogs myself, I only ask the person who does, to keep the SRTLFs in their pockets. They don't even know what they are.

The dog and the person showing them become really synchronized and read each other perfectly and the showing is very successful – thanks to the SRTLFs!'

SRTLFs and Plants

Lotta Naess: Orchids, Olive Tree, Christmas Tree

This is a story about an experiment with plants and trees.

I love orchids, especially when they are flowering. My problem is that I never manage to get them to reflower. I buy them in full flower and enjoy them, but then it seems as though they don't feel comfortable in my house at all. I can understand that, because during the winter we have very low humidity indoors.

Anyway, I have too many orchids with leaves like dried elephants' ears, no air roots and no flowers, so when I heard about a fellow Supercoherence practitioner in England putting the SRTLFs in a plant pot, I decided to put them every night on the window bench where the orchids were.

I am so glad I did, because it made me realize that plants also want to be coherent. Within a week four of them started to form beautiful new *white* air roots. That was different.

A week later, three of them had a couple of new leaves and then a few days later I saw the first shoot coming up from one of them.

Within eight weeks all four were flowering again and had fresh green leaves and lots of new air roots. *Lovely* and magical!

My sister came to see me one day and asked me if I wanted to take over three of her half-dead orchids, as she was moving and did not have the space for them.

'Oh,' I thought, 'time for another experiment. But this time it will be more difficult.'

These orchids were in an even worse condition than my poor orchids had been six months before. But I had nothing to lose. I put all three of them on a tray and put the SRTLFs on the tray every night for a week.

Then things started to happen. New roots started coming up, then new leaves and finally each of the orchids grew shoots. Within a month, one shoot was 20 centimetres tall and the other two were close to that. In another month all the orchids were flowering again. They were not hopeless cases after all and they seemed to like being in our house.

The week before Christmas I discovered that my olive tree had started to grow new shoots. It always rests at this time of the year but now it is more awake and alive than ever before.

The Christmas tree of the year was in and my husband took on the huge task of keeping it alive, watering it every morning for a week. On Christmas Eve, when it was time to open the gifts, we discovered something: all the packages under the tree were soaking wet! The tree had obviously not been drinking as much as we had expected. Nevertheless, all the green needles were still firmly in place on the branches!

Hmm, flowering orchids, growing olive trees and an un-thirsty Christmas tree with all its needles in place now, on 6 January, when it hasn't had any water at all since 24 December... *is the house coherent or what?*

Linear Science and the SRTLFs

How can these unbelievable results be explained to those who may 'justifiably' question how 'two little pieces of glass' can create miracles? The process does not sound logical or reasonable and certainly cannot be explained via mathematical formulae. So, is it voodoo, is it a scam, is it a money-making scheme, is it the placebo effect? These innocuous pieces of glass contain nothing that can be measured by the instruments of twenty-first century science and that may be a problem to seekers of 'proof'.

In this lifetime I am no mathematician – I need a calculator to do any but the simplest calculations. I know at one level that a hypothesis, a theory or a model of understanding is supposed to have a mathematical model underpinning it to make it understandable and acceptable to the scientific establishment. Yet can the laws of mathematics explain how one sperm + and one ova fuse and create a baby with a body that has many trillions of cells of organized intelligence, plus consciousness, thoughts and feelings?

To seekers of proof and certainty, as a non-mathematician I submit that you cannot now and never will find a mathematical model for a human – not with the most sophisticated computers, nano-technologies or tools of this physical reality. By their nature humans are part of the universe – infinite and ever-changing and therefore unknowable, except, maybe, through the Luminator and VRIC imaging, where you can see, for a moment, the truth of the whole, before it changes in an eternal flow of being and becoming.

Linear science talks about the burden of proof. I have to say that the burden of proof has to be matched by the burden of *understanding*. One will see and understand only when one is ready, willing and able, and not before. I do not, cannot make myself responsible for anyone's understanding and beliefs, and the constraints that may arise as a result. The only way of really understanding something as extraordinary as the SRTLFs is to experience them and the effects that they create in one's life.

Some may claim these effects are 'paranormal and 'anomalous', but what do they mean by that? It is simply that they do not obey the known laws of the science of 'dead matter', as the great scientist Dr Mae-Wan Ho calls it.

We have severely shortchanged ourselves by our unreasonable and stubborn determination to only believe what we can measure. We do not realize that we may not have the instruments or the parameters with which to make those measurements. It is OK to say 'I do not know how this is possible', but to say something is *impossible* because it cannot be understood or measured by the tools of modern science is patronizing, arrogant and counterproductive. As Einstein said, 'Not everything that counts can be counted, and not everything that can be counted counts.'

In any case, how does one 'measure' joy, love, happiness and grace? Why have we made the unimportant things important – money, possessions, power – and relegated to less important the really meaningful things such as loving relationships and lives of significance, meaning and happiness? Strange creatures, we humans!

For me, the gaping hole in the present scientific model is that it does not recognize the soul, feelings and consciousness and has no means of factoring these essential aspects of the universe into its calculations. As the neurophysiologist Sir John Eccles said: 'I maintain that the human mystery is incredibly demeaned by scientific reductionism, with its claim in promissory materialism to account eventually for all of the spiritual world in terms of patterns of neuronal activity. This belief must be classed as a superstition.... We have to recognize that we are spiritual beings with souls existing in a spiritual world as well as material beings with bodies and brains existing in a material world.'[13]

This shortfall leads directly to finding facts and gathering information without any thought of how, when and where that information will be applied. Knowledge without wisdom can have disastrous consequences. This resolute dismissal of the importance of feelings and the soul has brought our civilization to its present dire straits, despite all the technological advances of the twentieth and twenty-first centuries.

The Supercoherence system recognizes the importance of the invisible, intangible, unquantifiable but totally essential qualities such as awareness and feelings. It takes into account the fact that they are the key factors that shape our happiness in the moment and our destiny as a whole. The quality of our awareness and self-understanding enables us to know what is or is not right and appropriate for us, in the moment, making us the master and mistress of our destiny without reference to any external authority. It allows us to remember that we are a soul on a journey.

This breakthrough allows us to restore the soul to its pre-eminent place in our life and enables us to look at the bigger picture and to see, feel and know the magnificence that we are. And to live our life from that central understanding.

CHAPTER 12

The Supercoherence Frequency Toolkit

'I am that I AM.'

WHEN THE SRTLFS evolved into form, I did not think we would need anything more. But I was wrong. Other frequencies have come into form at various times between 2008 and 2011. They carry a different message and fulfill slightly different functions. So now the Supercoherence frequency toolkit consists of the Supercoherence Return to Love frequencies, three Supercoherence IAM frequencies – IAM Male, IAM Female and IAM Universal – and the Supercoherence Panic to Calm frequency.

I consider the SRTLFs, in conjunction with the Divine Mother image, the most important part of the kit. They are the most versatile and also in my view the most powerful. They clear the imprint of old trauma in the field better than any of the others and their principal goal and intent is to restore the system to love. But all of the other frequencies have their supporting role to play.

All the Supercoherence frequencies have been tested in the field of the

Luminator using VRIC imaging and are therefore calibrated to zero and create coherence in the field of the individual using them.

All of them affect all the levels – physical, mental, emotional, spiritual – all the time. This is because they work at field level, which encompasses and influences all levels simultaneously and continuously. At all times you are a whole being, and these distinctions, though convenient to help us understand things better, are in reality artificial.

The Supercoherence IAM Male and IAM Female Frequencies (SIAM Male and SIAM Female)

The Supercoherence IAM Male and IAM Female frequencies are simply worn round the neck or on the midline of the body and reinforce the coherence of the frequency of the wearer. They raise self-esteem and confidence, and when they are worn, you will see situations and people through the filter of your coherent self, and others, though they will not know why, will see and interact with you very differently from before. When the frequency is on your person, you are creating a coherent buffer zone. This is beneficial to all parties when interacting with you.

The Supercoherence IAM frequencies, as their name suggests, allow you to have a clear sense of self. If, for example, we are not able to speak up for ourselves with a difficult colleague, boss or family member, using the Supercoherence IAM frequency will give us the strength to do so. It gives us confidence and allows us to claim our rightful place in the world.

I would use these frequencies in the following ways:
1. Healing the ancestral Masculine/Feminine Line
2. To hold your own frequency.
3. To hold your own frequency when surrounded by the opposite sex.
4. To rebalance couples.
5. To ease loss and bereavement.

Holding your Own Frequency

If a person has low self-esteem or self-confidence for whatever reason, they will need the relevant Supercoherence IAM frequency to hold their own frequency.

We have seen this in several dramatic cases of young men with domineering fathers. After wearing the Supercoherence IAM Male frequency for just a month, they were able to stand up to them for the first time in their lives.

Lotta Naess: PF

PF was 47. He came from a wealthy family and had inherited the family business. His father was now 'retired' but had no plans to leave the firm, which was his life's work. He ruled with an iron will, whether his family or his business.

PF was quite a stressed person. He had tics and found it difficult to relax. He had big problems with his father, who often treated him with no respect, especially in front of their personnel. This had been common all his life and he didn't know how to change it.

His wife, who ran the finance department in the firm, told me about the situation. When I told her about the Supercoherence IAM Male frequency, she bought one instantly as a gift for her husband. The interesting thing was that he had no idea of the power of the gift. She never told him what it was. He just put it on and felt comfortable with it.

A few days later PF was discussing something with the personnel manager and suddenly his father came into the room, interrupted him in a rude way and tried to take over the conversation.

PF slowly turned around toward his father and said, 'Excuse me, but could you please wait outside until we have finished? If you have something to say we can discuss that later.'

His father turned around, went out and closed the door.

PF just stood there. He didn't understand what he had done. It had all happened so quickly. 'Did I say that? And it was so easy!'

The personnel manager gawped at him and said, 'You should have done that a long time ago. But better late than never!'

PF went straight into his wife's office and told her what had happened. She couldn't hold back any longer and explained about his frequency.

Now he never takes it off – he even goes to sleep with it on!

Jenny Hart: M.

M., a husband who could be difficult at times and did not wear jewellery, was surprisingly happy to wear a Supercoherence IAM Male frequency.

Almost immediately his wife announced that he had reverted to the man he had been when she first knew him. Now he loves to wear his SIAM Male frequency and puts it on every day – in fact he won't go out without it!

Jenny Hart: Three Supercoherence IAM Female Frequency Cases

A friend called me and asked if I could send her a Supercoherence IAM Female frequency for a friend of hers who was suffering badly from a broken relationship. I said that I would do so, but I would first like to put the SRTLFs on her friend's name, along with the Divine Mother photo. She gave me the name and I left the frequencies on for a few days.

The woman was pleased to receive her SIAM Female frequency, and when I enquired how she was getting along, I was told that as soon as she had started to wear it, her whole attitude had changed towards the loss of the relationship. She just felt different about it and could now cope.

Another client, who had been very amenable in the past and had never stood up for herself, was able to really stand up for herself, even though she was in a vulnerable position, with a friend who was constantly taking advantage of her. She was surprised and delighted with herself and said she could never have done it without the SIAM Female frequency. She wears it 24/7 and swears by it.

Another client claimed she felt 'blissed out' wearing it. She simply loves it.

Lucy

I had been feeling very vulnerable and low and under attack from people, but when I started wearing the necklace [SIAM Female frequency] I felt more at peace.

I hadn't been going out much, but decided to go to my son Jack's school fayre. The first thing that happened was that everyone I met was very nice to me and I had several comments from other women about my pretty necklace.

Then I was amazed, as a lady who had been absolutely awful to me and Jack about a year ago (her son had been bullying Jack and I had had to report it to the head, as Jack had been scared to go to school and had been covered in bruises) came up to me and smiled. Before, she had avoided eye contact and blanked me on several occasions when I'd tried to talk to her and she had sent her son to Jack's birthday party recently (with no card or present) without letting me know or saying thanks. So it was a shock when she apologized for sending her son to Jack's party without letting me know and made an effort to be friendly. Since then she has said hello to me every time I've seen her. To me, this is a miracle, as it had been a really upsetting situation.

About half an hour later, my next-door neighbour came up to me and was friendly. She had also been very unfriendly for a long period of time, but since then there hasn't been a problem, which has made a big difference to me. There have been a few other things too, like extra kind people in shops and just a general feeling of positivity from women in particular.

Thank you for introducing me to the necklace, as it has really helped me a lot, plus I love it… Things with Jack are so much better too – he is a lot more peaceful at the moment, which results in us being able to have a much more loving and peaceful relationship.

BU

"And there is the story of my granddaughter. I sent you a very short mail some weeks ago, as I was so astonished at what has happened.

Lisa, my granddaughter was on the one hand a very daring girl, she tried out new things quite easily. On the other hand, she was very shy with other people, she had little self esteem and didn't trust her creativity. I realized that we all, my mother, I, my daughter Maria and Lisa had the same pattern. We all felt unworthy, and somehow out of place. My mother, Maria and Lisa all had elder brothers who were difficult children and got themselves the attention of their parents. I had no siblings but my parents were such a symbiotic couple that I always had the feeling of not belonging. We all three did the family clearing and I do hope that we were able to break this unhappy chain. Maria and I we love each other, but our relationship was about the same as you describe yours with Meher. There was always something like a wall between us. It seemed that she had to protect herself and her life from me. Now Maria is more open towards me, it seems as if the wall has been torn down. She even asked me to go with her to a Meditation-workshop in the mountains! But the biggest change has happened to Lisa. Her insecurity always showed. She even stood there like a question mark, bent and her head down. Of course nobody wanted to give her a job. She has been searching over a year. After the family clearing and after wearing the IAM feminine frequency she got a job within a week. She has changed so much! She seems more sure of herself and is trusting her abilities, and it shows! She walks upright and her head is up and her eyes are shining. She is convinced that the frequencies helped her. And, oh yes, she has a new boyfriend, as the old one of course helped her to keep up her image of an unworthy person."

Jenny Hart: R.

R., a man who was kind and giving, too much so at times, as people took advantage of his good nature, suddenly had a family crisis. He found things hard to cope with and his health suffered. I asked him to hold the SRTLFs and later I gave him a SIAM Male frequency. He now wears it every day. He places it by the bed at night and puts it on in the morning. This is a man I would never have thought would want to wear anything around his neck!

His wife tells me that he is now more authoritative, which is a good thing for him. If he is asked to do something for a friend, he may now say he is sorry but not today, as he is rather busy. Before he would drop everything to go to the aid of anyone. He would still help an emergency of course, but he now does what is right for him.

Holding your Own Frequency when Surrounded by the Opposite Sex

If an individual is surrounded by a disproportionate number of the opposite sex either in the family or work environment, it is beneficial and indeed important for them to wear their SIAM frequency when they are in that environment. They will not know why, but they will feel more comfortable.

Lotta Naess: A Missing Father, a Domineering Mother and Grandmother, a Demanding Sister and the Supercoherence IAM Male Frequency

The parents of KN, 48, divorced when he was three years old. A huge conflict followed the divorce and KN and his older sister were only allowed to see their father on a few occasions every year. He grew up with his mother and sister and grandparents. His grandmother, who was a very strong and dominant woman, assisted his mother in raising him and his sister.

Years went by and the father did not show much interest in the children, probably because the mother and grandmother did their best to talk negatively about him. KN was often told, 'Watch out, otherwise you might end up like your father.' He never understood what he had to be careful about, so he developed into a child who never took any space. He always played by himself and was very quiet and calm. He never asked for anything. His sister was the opposite – a lively and adventurous little girl who had very definite ideas about how things should be. She was also very demanding.

In his early twenties, KN moved away from home to pursue his studies. When he was 25, he met his wife-to-be. Their marriage was harmonious most of the time, partly because KN never entered into conflict. He never stood up for himself in a strong way; rather, he avoided disagreements and in difficult situations he let his wife make the decisions. To her this was very confusing, as he had a profession that demanded otherwise. Her experience was that he behaved like two different personalities, one at work and the other at home. She could see that very clearly, as they had been colleagues before they married.

Though KN's mother lived far away, she did her best to interfere in his family life. His wife found her very controlling and manipulative. Her own parents seldom told her how to act; in fact she had been used to having responsibility and freedom from the age of only five or six.

This brought a lot of frustration into the marriage. KN never stood up to his mother and she went on and on and on… It was obvious that KN was afraid of conflict, at least in his private life.

Finally his wife decided to stop meeting his family. She was tired of being the one who had to stand up for her own family without being supported by her husband.

This was not the only trouble in KN's family. His sister, who had had a lot of problems in her family life, had divorced. At that point, for a lot of reasons, a major disagreement arose between the sister and the mother. The result was that the sister broke off all contact with both her mother and KN's family. This cold war continued for ten years.

Within a month of starting to use the Supercoherence IAM Male frequency, KN began to change. Suddenly he could meet his mother on another level. As he put it, 'I had to stand up for myself and my opinions. They are worth just as much as hers.'

He also stood up for himself in private and expressed his long-suppressed longing to ride a motorcycle. So he bought one, and shortly after that he bought a boat. The family lives near a big lake and he said to his wife, 'That lake has been crying out for me for many years and I feel really free on a boat. If I don't get one, I will regret it.'

The relationship with his sister also became warmer. While there were still disagreements between them, now he explained his opinion in a clear way and did not let himself down. She was astonished. She was definitely not used to a brother who told her what he wanted.

As KN said, 'Well, she just has to get used to it!'

Lotta Naess: NJ

NJ was very keen to try the Supercoherence I AM Male frequency. 'What will this little thing do for me?' he asked.

I said, 'I don't know, but why don't you try it out?'

I would have thought he was the last person to try it. He is very scientific and everything has to be proved – he wants evidence. The thing is that he is the only male in the family – he has two daughters and a domineering wife.

He put it on and wore it all evening. Before he went home, he took it off and gave it back to me.

'Now I know what it is to be a man!' he said.

A while later his wife told me that he had said to her, 'Strange, but I have been thinking about the blue stone necklace with the male frequency a lot lately. I don't know why, but I am thinking of having one of my own. Hmm, strange feeling!'

However, when he was offered it, he made a joke about it and did not take it further. His soul level wants it badly, but his intellect is afraid of it!

Lotta Naess: ÅN and LN

ÅN was 52 years old. She had three children with different fathers, had divorced twice and had also had several relationships throughout the years. None of them had worked out very well. She was living with a new man who was ten years younger than her and had never had a relationship with a woman before. He wanted children of his own, but ÅN felt that she was too old to start all over again with a new family. Yet she loved him very much and part of her would have liked to have given him a child.

When I saw her, her period was three weeks late. She was really nervous and when she had done a pregnancy test earlier in the day, the blue strip had cracked and she was going to have to buy a new one and do it again.

It emerged that ÅN suffered a lot from a lack of feminine energy. Ever since she was a child she had felt very 'boyish'. She was indeed a robust woman.

At the end of the session she broke down and started to cry. She was really in deep sorrow at her lack of femininity. Intuitively I took my SIAM Female frequency off and put it around her neck. I told her what it was, but she had great difficulty borrowing it for a few hours – not because she didn't want to, but because she didn't want to be indebted to me.

Later that day she sent me a text message:

'Lotta, I just got my period! It feels so good. And in a strange way I got the insight that I had always thought that I had to be small, thin and beautiful to feel feminine. That doesn't apply to me, but now I know that is OK! Thank you for lending me your frequency and standing by me today!'

I was pleased that my intuition was spot on!

My own experience of the SIAM Female frequency is actually similar to that of ÅN. In the last year I have had a lot of trouble and problems with my hypogastria. My period turned upside down a year ago and I was bleeding for three weeks and clear for one week – just the opposite of how it used to be. In March this year the bleeding stopped and I thought I might be menopausal. The mucous membranes in the vagina were very dry and gave me a lot of problems with burning and itching. Besides this, my candida infection returned. Life became a minor hell. The last time I visited my gynaecologist she also found eight quite big cysts on the ovaries.

I tried a lot of different medications, crèmes and gels, with and without oestrogen. Nothing helped.

Then Thrity gave me the Supercoherence IAM Female frequency in Stockholm. It was a Monday. On the Wednesday of the same week, my period came back. I had a real flow with fresh red blood. It continued for a week and then stopped. During the first days of the period I had a lot of pain. I put the Supercoherence Panic to Calm frequency on my second chakra and the pain disappeared in about 15 minutes. And it didn't come back!

When this period was over, all the other problems had gone too! It was pure magic! Now I am like a teenager again. My period is regular and all the discomfort has vanished. I can't describe how lovely this is. I was really out of the female frequency in many ways.

My position in the family (of a husband and three boys) has also changed. Now I feel more respected.'

Interestingly, I have received reports from four clients using the Supercoherence IAM Female frequency saying that their periods have regularized. These are all older women and their periods were previously irregular and not so clean, whereas now they are regular, clear and clean. However, that is a happy side-effect only; the SIAM frequency works at other levels which are equally if not more important.

Balancing Couples

In relationships between couples, very often there is one dominant partner. As a result the relationship can be lopsided and compromised. Over a period of time this is not beneficial for either partner and can lead to conflict, resentment and the eventual breakdown of the relationship. In my view an authentic relationship has a quality of intimacy and delight, plus the willingness of both parties to truly honour the needs of both themselves and their partner and respect their differences. This is easier said than done. To change a non-nourishing dynamic takes more than good intentions, though they are a start.

What we have found is that if both parties wear their respective Supercoherence IAM frequencies, the lopsidedness disappears, as both are able to literally hold their own frequency and have the courage and confidence to be true to themselves. Change for each one becomes not only possible but inevitable.

When true balance is restored in this way, the relationship either becomes authentic or falls away. The key of course is coherence – when both parties are coherent it is possible to have a coherent relationship.

Though we did not have the SIAM frequencies in their present form until 2010, we used the relevant Biolumanetics frequencies for many years and this process has been tried and tested for many years with couples using VRIC imaging.

If we initiated change using VRIC imaging and Biolumanetics and had an energetic solution for one partner that made them coherent, very often we found when the other partner stepped in and they were imaged together, the first person could not hold their coherence, as there was an energetic resistance to the change from the other partner. So we learned to give both persons in the dynamic their relevant Supercoherence IAM frequencies. When we re-imaged them, we would find that now the change was acceptable to both.

I think using these frequencies with couples strengthens the frequency of both parties and creates a sort of buffer zone and more energetic space for each to be their own authentic self – this is simply my interpretation of the phenomenon.

Easing Loss and Bereavement

This is an unusual way to use the SIAM frequencies. If a person has lost their partner, or a child either through death or separation, and is grieving and cannot function, they can keep the SIAM frequency relevant to that partner or child in the room or even under the former partner's pillow or on their photo. If the partner who died or left was female, for example, they would keep the SIAM Female in the room or under the pillow and vice versa. That way they will recover sooner and be able to function.

The Supercoherence Panic to Calm Frequency

The Supercoherence Panic to Calm frequency, also called SPTCF or SPtoC, is actually a combination of two frequencies, one for calming and the other for grounding.

When panic strikes, we lose our nerve and cannot hold our ground. All sense of balance and control is lost as the body goes into fight or flight mode. Its most dramatic effects can be seen in a panic attack. Put the SPTCF on the solar plexus area and the attack will stop almost instantly. There is, however, one caveat with the Supercoherence Panic to Calm frequency as far as its use in panic attacks is concerned: while the results are often dramatic and immediate, it does not resolve the underlying problem that caused the panic in the first place. In my view it is necessary to go deeper and neutralize the underlying trauma with the SRTLFs. So while the Supercoherence Panic to Calm frequency is a super tool for relief, it should not be considered a resolution mechanism.

A lot of unconscious fears are held in the solar plexus, belly brain area and this can feel tense and 'knotted' without any obvious reason. Using the SPTCF on this area will bring calm, clarity and insight as the unconscious emotional knots are loosened and released.

Here is some feedback on the SPTCF from a variety of Supercoherence practitioners and users.

OB

When I went to see Thrity I was facing a very, very stressful situation. In my business I was dealing with a guy who kept on asking for money and was threatening to take me to court. I was in such a state of shock over this that I could only read a few sentences of the legal papers, because I felt so nervous about it. There was such an emotional charge about the whole thing. In the morning I would be asleep and suddenly that man would come to mind and I would wake up.

Thrity and I did some VRIC imaging holding the legal papers (*see Plate 10*] which showed that the situation was a total mess [the images were incoherent]. I knew that already! But then I made some affirmations and held the legal papers again on my solar plexus, along with the Supercoherence Panic to Calm frequency, and what came out was much better [the image became coherent]. I went home feeling much, much more relaxed.

And the outcome of that problem, which could really have cost me several thousands of pounds, so it was no joke, was that I ended up being strong and negotiating with the guy and contacting his professional organization. We did some mediation and I had to pay some money, but we both ended up with no hard feelings. So my experience with the Supercoherence Panic to Calm frequency was very positive and allowed me to handle the situation with clarity. It taught me other lessons too, in business negotiations.

Jenny H.

I must say how wonderful the Supercoherence Panic to Calm frequency has been for me. I used to wake in the night feeling quite anxious and then I could not go back to sleep. Now if I wake and feel any anxiety I reach for my Supercoherence Panic to Calm frequency and put it on my solar plexus and I normally fall asleep almost straight away!

SS (India): A Hug from a Mother-in-Law – After 22 Years

In my culture girls are not favoured that much and when I was a child I suffered a lot because of my brother. He was always at the top of the class and I wasn't really encouraged and things like that. I developed an inferiority complex, which affected me throughout my life in different relationships, even after I got married, as a result of which I could not have a good relationship with my mother-in-law.

Gradually I became very sick and I went to Thrity, and with the frequencies [SRTLFs], slowly everything started to clear out. I started realizing I was the one limiting myself.

However, I thought one thing I would never be able to have was a good relationship with my mother-in-law. But then I went to India to visit her and she hugged me. That was the most amazing thing, because in India mothers-in-law generally never hug daughters-in-law and my own mother-in-law never hugs my two sisters-in-law. And now she has started always hugging me! I have been married 22 years and this has just started happening in the past year.

But even though she was hugging me, I was a bit resistant towards it. So I started to use the Supercoherence Panic to Calm frequency and something changed – one night I suddenly felt such tenderness and love towards her and such appreciation. When I got up the following morning, my husband told me that my mother-in-law had rung up to speak to me, and that was such a coincidence.

Now all the harshness and bitterness has just dissolved. I wanted to come to this place of love and the SRTLFs have done that.

Jane Cook: The Hangover from Hell

My friend had been out on the razzle and had too much wine to drink. The next morning she had the hangover from hell – headache, slightly blurry vision, nausea. I said, 'Hang on, I have just the thing for you.'

I got the Supercoherence Panic to Calm frequency out and told her to lie on the sofa. I put the frequency on her forehead over the third eye point for five minutes. Then I removed it and gave her the SRTLFs to hold in her hands for five minutes, then let her get up and get on with everything.

About an hour later I asked, 'How is the hangover?'

Above the noise of the TV and hoover she replied, 'What hangover?'

Jane Cook: NM

After a long day at a family gathering NM, 33, had had a few too many alcoholic drinks and the next day had woken up feeling tired and hungover. She not only felt awful but had a problem with her eye, which was irritated, inflamed and itching.

First of all she had ten minutes of holding the SRTLFs and immediately said she felt calmer and more organized. Then I got her to lie down and hold the Supercoherence Panic to Calm frequency over the bad eye for five minutes or so. She had a busy day ahead of her, so then had to dash off.

Later in the evening I phoned to see how things were and to ask about the eye, as it had been particularly painful and she had been worried something was in it.

She seemed surprised that I had phoned and just told me that everything had been fine. She had forgotten about her hangover and her eye must have got better as well, as she had forgotten about that too.

Jane Cook: JH

JH, 70, was sent to me with a great fear of flying. In the past he had travelled a lot, but always by sea. Now his wife wanted to see the Great Wall of China before she died and wanted them to fly there together.

JH held the SRTLFs and made some statements with them, including 'I always love and enjoy flying.' He felt perfectly calm when saying this, even though he did say he felt 'a bit weird'.

He came to see me three times. The third time I tried the Supercoherence Panic to Calm frequency whilst doing a mind trip as if we were on a plane. He said he felt great and calm. He asked me to use the Supercoherence Panic to Calm frequency on his photo on the days he was travelling, which I did, and he has since told me he managed very well – no anxiety at all plus a happy wife.

Jane Cook: NJ

NJ, 44, was a keen athlete and rowing fanatic and trained two or three times a week. He was very careful about his diet and took an interest in alternative therapies. His worst nightmare was a visit to the dentist. He could get close to a panic attack when he had to go. He asked me for help.

He thought it stemmed back to his childhood when, because of overcrowding, he had to have a number of teeth removed. They were taken out two at a time every school holidays. At first he was offered gas, but he could not cope with the mask covering his face, he pulled at it and I think let in some air; anyway, he felt considerable pain with the first two extractions. After that, each visit was a nightmare, causing vivid dreams before and after the visit. The other extractions were done with injections, but the dentist had no sympathy with NJ and said he should 'be a man about it'. NJ thought he was about 11 when this happened. The fear had dogged him ever since.

I thought we could help using the Supercoherence Panic to Calm frequency. NJ sat and held it in the dentist's waiting room and described going from 'total nervous wreck' to 'complete calm' in less than 30 minutes. He put it in his pocket and was able to sit in the dentist's chair to be examined and even endure the scraping and poking, which previously he had not been able to do without extreme difficulty and 'gritting his teeth'.

Gabriella Angus: Two Clients

I had two clients working with the Supercoherence Panic to Calm frequency (in a meditation group). The first client was very anxious and it calmed her down to the extent where she described herself as 'calm and peaceful'. It also enabled her to relax into the heart energies of the meditation.

The second client was full of rage. Meditation and acupuncture had done nothing to help him calm down, so I got him to hold the Supercoherence Panic to Calm frequency on his solar plexus. As he held the frequency I spoke to him directly, telling him that

I completely respected him and that no matter what he thought, I held him in high esteem. All of a sudden he melted and said no one had ever said that to him before. He calmed right down as he got in touch with the suffering underneath the anger. He said he then felt able to express himself clearly to the group. Amazing.

So what I realized today was that the frequencies create a space for healing messages to be received.

Grief and Bereavement

One of the greatest traumas we can suffer is the death of a loved one. This is especially so if the one who 'died' was young, a child or a sibling or lover. Worse still, the death may have happened as a result of violence or, worst of all, suicide. Feelings of overwhelming grief, sadness and guilt can take over for years and make joy impossible. If not addressed and mitigated in some way, they can destroy the lives of the living. Whole families can be devastated by these 'tragedies'. While it is natural to feel grief when someone we love dies, excessive grief is another matter. And as you know by now, time does not heal.

Life is a precious gift and is for living, not simply for making a living.

The SRTLFs and/or the Supercoherence Panic to Calm frequency can help find the way back from grief and guilt to life, laughter and function simply, easily and quickly. What happens is that while the grief is neutralized, the love remains, and it is possible to honour and celebrate the life of the one who has left.

Dilnaz Gilder: MV

MV, 33, came from a close-knit traditional Indian family and her only brother had died suddenly the previous year of a massive heart attack at the age of about 30. This had left the entire family in a state of shock.

On the first anniversary of her brother's death, MV was thinking about him and missing him a great deal and was unable to do her work as she was crying throughout the morning. When I met her, I decided to introduce her to the Supercoherence Panic to Calm frequency. I told her briefly about it and she was very open to using it.

After holding it against her solar plexus for about 20 minutes, she told me she was able to remember her brother without the accompanying trauma, sadness and tears. It was lovely to see a smile on her face again and she was most grateful for the ease with which she could let go of the pain she felt.

Later we spoke again and she was able to understand that although her brother was absent in the physical, he was present in another realm.

Sandra Fiquet: Three Cats

We had two cats, Mogwai and JymJams, both females, and they got on well until Mogwai had kittens, four females and one male. After this, JymJams often attacked the females, including Mogwai, if they came too close to her. She never seemed to be annoyed with the male kitten. Due to lack of space, we had to give the kittens away, but nobody seemed to want the male, so we kept him and called him Snowy. Then we noticed that even after the female kittens had gone, JymJams was still attacking Mogwai if she was too close to her, which we thought strange, as they had got on before the kittens appeared.

For whatever reason, JymJams had been very nervous since she was a kitten herself. When Snowy came on the scene, he and his mum appeared to gang up to tease her every so often, then JymJams would retaliate and so on. It wasn't on a regular basis, but often enough, and one cat or another would end up looking a little bit worse for wear.

Sometimes JymJams would strike first out of fear when the other cats were just minding their own business. Then she tried to avoid being in the same room as the other cats and she no longer stayed on the sofa with us if either of the other cats was there with us.

We were planning to go away for about eight days and I was concerned that the cats would get even more into tease-fights when we weren't there, so I put all their photographs in a line and put the SRTLFs at each end with a picture of the Divine Mother at each end too. And I also put the Supercoherence Panic to Calm on JymJams' photograph in the middle.

On our return, I kept the frequencies on the photographs for maybe a couple more weeks. I don't know why; it just felt right.

Ever since then, JymJams has been standing her ground a lot more with the other two cats and their teasing has reduced a lot. When Mogwai or Snowy are on the sofa, JymJams also claims her comfy spot there now, even when the other cats are together. They allow her to be there too. And sometimes they even sleep side by side.

Another fighting ground used to be on top of a bookcase at the window. Whichever cat was there was king. Not anymore. They now share that spot and every now and then JymJams watches the world go by in the company of Mogwai or Snowy.

Snowy the Cat and the Supercoherence Panic to Calm Frequency

Eight months after Snowy hurt his leg muscle and recovered twice as fast with the SRTLFs as with a 'traditional' anti-inflammatory (*see p.000*), he hurt his leg muscle yet again. It seemed quite a bit worse this time, as he wasn't putting his paw down at all and was hopping along on three legs.

I noticed it first thing in the morning and I put the SRTLFs and the Divine Mother picture on his photograph straight away. Then a thought came in my head: 'What if I put the Supercoherence Panic to Calm on the injured paw on the photograph as well? Luckily, the photograph I had was showing all the paws. I thought it would be an interesting experiment, so went ahead with it.

The next day around lunchtime, Snowy was walking normally. He flinched slightly when he tried to run, but by the evening he was running normally. Considering his injury had seemed worse this time around, I was astounded by the result.

So his recovery rates for walking normally were:

1 week with the anti-inflammatory from the vet.

3 days with the SRTLFs and Divine Mother on his photograph.

1.5 days with the SRTLFs and Divine Mother and Supercoherence Panic to Calm frequency on the injured paw/leg on his photograph.

JymJams the Cat and the Supercoherence Panic to Calm Frequency

Every year around 5th November, JymJams has been terrified of the fireworks sounds outside. She has always sought refuge under the futon upstairs, only daring to emerge to eat and to quickly 'do her business' outside. Each year she has stayed under there for three or four days.

This year as soon as the sound of the fireworks started, she was under the futon again. So I found a photograph of her and put the Supercoherence Panic to Calm frequency on it, right in the middle.

She became much calmer and came out, and, although a little jumpy when a firework was particularly loud, she stayed with us downstairs throughout the firework season and when we were upstairs, she didn't go under the futon once.

When the firework season was over, I kept the Supercoherence Panic to Calm frequency on her photograph for a few more days, as it felt right to do so, and I noticed an additional change. Normally when she is on the sofa next to the front door and the doorbell rings, she jumps off the sofa and stands by the cat flap, ready to run out. Now, each time the doorbell rings, she stays on the sofa and simply looks towards the door in an inquisitive way.

A couple of friends visited, sat down on the sofa next to her and commented how amazed they were to see her so calm. Normally they only catch a glimpse of a fluffy tail running away.

Thrity: Emma's Cat

My friend's house was recently broken into while she and her husband were out of the country for the weekend. The burglar alarm went off and the thieves were there for just a few minutes and did not get anything.

Emma has a cat which is very timid and does not like strangers – a typical scaredy cat. When the house was invaded, the cat must have heard the door being forced and the loud noise as the burglar alarm went off, seen or heard the strangers in the house and run away.

Within a short while, Emma's brother came over to make sure the house was secured again and discovered that the cat had disappeared. He and a friend went looking for her, but could not find her. He knew that his sister would be terribly upset about her, so he phoned Emma's husband to let him know about the situation. While they were on the phone Emma herself came in and realized what had happened. By this time the cat had been missing for several hours.

Emma took out her BlackBerry. She has several photos of her pet on it. She put the Supercoherence Panic to Calm frequency on the cat's photo and within 15 minutes there was another call from her brother – the cat was back.

The story does not end there. The next day Emma took the Supercoherence Panic to Calm frequency off the photo, as she needed to use the BlackBerry, and the cat disappeared again. When the frequency was put back on the photo, she reappeared within minutes.

Coincidence, placebo effect or miracle of the frequency universe? You decide.

Jane Cook: Mrs. Orchida

When Mrs. Orchida the orchid was bought in a sale, although she had about five flowers, they were very pale pink and did not last long. She was placed in the kitchen on the side close to the window and seemed fine to start with, but as time went on she appeared to get more and more unwell. I tried wiping her leaves with damp cloths and watering her shoots and roots, but she just deteriorated more and more. This went on for about six months.

I then moved her into the back bedroom, as I found her depressing to look at. I kept an eye on her, but not as often. She got worse – her roots went brown and started dying, her leaves split down the centre and had brown patches on, and last of all, they began to lose their shine. Then someone came to stay, so she came back into the kitchen to clear some space. This was in March 2011. I looked at her in despair; I thought she would have to go. But just as I was making some coffee, a thought popped into my head: 'What about using the Supercoherence frequencies?'

First, for about 20 minutes, I put the Supercoherence Panic to Calm frequency in her pot, because I was sure she was stressed! Then I left my SRTLFs overnight in her flower pot for the following five to six nights.

Nothing happened, but I had to wait and see just in case. I waited and waited – nothing.

A whole month went by and I was starting to give up hope when to my amazement a small green shoot began to appear right in the centre of all the dilapidated leaves. It was tiny, but at last there was a change. I gave Mrs Orchida another night of the SRTLFs. The shoot grew slowly, but I could see it was forming into a leaf. When it was nearly half formed, a small grey root appeared from below the base of the leaf stem. This grew quite quickly, about an inch in a week. I was fascinated.

By the end of April the leaf had formed and some more roots had appeared and then there was what I thought was a brown shiny root poking out from underneath. This root also grew quite quickly, but it grew upwards and headed towards the window. In a month this had grown over six inches. It seemed to just keep growing and then I noticed some small nodules forming along it and gradually they began to form into little bumps. There was nothing more for a week, then they stared to grow into little shoots, and then the shoots began to form small buds. I thought they might become flowers.

To my total joy and amazement, they did grow into flowers, but not the weak pale pink ones Mrs. Orchida had had when she last flowered – these were strong and dark pink and perfectly formed. Every one was the same, every one was perfect, right down to the identical little lines inside, the beautiful whiskers on the outside, the little veins running through the petals and the slight shimmer of stardust coating the back of every flower. We thought she was going to have sextuplets, but in the end she has ended up with undecaplets – 11 identical flowers, all perfect and correct.

She is totally awesome and still flowering as I write during the second week of September. Also, she has replaced two of her leaves with two new ones whilst still holding onto her two large split ones, which have lost their brown blotches and are shiny green despite still being split down the centre along the stem.

She is my shining example of what can happen when using the SRTLFs – she has responded to them by producing perfection.

Angela McArthur: LCM

LCM had been experiencing panic attacks for four months, centred around the break-up of a relationship. This had been adversely affecting her sleep and as a consequence her work was suffering (she is self-employed in a very demanding role). She was instructed to use the Supercoherence Panic to Calm frequency as and when needed.

'I was astonished by the effectiveness of the stone. I was in a blind panic – short of breath and feeling the world was a place I didn't want to be in. After using the stone for just a few minutes, I was calmer and more at peace. I have continued to use the stone and over time my calmness has returned.'

Judy K.

I have been using the Supercoherence Panic to Calm frequency to clear chakras. I usually ask my clients where they would like to have it placed. Most of them want to have it on the heart chakra. I sense that it aligns and clears old pain and trauma and opens the heart for more compassion towards self and others. I use it frequently on my own heart. The heart chakra clearing is very powerful. It frees up pre and post-natal trauma and early childhood pains and generates more love for self and others.

I have also used the Supercoherence Panic to Calm frequency on the sixth chakra to clear old beliefs or excessive worries and thinking. It works great there.

Also, I use it on surgical wounds and it helps ease the pain.

Oh, by the way, it worked with a client of mine who was in the last trimester of a pregnancy when her husband was diagnosed with cancer. She was in shock, but we put the frequency on her heart as she requested and then I put it on her navel for the baby and I felt and saw the return to calm for her and the baby.

Before using the SPTCF for the baby, by taking his pulse I found that he was in shock and his biorhythm was chaotic. Afterwards, it had calmed down to almost normal. I was able to take his pulse while he was in the womb because babies have their own energy system right before conception so they can take form in the physical world. Chinese pulse-taking and my own sense pick it up.

I also felt a divine presence throughout the pregnancy – the Divine Mother was there. It was such an experience for me to witness that. I was being healed by that presence. The baby is very special to carry that aura.

I also treated him after a traumatic birth – he was pulled out of the womb with forceps and was screaming a lot. It felt as though he had a headache because of the forceps pressure, so I put the Supercoherence Panic to Calm frequency on his head. He smiled and has slept well since then.

Jane Cook's experiences with the Supercoherence Panic to Calm frequency:

MB

When MB, 71, wakes up during night with cramps in her legs, she places the Supercoherence Panic to Calm frequency on the spot and the cramp ceases immediately. She has done this on a number of occasions.

AR

AR, 42, enjoyed jogging but had been suffering with cramps. One day when she was running past the house she called in with bad cramp in her left calf. We put the Supercoherence Panic to Calm frequency on it and it went immediately. We have done this now on several different occasions and it has worked every time.

JN

JN, 3, suffered a great deal from hiccups, and suddenly more so when his baby sister was born. They were stopped every time immediately with 'Granny's magic glass' – the Supercoherence Panic to Calm frequency.

JC

Whilst in the garden, JC, 54, got either bitten, stung or scratched. She had an immediate allergic reaction: her left wrist and hand began to swell and a rash appeared going up the inside of the arm ahead of the swelling, which also started spreading up the arm.

She was already carrying the SRTLFs in her pocket, but she was alarmed and went in to get the Supercoherence Panic to Calm frequency. She placed it on the spot of the bite/sting/scratch and held it there. Ten minutes later, the arm had calmed down – no swelling, no rash, all back to normal. The swelling and rash did not return.

MS

MS, 68, was over in London from Ireland. He was suffering from stress caused by certain family obligations and decided to stay on for a couple of days to recover before returning home.

On the second morning he woke up quite alarmed, as a very severe rash had developed all around his navel and was spreading across his stomach. It was four to five inches across and two inches wide. It was also extremely inflamed and itchy. He was worried that it might be shingles. I asked him if he had had anything like it before. He said he hadn't.

He was open to trying something a bit different, so I gave him the Supercoherence Panic to Calm frequency to hold. I told him it would probably take a few minutes, but it should help.

After 20 minutes, the entire rash had disappeared, all the itching had stopped and MS could hardly believe it.

We never knew what the rash was and he has never had it back again.

Lotta Naess's experiences:

JN

JN had been away for three days on a school trip with his class. They had done a lot of fun activities like horseback riding, river rafting and so on. They hadn't slept very much and he was really tired when he came home. He complained about his 'aching eye' and I wasn't surprised. I was afraid he might be starting one of his migraines.

As he was lying down on his bed, I put the SPTCF on the eyelid of the aching eye. It was only two minutes before he was up again! The migraine attack was neutralized at the speed of light.

VN

VN, 18 and a little bit skeptical about the frequencies, had had terrible hiccups for two days. They stopped for a while, but kept coming back again and again. I suggested that he put the SPTCF on his solar plexus.

The hiccups stopped instantly and did not come back! Great!

MPC

My son's girlfriend, MPC, 16, showed up with a terrible headache. This was not unusual for her. She asked for an aspirin, but I offered her a frequency. She was very open-minded and answered, 'Why not?'

She lay down on the sofa and I put the SPTCF on the spot on her forehead where the pain was almost unbearable. At the same time she held the SRTLFs reversed.

After ten minutes on the sofa, she got up. The headache was gone. Faster than aspirin.

From Mumbai, Supercoherence practitioner Dilnaz Gilder also had good results with the Supercoherence Panic to Calm frequency and headaches:

PTCF and Headaches

My colleague, FM, came to me asking for two aspirins because she had a headache. I told her I didn't have any and offered her the Supercoherence Panic to Calm frequency instead. She was quite skeptical, but was willing to try it nevertheless. So she stood there chatting while holding the frequency to her forehead. In a few minutes she returned it to me, thanked me and left – the headache had gone!

I had some friends come over for dinner and during the evening their teenage daughter asked if I had a Crocin or Tylenol, as she had a headache. I told her I didn't, but gave her the Supercoherence Panic to Calm frequency to put on her forehead. She was quite open to doing it and within 15 minutes said she was fine and returned the frequency.

My friend's mother suffers from migraines. As soon as she feels one coming on, she has to take her medication otherwise it becomes so severe that she throws up. One day she held the Supercoherence Panic to Calm frequency and the migraine disappeared after about 30 minutes. She now uses only the frequency to deal with the migraines and is completely off the medication.

2 airline captains in Scandinavia report success using the Panic to Calm frequency with passengers who are afraid of flying. They simply ask the panicky passenger to hold the frequency in their hands and have a chat with them. It works every time.

I have left the Supercoherence IAM Universal (SIAM U) frequency for another chapter. You will see why when you get to it.

CHAPTER 13
Tales of Transformation

'Because of time and space, the material result will reveal itself only later, but it cannot fail to come. If you transform yourself, matter likewise transforms itself.'

Talking with Angels

THESE CASE STUDIES or stories come from various Supercoherence practitioners. Here is one from Angela McArthur's casebook:

AL

AL had been living with her boyfriend in London for three years. She was a primary school teacher and Reiki master. Although she had an underlying sense of 'something being wrong' she did not have any acute issues that she wanted addressed.

In my opinion AL had a huge sense of guilt, and vacillated between this and a corresponding anger or resentment, which manifested as criticism or sniping at those close to her (namely her boyfriend and her family in Brazil). She was introverted and insecure, and her current relationship afforded her safety and security. However, it was unsatisfactory for her; she was almost entirely sexually inactive and blamed her partner for his complacency in not addressing this area of the relationship.

During her use of the SRTLFs she experienced a greater degree of calm and acceptance of others, not feeling the impulse to project her guilt in the form of blame. After using the Supercoherence IAM Female frequency, she decided to leave her partner and began seeing other people. This was positive for her, although she experienced much upset along the way and was unsure whether she had done the right thing.

In her words:

'Whilst I was using the SRTLFs helpful people would pop up – the intent plus the SRTLFs seemed somehow to equal synchronicity. Some situations could be explosive, but I'm choosing not to act from anger anymore, rather from a place of love. I'm not holding as much resentment as when I left my partner in July of this year. I am more able to stand up for myself...

Previously I'd sometimes been intolerant with my class, but now I'm very aware of my intolerance as it's happening and I have an internal dialogue. I'm a bit frustrated by being a teacher, but I realize the kids are seeking love and approval. During a recent parent–teacher evening, I wasn't fearful as usual and didn't react to parents who were threatening or intimidating.

In reversing the SRTLFs I felt more tingling in my hands. They relaxed me.

The SRTLFs helped me to find my feet in Brazil when I returned home over the Christmas period. I was all over the place in my mind and came back destabilized, but my own spiritual practice and the SRTLFs have comforted me.'

From Jane Cook's casebook:

CJ

CJ, 55, came to me quite distraught. She had been having some very big problems with a work colleague. It had started with a slight dislike of this lady and by the time she came to me had grown out of all proportion, to the extent almost of hatred. CJ just could not stand the sight of her colleague and cringed every time she saw her. This did worry her, as she had no idea why it was happening. She had not felt this strongly about anyone ever.

She asked if we could try using the SRTLFs. She had brought along a picture of the colleague. She sat down quietly with the SRTLFs, green in the right hand pink in the left, for five minutes to get quite calm. Then we added the Divine Mother picture and the picture of the colleague for three to four minutes in each hand whilst also holding the frequencies. At the end of the session I assured her that the SRTLFs would have done the job and she left quite happy that they had worked and keen to see what happened the next day at work.

The next day, although there was some improvement in how CJ felt when she saw the colleague, it was plain she still could not stand the sight of her. After work she called in, full of woe. I asked if she would mind if we tried again. She agreed, so we repeated the same process as the day before. CJ left happy again.

To her surprise, the next day she felt even more hostile to the colleague! Luckily she was not put off and came back to me for more SRTLF sessions. In fact altogether she had five sessions in a row.

After session number five, which was on a Friday, when she went to work on the Monday she said it was like a miracle: she met the colleague, looked at her, even peered at her, but no way could she experience the feelings from the previous week. She was totally amazed.

To this day she works quite happily with this woman opposite her all day and has not had even a twinge of her previous feelings of hatred.

EWM

This sweet elderly lady, aged 90, had been suffering from incontinence for a little over six months and was rather afraid it might get worse. She held the SRTLFs and Divine Mother photo for ten minutes, first with the DM in the right hand and then in the left, and said it felt very soothing and she felt happier.

She was apparently getting worked up about moving from her home into a care home. She was keen to do it, but was anxious in case anyone found out about her 'little problem'.

We decided to meet for five sessions, one session a day for five days. She agreed and over the week there was no obvious change. On the last day

I asked her to do the same as before but to make the statement 'I am totally free of my incontinence.' She did this twice once for each hand.

Since then she has phoned to say she is perfectly dry, even going through the night without getting up!

DB

DB, 65, lives in Devon and is a financial advisor. He suffers from anxiety and depression. Although he struggles to keep on top of it, he does find that it interferes with his life. Sometimes he cannot eat properly because of digestive problems. When he gets depressed he does not have any idea why. He is married with three children, two from his first marriage and now a little girl from his present marriage. He is 'happy' with everything but is plagued by this problem of depression. He had some counselling years ago but that went nowhere and the anxiety and depression continued. He was given my number. We have been working over the phone and with remote SRTLFs. We cleared the family over a few days about a month ago and since then I have been busy and away a lot, so it is only now that we have had time to have a good catch-up chat on the phone.

D says he just cannot believe what has happened – his world has been spun around and put on a new course. He is now only working for his old clients. In the rest of his time he has taken up golf and yoga! Both are new activities and he loves them. In fact he thinks that he now loves *everything*, including himself and his family, more. He has hardly thought about the depression – all the anxieties have lifted and he and his wife and child feel so free.

From Lotta Naess's casebook:

JN

Today my youngest son, JN, 13, came home from school crying. There had been a conflict between him and two of his new friends at school. He was really, really upset, so I gave him the green SRTLF in his left hand and asked him to tell me exactly what had happened. He stopped crying very shortly. Then I gave him the pink SRTLF in his right hand so he held both reversed while he was telling me the story and for a while after.

He calmed down and felt a bit low. He was hungry, so I made him a sandwich.

Later in the afternoon I asked him how he felt about the conflict. He looked at me and said that he wasn't even thinking about it anymore. 'It feels like nothing,' he said.

Next day he went to school without worrying about it. Everything was back to normal and he was obviously not affected anymore.

JN was at a tennis camp when he got into trouble with one of the other participants, a boy called Kevin. This boy had been fooling around, teasing the others and spoiling the game for a while. The camp leader had told him off several times but he didn't stop. Suddenly JN had enough and told him to stop it, otherwise he would hit him! This was not a very good thing to say, but he lost his patience.

Kevin got mad. He kicked JN in the stomach and slapped his face, then ran away.

A little later JN called home. He was crying and felt that it was his fault since in a way he had threatened Kevin. And of course he was hurt and in pain.

At first I didn't hear what he was saying, but while listening to him I put the green SRTLF on the left side of his photo. Shortly after he stopped crying and went on telling me the story. I put on the pink one on the right side of his photo, so both SRTLFs were there reversed.

At the beginning of the phone call, he wanted us to pick him up – he wanted to come home. This was not possible, as the camp was four hours' drive away. I turned into a big heart with ears and a very small mouth just to be there on the phone listening.

Half an hour later after, JN felt balanced again. He said that he felt alright and we decided to talk to each other again before bedtime.

After a few hours I put the SRTLFs the right way on the photo and my intention was that the boys should become friends again.

Later that night JN called to say good night. I asked him how he felt and it was fine. Kevin had said he was sorry to him and he had said, 'I am sorry too. I shouldn't have threatened you.'

Autumn has been like a roller-coaster. JN started a new school and got new teachers, completely new classmates and a lot of new subjects. He needed a lot of support.

When I put the SRTLFs and SPTCF on his photo, things took a new direction. It seemed that a lot of fears loosened up and he was much more comfortable with himself. This has stayed with him and he is also very loving with a lot of hugs and telling me he loves me. Of course he still has his ups and downs, but nothing we can't handle.

At the end of the first semester he told me that he was very fond of a girl in his class called AC, but all through the autumn her best friend, JB, had done her best to keep them apart. AC was not allowed to talk to JN or even sit beside him. JB had total control over her friend. After several months JN was sick and tired of JB and finally he told me about it and we talked about how he should try to handle it.

Late that night the voice within me told me to put the frequencies on JN and JB. I wrote out JB's full name and put the piece of paper on JNs photo together with the Divine Mother photo, the SRTLFs and the SPTCF.

Next day, when we were having dinner I said to JN, 'By the way, how did it work out with AC and JB today?'

'She asked for forgiveness,' he said shortly.

'What! How come?' I asked curiously.

'Well, five minutes before the first morning lesson she came up to me when I was getting my books from my cupboard. We were all alone and she said, "I have been stupid. Can you forgive me?"'

'And what did you say?' I asked, as I felt tears rising in my eyes.

'You are forgiven!' JN said.

It was as simple as that. I was overwhelmed! It had been less than eight hours since I had put the frequencies on their photos and names.

KN

When I first started using the SRTLFs, my husband, KN, 46, was pensive but at the same time he joked about them. After a while he wanted to hold them.

I was waiting for something yet to come.

A few months later it was time for one of our son's confirmation. While preparing the invitations my husband suddenly said, 'Maybe I should send an invitation to my sister?'

I answered, 'Yes, do so.' But at the same time I thought, '*What* did he say? She hasn't visited us for ten years!'

He sent her an invitation and two days later she said yes!

KN often get herpes simplex virus on his mouth and two days before the visit he noticed that it was breaking out again. So we tried an experiment: I put the SPTCF on his lips, the I AM Male on his chest and he held the SRTLFs reversed.

I integrated the IAM Male frequency because, according to Lise Bourbeau's studies in the book *The Body Is Telling You: Love Yourself!*, the HS virus has to do with a deep inner conflict with someone of the opposite sex. KN has had a complicated ongoing conflict with his sister for many years.

Normally it takes weeks for a HS outbreak to subside, but this time it was over within a week. Interesting!

His sister duly visited us, first attending the confirmation in church and then coming home to have dinner with us. That visit, I am sure, was a result of my husband holding the SRTLFs for a while. Probably her field felt the configuration in his field and started to connect in a positive direction...?

After this KN started to use the SRTLFs more regularly and since then his dry hands, cracked skin and sore back have all cleared up. This physical healing has come from the alignment with the ZPF, I just know it!

VN

One of our sons, VN, 18, was going through a very busy period at school. There were a lot of tests in chemistry, physics and mathematics. He was under quite a lot of pressure and he asks a lot of himself. This makes him stressed and he finds it difficult to relax.

Today he took the SRTLFs with him to school. Directly he came home, he told me that he had felt much calmer and more relaxed during the day.

'You know, Mum, even if I don't do anything for a while the world keeps spinning around!' he said.

What a wonderful insight for a teenager.

MPC

My son's girlfriend, MPC, 16, was very upset one day because she had been treated very badly by two of her teachers. She had had difficulties with her schoolwork and a very busy time in school, but there was no understanding at all when she delivered her homework a day late. Her teachers were both arrogant and sarcastic, even though she had done her best. MPC felt misunderstood and sad, she had tears in her eyes and was very close to crying.

Her family had immigrated to Sweden from Chile and I understand that there have been a lot of worries about their future that have affected her negatively as well.

She had used the SRTLFs before, so I asked her to hold them while she was telling me all about it. She held them reversed, along with the Divine Mother photo. After a while I asked her how he felt. She felt calmer inside and after ten more minutes she decided to do some homework. She kept the SRTLFs in her pockets for an hour.

Two days later I met her and asked her how she felt and how she was doing in school. She looked at me in a peculiar way and said, 'I'm just fine! Why are you asking?'

I reminded her about our little chat and the SRTLFs.

'Oh, that!' she said. 'I've forgotten all about it. I mean, I remember it of course, but it doesn't matter to me anymore. That's odd, actually – I always get stuck on things that affect me emotionally, but not this time!'

At the end of the semester she received a scholarship which took her to England for a week. Now she has been accepted for high school studies in society science, the course she wanted the most! She has also been lucky enough to get a job in a restaurant during the summer holiday, so she can earn some extra money. Life is suddenly easier for her and we have been talking a lot about what the SRTLFs really are!

LA

My father, LA, is 71 years old. His life has been full of working, doing and 'musts'. He is a very restless man who always has to be doing something. He is an incurable perfectionist and has always had a very short temper, to say the least.

Ha has had several heart attacks and has also undergone heart bypass surgery. He has suffered from depression, too, especially after the surgery and after a very serious accident: while cycling, he was hit by a car travelling at 70 kilometres per hour. The only reason he survived was because he was wearing a helmet. It took him several years to recover and he is still a little 'crash-damaged' due to frontal-lobe bleeding.

The first time he held the SRTLFs was in December 2009, and from then on he held them maybe once a month over a period of five months. Today he has his own SRTLFs and uses them daily.

There have been several what he refers to as 'notable changes' in his life:

Since he suffers from sleep apnoea, he uses a special kind of oxygen mask while sleeping. He has very seldom slept all night, but after using the SRTLFs for a week he suddenly started sleeping right through, not even having to go to the toilet to urinate. He also started taking an afternoon nap. That was never possible before.

All his dark dreams have changed to dreams of the sweet kind.

His restlessness has gone and a kind of calmness has rolled through his body and life.

A lot of synchronicities have been happening and things in his life are falling into place without effort.

He now views the people around him as 'good guys' rather than opponents.

'Is it the frequencies that are making me accept myself without having to be the best all the time?' he asked me. 'I couldn't like myself earlier in my life, but I think I am starting to do that.'

For several years LA had a constant headache at the back of his head on the left side. He had learned to live with it, but when he started holding the SRTLFs more frequently it first reduced to half the strength and after a week it had gone entirely.

He commented recently:

'The headache is still gone! Unbelievable!

Since I have been using an oxygen mask during the night, I have had a big problem with a very dry throat. It is also difficult to open my eyes properly before I have washed them thoroughly. It is as if the lids are pasted down with glue. Suddenly both my throat and my eyes are back to normal again. Is this some kind of magic?

I still feel so peaceful inside and I wonder if it will go on like this or if it is only temporary.

Every day when I exercise on my stationary bike, I follow my cardiac rhythm on a display. Every fifth beat has always been a kind of double beat. My doctor says it is nothing to worry about, but now this double beat has been gone for three days and the rhythm is very even.'

IA

My mother, IA, 72, held the SRTLFs for the first time in December 2009. Since then she has only held them a few times.

She has worked very hard in the family business all her life. Her husband is very dominant, which has made her very compliant and afraid of conflict.

She has suffered from high blood pressure for ten years and takes medication for it. She also has goitre and lichen ruber planus, a disease of the mucous membranes of the mouth. All three are connected to stress.

In March 2010 she became very ill. Her whole body ached. At the hospital the doctor diagnosed PMR (*Polymyalgia rheumatic*). It is a state of inflammation of all the muscles and it was treated with cortisone.

According to Dr. Geerd Hamer from Germany, a New Medicine doctor, a state of inflammation is the body's first step in reconstructing itself – it is the result of the body's resolution of a deep inner conflict. As soon as the body starts to heal, the disease will appear. The biological task of the disease is to 'paralyze' the person to make optimal healing possible. Dr Hamer also says that warm diseases, like inflammation and infections, indicate that the conflict is solved and the body is in a healing process.

The background is that my mother was excluded from her biological family over 30 years ago, as the result of a disagreement. Her parents died with the situation still unresolved, and her six brothers and sisters still have no contact with her.

My conclusion is that when she held the SRTLFs for the first time in December, she aligned with the ZPF and became coherent. Imprints started to neutralize. Then it took a while for the healing process to reach cell level in the physical body and when it did the body responded with PMR as a confirmation that she was a holistic being that was being healed on all levels from the ZPF to the physical body.

My mother's feedback to me is that her mind is much clearer now. She feels much calmer and sees things from a new point of view. Earlier she held herself very tight in all situations and always had to have control over everything – that has loosened up a bit. All this within a few months!

Three weeks after starting the cortisone medication, one night she found it difficult to breathe. At the hospital they gave her morphine intravenously and sedatives. Next day she still couldn't take a deep breath, just small nips of air. It felt as if an iron belt had tightened around her ribcage.

Next morning, at breakfast, a voice in my head told me to put the SPTCF on her photo. Why didn't I think of that earlier? I did it instantly. An hour later I called my mother to ask her how she felt. She told me that suddenly, just half an hour before, something had loosened up around her chest and she had been able to take a deeper breath. That was half an hour after I had put the SPTCF on her photo.

I kept the SPTCF on the photo for the rest of the day. In the evening I put the SRTLFs there and left them overnight. She left hospital two days later, without a diagnosis.

A few weeks after that the next physical problem appeared: both feet swelled up. Again, the doctors could not find an answer to her problem. I paid her a visit the same day to lend her my IAM Female frequency.

Next morning I called to check on her. She was overwhelmed. When she had woken up, she had found her feet were back to normal again!

Now my mother has got a set of SRTLFs and uses them daily. As her soul heals, she has also been experiencing a lot of positive things in her relationships. This is her story about visiting an old uncle:

'Because of my background, being excluded from my biological family, it has been important to me to keep contact with an old aunt. I talk to her once a year and send her a Christmas card.

Last autumn she died and I sent a Christmas card to her husband, "Uncle" Folke. My family never liked him very much, because he and my aunt had a lot of problems in their marriage and they all took my aunt's side. I must say that I was never very fond of him myself.

One morning in June I woke up and felt that I had to go and see him. I don't know where the idea came from, but I did it.

I bought some pastries and went to the care home he lived in. He didn't know that I was coming and I hadn't seen him for five years. When I went into his room I gave him a hug. When he put his arms around me I could feel his love streaming into my chest and I felt the same way about him. We had two wonderful hours together, talking about life. He is 96 years old and crystal-clear in his mind. For the first time in my life I discovered what a nice person he was, loving and full of sympathy! When I left we both cried, because it felt so good just being together.

In the car on my way home, I felt such happiness in my soul. On my way to the care home I couldn't have imagined how this visit would turn out. I, who always thought my uncle was an old, stupid and selfish fool, understood that I hadn't known him at all – only others' judgements.'

This is her view of her relationship with her mother-in-law:

'Through the years I have always tried to do my best in my relationship with my mother-in-law. She became a widow when she was 56 years old and our family have always taken care of her. Today she is 90. I have never said no to her and have always tried to please her. I have felt sorry for her. Two years ago she moved to a care home, but she has never liked it and in the process she has tied me even more closely to her. She wants me to visit her every day.

Suddenly, this spring, I realized that I had to cut the bond, otherwise I would go under. It became very clear to me that I had let her live her life through me/us and bind us closer together. This was wrong. My mother-in-law had ruled my life, but I haven't seen it until now. I could see that we were separate individuals who both had to live our own lives. It wasn't easy to cut the ties, but I was astonished by how smoothly it went. It felt good and, after all, it is the way it should be.

My special relationship with my mother-in-law has not been very easy for my sisters-in-law. I have been favoured in front of them and they have felt neglected. One day I called one of them to really talk about what has been going on in the family for all these years. After talking for an hour and a half, we felt relieved. It felt as if I had a new sister. We told each other that we loved each other very much.

Afterwards it felt like being born again!'

I can only confirm the beauty of the system over and over again. It is fantastic to hear what happens to people when the imprints in the ZPF are neutralized and the soul starts to heal!

All these things happened in my mother's life between December 2009 and June 2010. Wow!

And suddenly she has started to read spiritual books. This is wonderful because she has never read any kind of books before, only 'gossip magazines'. Now she is reading book after book after book! Lovely!

The following month I gave her instructions how to clear her past. She decided to start with her siblings, since there is a lot of old stuff hidden there. I also taught her how to put the SRTLFs on a photo. She was very eager to get started.

Just a few days later her husband had a minor stroke and went to hospital. While he was eating his dinner, a lady approached his table.

She said, 'Hello, LA, how are you? What are you doing here?'

He looked at her and after a few seconds he recognized her. It was Beryl, one of his sisters-in-law. And she had neither spoken to him nor as much as looked at him during the previous 32 years. In fact, following an argument with her sister, she had been completely outrageous and done her very best to blacken his and his wife's name with the whole family. It was as a result of this that they had been excluded from the family, who had all either taken Beryl's part or just kept quiet.

Now, Beryl was standing in front of him, asking how he felt! What on earth had happened?

He told her, a little carefully, about the stroke. Then he asked her what she was doing there. She was visiting her husband's brother, who also had had a stroke. Then she said that someone had told her that IA had been in very bad shape over the last six months, and before leaving him, she asked him to send IA a greeting from her.

When IA heard all this, she had to sit down for a while. Could it be that clearing the past with her sister had led to this situation? In less than a week the SRTLFs had dissolved a 32-year-old conflict affecting a whole family!

It will be interesting to see what follows when the two sisters meet in person!

SA

SA, my grandmother, is 90 years old. A year ago she had to move into a care home, but this wasn't easy for her. She was frustrated at losing her independence and irritated by the nurses and carers not doing things the way she was used to.

The manager had complained to my father about her bad temper on several occasions and my father had tried to talk to her, but without success.

One day when he was visiting her he brought his own SRTLFs. He told her that they would be good for her and would help her to be calm and peaceful. He asked her if she wanted to hold them. She said it might be worth trying – though she really meant that nothing was wrong with her, only with those who were working at the care home! However, she said the SRTLFs were indeed nice to hold and very beautiful to look at.

My father took them with him every time he visited her, maybe twice a week. She held them for a while and she liked it.

A few weeks later the manager called my father again. This time she told him his mother had been so calm and gentle lately. 'We are not having those problems with her bad temper any longer,' she said. 'I suppose you have talked to her about it, and I want to thank you, it really helped.'

Now SA wants a set of her own SRTLFs because they make her feel so good.

LL

LL, 49, grew up in a lot of different places. Her father was a veterinarian and while he was working for Swedish International Development Authority in South America, her mother developed breast cancer. She left the family for treatment in Sweden. This caused a huge blockage in LL and created a life-long pattern: she is afraid of being left, so she is always the one who leaves others first.

Two years ago she divorced her second husband. She had no children from her first marriage but has three from her second one. Her middle child, Sophie, died seven years ago, at the age of ten. She had a brain tumour and in addition she had learning difficulties due to a broken chromosome. She could not speak at all; the only way to communicate with her was by reading her feelings. LL had become very good at this.

Since the death of her daughter, LL had really developed spiritually. When I first told her about the frequencies she said they sounded fantastic, but she already felt coherent, so this wasn't anything she needed. She had cleared her soul over and over again through the years. But somehow, a situation came up that forced the issue and to cut a long story short, she agreed to hold the SRTLFs.

Seven years before, when Sophie had been in hospital in the final stages of her cancer, she had been in a terrible state. She had been throwing up blood in cascades and LL had not even been allowed to hold her because the little girl cramped and panicked. At this stage LL was exhausted and had no strength left. She made a decision to go home to her other two kids and left Sophie with her assistant and the nurses. That had been her last contact with Sophie. She had fallen unconscious while LL was at home and died five days later.

Since that decision LL had suffered from guilt at not being there for her child when she was in such a condition. The interesting thing is that she thought that she had resolved that. But the morning after holding the SRTLFs, she woke up and just understood that she was forgiven for that decision. A feeling of complete relief and calmness was present inside her. She started to cry with happiness.

When telling me this, she added, 'I have managed to clear a lot of things by myself, but only the SRTLFs have been able to take me beyond myself to release this guilt that was stuck in my soul. I feel free!'

Later LL found a spot on her neck that looked just like one she had had cut away from her chest the previous year. That had been malignant melanoma. She called me, very upset, and I asked her to hold the SRTLFs reversed. At the same time I wrote her name down and put the SPTCF on it. After a few hours she called and told me that she had had chest pain and felt deep anxiety. While this was going on in her body she had come in contact with feelings of desolation that she recognized came from that time very long ago when her mother left the family for cancer treatment in Sweden.

The feeling of desolation led to a very strong desire to be loved.

Suddenly LL understood that it was something she had longed for since her mother closed her heart in fear – fear that if she loved LL without limits she would cause her a lot of pain if she died of the cancer. This feeling from her mother was planted in LL and led her in the same way to leave others before being left herself.

This pattern had been repeated in a lot in her life, for example at the hospital with Sophie and in leaving two marriages behind. She had also left her son to live with his father. She had been afraid that he would choose to live with his father, and then she would be the one who had been left. So she made the choice and left him.

When she had recovered, she felt a big emptiness inside her and also understood that the love of a mother had been the biggest and most difficult feeling for her to handle – so far.

The SPTCF hooked into these feelings in a deep layer and the SRTLFs cut like a laser through the knot and released energy from the imprint in the field.

I told her to get an appointment with a doctor to check out the spot on her neck, but by the time she went, two weeks later, it had almost faded away. Tests showed that it was not malignant melanoma.

LL worked part time as a massage therapist. One day something new happened: she started to emit light from her hands while massaging a client's back. A feeling of holiness appeared when she was circling her hands on the client's feet. She also felt that she was creating something new and felt very different, more like a 'giver'. After the treatment the client felt born again!

When LL visited her parents for the first time in two years, it was a very emotional stay. There had been a lot of disagreements with them since her divorce about how she should live her life. But when she looked at her 83 and 84-year-old parents, she was filled with gratefulness and joy. It was a very strong experience to see them both so alive and healthy in spite of their age. And she saw them in a new kind of way. All the old shame and blame had melted away.

LL is convinced that all these things are the result of being coherent. She is now using the SRTLFs daily.

JNW

JNW, 45, was married to Jack, who worked abroad in many different countries. He was not registered in Sweden and came and went very irregularly. They had two teenage children.

During the children's first years, JNW had lived together with her parents in her childhood home. As the children grew she and Jack had bought the house and her parents had moved. JNW had been a housewife all these years, but recently she felt she had lost her creativity and become apathetic. Seven years ago she and her husband had had a crisis in their marriage. They had never sorted it out, and fears, feelings and assumptions had been swept under the carpet.

JNW had a very special relationship with her family. Her older brother had been trapped in a religious sect and brainwashed 20 years before. Professional deprogramming had failed and he had never re-entered normal life. He lived in a special home and was on strong medication to keep the voices in his head away. This tragic family situation had made JNW her parents' 'only child' and tied her very closely to them.

JNW was overweight and had a problem with an aching knee, gastritis, an irregular heartbeat and aching feet. She also had an irritating problem: she kept calling her dogs by the wrong names.

During our first session JNW held the SRTLFs. A few days later she was out in the forest with her dogs and suddenly she had the feeling of being 'sober'. It was a very strange feeling. As she walked on, things in her life seemed so clear and she saw them from another angle. And yet in another way she felt confused.

She also noticed that she was calling the dogs by their right names more often and the tight painful bond over her feet was gone.

In the supermarket she also registered something unusual. Normally while passing through the aisles, she scanned up and down to see if there was someone she knew there, someone she had to say hello to. She had always been afraid that she would meet someone and not see them and they would feel ignored. This time she just passed through the store, putting groceries in the shopping cart without feeling the need to look out for other people. It was one of the most effective shopping rounds she had ever done!

In the next session she was taught to clear her past. A few days later she reported:

'I went to visit my mother, as I do every day. She is not feeling very good at the moment because my brother is in a terrible state. She is so filled up with shame and blame about all the things she didn't do for him when he was a little boy. She gave her own career as an opera singer priority and left him a lot with his grandmother.

My mother is of a very dramatic nature and always tells people what's right and what's wrong. We were sitting at the kitchen table talking when I mentioned that I was doing this thing with frequency transformation. I regretted it at once because I knew she had so many preconceptions about things, due to what had happened to my brother Johan earlier in life, and she was very critical of alternative stuff.

I immediately prepared to defend myself, but she did not react as I expected. She was curious about the frequencies and started to ask me a lot of questions. I told her about the information sheets about the Supercoherence system and offered to bring them next time. "Please do so," she said enthusiastically. "Maybe this could help Johan!"

When it was time for me to leave, the last thing she said in the hallway was, "Don't forget the papers about the frequencies!"

I went out to the car, sat down for a moment, overwhelmed by her reaction, before driving home.

I did clear the past with my mother's photo a few days ago and I'm sure that had something to do with it. She has never been so open-minded about anything that has interested me before!

When I saw JNW again she was a very good mood. In the last weeks she had felt alert, vital and clear. Ninety-five per cent of the time she had even been calling her dogs by their right names! Her gastritis had gone and the irregular heartbeats were happening less frequently. She told me that when they started she just held the green SRTLF in her left hand and that worked fine.

Her creativity had increased a lot lately. She had been inspired to do some gardening, which she hadn't done for years. One day she wanted to bake bread, which was unusual. She also felt as though nothing could knock her off-balance: 'It is as if I don't have any feelings at all anymore, just a big sense of calm and peace.'

That's what it is to be coherent.

SF

SF, 46, was happily married with a 14-year-old daughter, who was a test tube baby. SF and her husband had tried very hard for years to get a sibling for her, but none of SF's frozen eggs had, sadly, been fertilized.

SF and her husband ran a large factory. Her father-in-law had started the business about 40 years previously and SF and her husband had taken it over five years before. However, her father-in-law still retained a lot of influence in the firm. This affected both SF and her husband, PF, in a very negative way, since he was dominant, disrespectful and arrogant.

SF was a perfectionist and suffered so badly from migraines two to three times a week that she threw up and had such difficult cramps she couldn't stand up.

At her first session she held the SRTLFs and immediately bought a set to do the work daily.

When I saw her three weeks later, she had only had one migraine attack in that time. When the pain had started she had held the green SRTLF in her left hand and gone to bed. She had slept for a few hours and when she had woken up the pain had gone and she had felt fine.

A big change in her emotional life was that she was not responding to her father-in-law's harassment with anger or frustration anymore but with pity. She realized that she cared about him a lot, but he didn't accept the love she showed him. I recommended that she put the SRTLFs on his photo when not using them herself.

She had also had a new experience at a meeting with the company's accountant. She was normally very stressed over these meetings because she always felt that she was inferior to the accountant. That feeling was often the start of a migraine attack and she often had to go home and go to bed afterwards.

This was the first meeting since she had started to use the SRTLFs. It went smoothly and easily and she didn't get even a hint of a headache!

Her father-in-law had also done something remarkable: when he had finished work he had gone into her office, smiled at her, said goodbye and started to talk about a funny book he had been reading. This might not sound unusual, but he didn't say goodbye very often, definitely didn't smile and had never before recommended a book to her!

SF's biggest interest was going to dog shows with her poodle, Bosse. One day, when she was driving to a show, a migraine hit her like a hand grenade. She had to stop the car. She took the green SRTLF in the left hand and started to visualize that she was bathed in white light. It took 15 minutes, but then the terrible attack was over. She drank a little water, started the car and drove on. Amazing! Better than any pills!

She loved her dog and felt that she would like to buy another one. Her husband was not very keen on it, but when they spoke about it, for the first time SF really stood up for what she wanted. She was sure that had to do with the Supercoherence IAM Female frequency, which she had been using for a week. A month later she bought another dog, Berta.

SF and her family lived in an old house. They had been restoring it for many years and it had cost them a lot of money. There had been a lot of problems on the way and they had been talking about selling the house. One afternoon SF took the SRTLFs in her hands together with the Divine Mother photo. She walked around in the house from one room to another and let all her feelings come out – frustration, anger, worry, love of the house, happiness, irritation, sorrow and so on. She went to bed exhausted without knowing what she really wants to do. The last thing she did was put the SRTLFs on a photo of the house.

Next day her husband came home and told her that he had been thinking a lot about what they should do with the house. He suggested hiring a firm to finish the restoration instead of doing all work by themselves. He was sick and tired of it but did not want to sell the house and move away.

SF felt they were coming home and allowing themselves to stay there. She believed that walking around the house had neutralized the old blocked energy and let things come to them from a new point of view.

LD

LD, 30, was a social worker who loved travelling. She was an only child and worried a lot about her mother, who had MS and had had anorexia when she was younger.

LD had the opposite problem: she was overweight and suffered from bulimia on and off. She was longing for a relationship but the people she got involved with all seemed to have problems and needed to be 'fixed'. And then, when she had helped them through their problems, they would break up with her.

Three days after she had held the SRTLFs for the first time she gave the following feedback. She was also fascinated by the IAM Female frequency I had around my neck and I let her carry it while she was telling me her story:

'I really feel different in a positive way, but I can't explain how. There is a new kind of calmness inside. I am also very tired, and very awake in a way. It sounds weird but that's the way it is!

I have felt lucky the last few days and normally I only get that feeling when travelling. I have also noticed I am not as affected by bad weather as I usually am. I usually feel low when it is raining, but not today!

I'm very curious to see if these feelings will last.

I have also had an interesting discussion with my mother about our complicated relationship to food. She admitted that she had never dared to take enough space in her family, because no one was allowed to be better than anyone else. I feel exactly the same about her! I am afraid of being successful and am often holding myself back because I don't want to hurt my mother by being better than her. She has always had to fight to make a living and in a strange way I want her to feel that she is doing well enough.'

A week later she e-mailed:

'I haven't been myself lately. I am arrogant, irritated and sometimes angry. I'm standing up for myself in a new way, and I don't know if it feels positive or not! Today I over-reacted to things. What is this? How is this possible?'

I explained that when imprints were neutralized, energy that had been held in the field was released and that meant you would meet a side of yourself you didn't know was there.

Before our next appointment, she went on a week's holiday with her father. It was a complete disaster. At one point she had to take him to hospital since he got so drunk he fell in the hotel entrance and hurt himself badly.

His problem with alcohol became all too clear to her during the week, but she felt that she could meet him without a lot of fear and anger. She was convinced that hadn't been possible before using the SRTLFs. She was even wondering whether she could support him instead of cutting him out of her life. It seemed as though fear was turning into love!

In September she started using the Supercoherence IAM Female frequency, which really helped her to stand up for herself. She felt she needed time out from her relationship with her mother, just some space and time of her own, and she was able to tell her mother without shouting and getting angry.

Her mother felt hurt and abandoned, but LD was convinced that she actually also needed time on her own.

Something else had happened too: LD was in love.

By New Year, though, she had made a transformational decision:

'I had been dissatisfied with my job, mother, earlier boyfriends and other relationships for a very long time. It felt as though I had come to a dead end. I looked at myself and saw someone in the mirror I did not know. Enough! Suddenly I realized that I had never listened to my heart. When I went back to work after New Year I gave in my three months' notice.

I have such a strong feeling that something else is waiting for me out there, but I can't explain what – not even to myself. I just have to wait and see what turns up. I know this sounds crazy, but it is the way it is.

I have told both my parents that I want "time out" from my relationship with them, and even though I thought earlier I had met my soul mate, I am taking a break from that too.

It is as though an explosion has happened on a soul level and caused all this. It feels like a deep cleansing process. All the old shit has to come out! It's as though my soul has been turned inside out. This is not fun, but necessary, I guess. The "crystals" must have reset me to zero – I'm certainly not acting the way I used to. Maybe it will take a while to adjust.

Something new will come out of this when my soul starts to heal.'

CJ

CJ, 47, was one of four sisters and brothers and grew up on a farm. Her parents were working all the time and there was little time left for amusement. She was divorced from her husband, who had had problems with alcohol, and had two children, who were grown up but still needed some economic support since they were studying. She worked as an assistant to a little autistic boy. She was living with a new man and was very happy with him. Her relationship with her two brothers was not so good. They had always complained about her and told her she was worthless.

After holding the SRTLFs, she gave me the following feedback:

'Since I held the SRTLFs 10 days ago I have felt a lot of sadness. But at the same time I feel euphoria! How can this be? It is a little confusing! The healing spots on my hands are burning all the time... Suddenly I am seeing things from a different angle – both big and small things. And in spite of everything, a kind of calm and peace has come over me.'

I felt her sadness had to come out and be released so new energy and positive feelings could arise. She used the SRTLFs daily and the following month reported:

'My dreams have been extremely powerful lately; I am convinced it has to do with the frequencies. Things are falling into place and I see things I have written or read in a new light. They suddenly have another meaning. I also feel very peaceful and calm. There is also a lot of synchronicity in my life, which either wasn't there before or I didn't see it! This is so exciting!'

A month later CJ explained that she was experiencing her feelings much more strongly than before. That was new to her. Things around her were still falling into place very easily and a deep calm was spreading within her. She perceived that she was part of a big plan and that was a good feeling!

Her sister had visited her and whereas previously they had just been polite to each other this time they frankly enjoyed each other's company. When her sister went home, CJ wondered about that. Then, while clearing the cups and plates from the table, she discovered the box with the SRTLFs in lying there under a newspaper.

Five months after first starting with the SRTLFs, CJ found her work situation improving. In the previous six months she had felt used and that others had taken the credit for her ideas, but suddenly she was the one who was implementing her ideas. It just happened – she didn't know how.

After clearing her past with a lot of family members she felt more confident about how to handle her relationship with them and besides she had been given much more respect than before.

She could look at herself with new eyes and appreciate her own qualities. A big step forward was that she was now daring to admit when she needed help or had a problem with something.

She put the SRTLFs on both her children's photos for a while. They were very different and did not get along very well. But then her daughter decided to move to the same town as her brother. She asked him if she could move into his place to start with and he said yes! CJ was astonished. That was something she wouldn't have dreamed of in her wildest dreams!

A-LE

A-LE, 36, was a very, very shy woman. This had been a problem for her as far back as she could remember. She called me after reading Thrity's book about supercoherence. It was definitely not her kind of book, but it literally fell on her from the bookshelf when she was visiting the library. When she tried to put it back again, it didn't fit in anywhere. So she borrowed it and read it. This was the beginning of her soul journey.

During the first session I only managed to make eye contact a couple of times with A-LE. She was very difficult to get close to and was not willing to share information about her life.

It seemed she had always been very lonely. She had no friends and she lived alone except for a cat. She was very close to her sister but now her sister had a boyfriend there wasn't much time for them to get together. She also had a brother but they had little contact. Sometimes she visited a cousin who lived close to her. Her father had died 15 years before and she described her mother as a very shallow person who never listened to her and always flitted from one thing to another.

She had had the same kind of job for the last 12 years. Her boss was very cold and serious. Her fellow workers were nice to her but she really wanted to do something else with her life. In her spare time she went to the gym or the library. She had spent many hours trying out different therapies to help with her shyness. None of them had worked out so far.

She started to work with the SRTLFs immediately.

Three weeks later, when she rang to make a new appointment I did not recognize her voice at first. She sounded so clear, open and happy. She had cleared her past with all possible relations, even with a photo of her old class from school. She suddenly told me that she had been bullied at school.

She said she felt calmer and found it easier to get closer to other people than before. When I met her, she looked different, seemed happier and looked me in the eye more often. Suddenly she told me that she had booked a ticket to Thailand! This was something she had dreamed about for a long time and now she was daring to do it, and on her own.

Three months later A-LE was back from Thailand and very satisfied with her trip. She felt very well, very stable and calm.

She had put the SRTLFs on her boss's photo and since then he had been much more pleasant and had even smiled and joked with her.

A-LE had also asked her sister to make more time for her and even confronted her mother and asked her to listen to what she had to say. She had done it in a very clear and controlled way. And the best thing of all was that it had felt so good.

Now she was ready for something else... like a relationship. Her next project would be to buy a computer and look for someone on a dating site. Her creativity was flowing!

SH

The first time I met SH, 43, was together with her husband, DH, 50. He had recently been diagnosed with ADHD, but it had been affecting their marriage for over 20 years. He had always been overactive and had difficulties with mood swings that affected SH tremendously. They had tried everything and were now contemplating divorce. But DH loved SH and did not want to live without her. He said that the diagnosis had been a kind of relief to him and now maybe he could understand himself and his behaviour a little more easily and do something about it.

SH had one grown-up son from an earlier relationship and two sons, 15 and 17, from her marriage to DH. The youngest of these had also been diagnosed with ADHD. He had problems with his social behaviour, especially at school.

Trying to avoid conflicts and fend off possible outbursts from her husband and son made SH very tired. During the previous two years she had also had a severe dry cough problem. She couldn't go anywhere without her water bottle in case of a fit of coughing. Her doctors hadn't been able to find any reason for her problem and thought it was psychosomatic. She was seeing a psychotherapist.

When SH first took the SRTLFs in her hands, a very intense generation of heat took place and suddenly she felt pleased and happy. She started working with them and also carrying the SPTCF almost all the time.

When I saw her a month later, the most surprising thing was that her terrible coughing attacks had stopped. She also felt more upright and firm in the way she was acting. Something else she had noticed was that people were around her 'like flies on a lump of sugar' and often confiding in her.

One remarkable thing that had happened was that she had gone through her huge wardrobe and completely cleared out all her old clothes. This had not been done for years. Talk about released energy transformed into creativity!

Four months after SH first started working with the SRTLFs, her psychotherapist commented that she had never met anyone who had recovered so fast from being on the way to a total breakdown.

SH and her husband had also decided to make some changes in their lives. Instead of divorcing, they were planning on moving a little closer to their home town. SH was also looking for a new job.

A month later they had sold their house, bought a new one and got their children in a new school which even had a programme for pupils with different disorders and could offer support to their younger son. SH had got a new job and would start when they moved house.

Unfortunately, her coughing had come back. It was not as intense as before, though, and she was happy to work a little bit more with the SPTCF. Overall, she was delighted with everything that had happened since she had started using the Supercoherence frequencies.

DH

DH, 50, was married to SH [*see above*]. All his life he had lived very intensely. His childhood had been hard and he had found it difficult to get along with his parents and siblings, as he was very demanding. Later he had run his own office equipment and interior design business but a few years before he had sold the company and was now an employee in his old firm but in another town. His marriage was falling to pieces and he had almost no patience with his children. He had recently been diagnosed with ADHD. He was willing to try anything to understand himself better and get his relationships to work.

When he held the SRTLFs for the first time, he became completely calm. This was new. He had to lie down on the sofa. He commented, 'Maybe I can stop my medicine!'

He almost passed out!

He was very attracted to the IAM Male frequency and found that with it he could stay focused for a longer period than he has been used to. He also felt much calmer.

Over the next month he became very excited over a new project he was working on, but unfortunately the architect he was working with didn't share his ideas. DH had no idea how to get round this, but to his amazement she opened up their next meeting with plans and suggestions which were almost identical to his. This had never happened before. They connected and got very close and the project ran smoothly. This was all new to him.

Four months later, DH and his wife had come to the decision to move closer to their home town. After a re-organization in his company, DH was looking forward to a new job assignment. He still had his issues but he carried the SRTLFs in his pockets all the time. He felt they made a huge difference. Without them, he said he felt naked in his soul.

A month later I received an unexpected phone call from DH. He was very upset. Lately he had been feeling pressure in his chest and found it difficult to breathe. He had been to the doctor but there was nothing physically wrong. In his new job he often held lectures in front of large audiences, but suddenly he found he was forgetting his words. He was also very sensitive; he couldn't even bear to hear his sons chewing crispy bread. And without the frequencies it was even worse.

He also told me that he had never talked to anyone before when life had been tough. It had been a big step to pick up the receiver and call. I had been the only person he could think of. I was humbled.

There had been so many changes in a very short period – selling the house, buying a new one, planning the big move, finding a new school for the children, taking on a new job assignment and adjusting to the new frequencies – so I suggested that DH carry all four frequencies at the same time to calm down the tangled energy and connect to his Self. He listened carefully and I felt that he understood.

I also asked him to give himself some time for reflection on his own. If he fell apart he couldn't do anything for others, so taking good care of himself was an important step.

That was in January. Now, at the end of April, DH is more calm and centred. Things have fallen into place. He says:

'I carry the SRTLFs in my pocket all day. They keep me calm and make me see things more clearly. I need them to stay firmly on the ground and to feel safe. The SPTCF is necessary to keep me from blowing up in a stressful situation. I want to be a good manager and husband, of course, and this is the perfect tool to use in relationships.

As for my IAM Male frequency, I can't say what it does for me. But I can say that if I discover on my way to work that I have left it at home, I turn around, drive back and get it. If I am without it, it feels as though a part of me is missing – and maybe it is!

The last three weeks I have put the Divine Mother photo in my shirt pocket every morning. I guess she helps me to be more connected to love.'

DS-W

DS-W was 16 when I met him for the first time. He was a lonely young man with few friends. He found it hard to express his needs and tried to accommodate others as much as possible. He seldom reacted aggressively and spent a lot of his spare time playing computer games.

He had just started a new school. Six months before he had had trouble with a sore scalp and a swollen, inflamed knee which was filled with fluid. He had been diagnosed with a kind of rheumatic disease and treated with cell toxins.

I felt that this young man needed to stand up for himself and raise his self-esteem. He started to use the SRTLFs and Supercoherence IAM Male frequency.

The next time I saw him he seemed more open and relaxed. He had joined the school choir and made some new friends. His mother told me that he had also found his own style, both his own clothing style and a new way of presenting himself.

He had also learned how to stand up for himself. For example, at a big party, a lot of his friends were talking about what to drink and how much. When he was asked, he simply answered, 'I don't drink.'

He was one of the few who didn't drink alcohol at all at the party, but none of his friends made a big deal about it. Group pressure is very common among youngsters, but he was able to follow his heart.

EA

EA, 27, lived alone. Her parents had divorced when she was six and she had lived every second week with her father, who had soon remarried. She had a brother and got a new sister as well. Those years were hard for her. She couldn't get along with her stepmother and never felt comfortable in her father's new home. School was difficult, she could not concentrate and she had to spend a lot of time doing homework.

After school she had moved around a lot and done a lot of different jobs. When she came to me, she had a job that was OK, but not one she wanted to have for the rest of her life. Since she was very sporty and competed in cycling and swimming competitions she had done a lot of mental training which had led her to explore different self-development techniques. In spite of that, she was not satisfied with her life. She felt she was living a mediocre life and wasn't getting anywhere. She couldn't see what was stopping her from moving forward and didn't know what to do.

She started to work with the SRTLFs and was also very attracted to the SIAM Female frequency.

Two months later she was experiencing a lot of synchronicity in her daily life. She thought it was very uplifting that she could see this. She sensed serenity, too, but there was something stopping that feeling coming through.

After a while she confided that just over a year before she had had a date with a male workmate. Something had gone wrong and he had tried to rape her. When she had told her boss about it, everybody at the workplace had got involved and sided against her. She had hired a lawyer and it had ended up with her workmate having to quit, but EA had also had to change jobs because the situation had been unsustainable between her and the colleagues who had taken the man's part.

After this episode she had been approached several times by men but had never let anyone get close to her. She had felt no attraction at all, not even towards nice, gentle, men.

She also felt something was holding her back from expressing herself.

We agreed that she should concentrate on clearing her past with those involved with the sad workplace events and looking at her life and what she wanted to achieve.

'I can feel that there is a completely different calmness inside me!' This was EA's first comment when we met a month later. 'A few days ago a friend said to me, "Is everything OK? You seem so calm." I heard myself say, "Yes, I have nothing to get stressed about." As I said that, I realized that it was a very unusual comment from me! A funny feeling!'

EA explained that she had been in a very happy mood and people had suddenly been attracted to her – both men and women – and had started confiding in her. She was surprised because that had not happened often in her life.

A physical change was that her 'sweet tooth' wasn't bothering her anymore. Before she could eat sweets and chocolate unstoppably. But the craving had just gone.

I must say that she felt like a freer person, compared to the first session. She had got another look in her eyes and her body language and energy flow were much more obvious. My impression was that she was enjoying life now that she was allowing people to get closer to her.

The following month I received a phone call from her. She was exhilarated and told me that she had been in Switzerland visiting her brother, who lived there.

'It is completely astounding how people are gathering around me!' she said.

Wherever she went, people were going up to her, wanting to sit beside her, talk to her, dance with her or just be with her – and see her again. Her social life had really changed. I believe that people were feeling her coherence and wanting to be part of it.

She also told me that she had lent her SRTLFs to a very good friend, but had only managed a few days before her world started to wobble. That made it plain to her that they really worked.

'It's not that I doubted it,' she said, 'but it was such clear evidence to me.'

AB-B

This lovely woman was in her late thirties. She was very down to earth and lived close to nature. She bred sheep and used the wool to make her own handicrafts. She was married for the second time and had two small children from that marriage. Her husband was about 10 years older than her. They had had to use *in vitro* fertilization to have their first child; the second had come naturally just few years later.

AB-B felt that her life had stagnated. Her creativity had decreased and she felt stuck. She had suddenly got a lot of physical symptoms: her left heel hurt, which made it hard to walk when she had been sitting for a while, she felt dizzy on and off and was prone to colds. She felt out of balance.

She and the children loved their life in the countryside, but her husband had taken a job on a five-year contract and wanted to move shortly. There had been a lot of turbulence around this issue and her husband had threatened to leave her.

Two and a half months after starting work with the SRTLFs she wrote:

'Time is passing by very fast and it feels as though *a lot of things* have happened since I visited you in November.

I must say that I am focusing better and am more present now than I was before. I just drop everything around me and follow the flow in what I do. The result is that I am less stressed. It is very liberating to release a lot of unnecessary "musts".

It also feels as though I am seeing things from a new perspective. I look at my environment from another angle – as if I have new eyes or have cleansed my glasses! Cool!

When I go to bed at night and hold the SRTLFs, they are pulsating in my hands as though life is flowing through me… I fall asleep very quickly and sleep very well all night.

I am working on clearing my past with my loved ones. It took time before I got started but now I work with them one by one. It is as if I can breathe more easily with everyone I clear with.

As you can see, I am very satisfied to have achieved so much in such a short while!'

When AB-B cleared her past with her grandmother she gained a huge insight:

'I have always heard that I am a copy of my maternal grandmother, but I now realize that I have a lot more in common with my father's mother. I can also see why my mother always pointed out my similarity to her mother: because she did not get along very well with her mother-in-law and didn't like her. I think she was afraid of me being like her: earthy, close to nature, fond of animals and handicrafts. Exactly what I am!

The clearing gave me this insight. When I cleared my past with my father's mother too, it was like letting a waterfall of energy loose. A lot of new ideas popped up in my head and there was a flow of creativity. It felt as though I had been tied to her for many years and was now set free. Wonderful feeling!

When clearing the past with my ex-husband I felt a lot of sorrow. I cried rivers of tears over the failure of my first marriage. I did not know there were so many hidden feelings inside me, because I had almost forgotten about that relationship. After that outburst I felt completely calm.'

Several months later she reports that her relationship with her husband has become a lot closer. He is not threatening to leave her or insisting on selling the farm, his job has stabilized and her business is doing well. She continues to use the SRTLFs regularly.

KR

KR, 50, has had a hard life. He was an only child. His father had a stroke a few years before and died instantly. KR was worried about his mother, who suffered from dementia and was living in a care home.

He was also carrying guilt from the past. While driving drunk he had been involved in a terrible accident in which his girlfriend and one of his male friends had died. The car had turned upside down in a field and he had tried to save them by pulling them out, but failed.

This tragic accident had a huge impact on his life. He had desperately tried to deaden the fearfulness and anxiety within and drown the shame and the blame that were chasing him. He started to drink.

After several relationships with different women he met the mother of his son, MR, today 22 years old. They got married, but after suffering his addiction for many years, she left, taking MR with her, and divorced him.

A long period followed of being addicted to everything possible: alcohol, cigarettes, hashish, cannabis, amphetamines, poisonous fungi and cacti, anti-depressants and so on. KR used everything possible to get high. This ended tragically in 2008 in a suicide attempt.

KR was currently taking tranquillizers for anxiety and OCD and had been treated at a psychiatric clinic on several occasions during the past two years. He was on a programme to reduce his medication.

He lived with his son but it was a difficult relationship. He was still working but was afraid of losing his job. On the other hand, he wanted to do something else anyway. His deepest wish was to find inner peace.

He had read Thrity's book and even though he had found it difficult, he felt that this was the way to go. He told me that when he had been driving to meet me, he had passed under a viaduct and as he had done so, the radio had been playing the Beatles' song 'Let It Be'. He had a strong feeling that he was letting all his old stuff go and heading for something new.

He started working with the SRTLFs.

Three months later I hadn't heard from him. After several attempts to get in touch without success, I sat down with the SRTLFs and affirmed that he would call me. He did, two days later.

Unfortunately his son had lost the pink SRTLF after using it when sleeping on the sofa. They had turned everything upside down, but no pink

SRTLF. His son was heartbroken and in spite of their lousy finances they were determined to get a new set. 'By chance' I had an extra set available.

I told KR that I had tried to get in contact with him. He explained that he had changed his phone company and therefore also his phone number. We decided to have another session when he came to pick up the SRTLFs the next day.

When he walked through the door, he looked different. His eyes were more open and clear. He seemed 'cleaner' and more present in his appearance. He told me:

'One night at the end of January I was sitting by the fire when I realized that it had been a very long time since I had felt this good. Suddenly I threw all my tranquillizers into the fire. I felt that I had had enough of drugs in my life. That was the end of it. I felt so relieved.

Since then I haven't used anything but a sleeping pill now and then, because I work the night shift and it can sometimes be hard to go to sleep when it is daylight.

And I tell you, my finances have never been as bad as they are now – ever. But I know I will work it out.

I have started up an internet website where I'm selling all my old books. It isn't making me rich, but it is a way of getting rid of a lot of old things that are taking up space at home, and since I need every penny it is better to sell them than throw them away.

I am cleaning out a lot of old stuff in my home and that feels good.

I'm also looking forward to spring and summer and driving my big American car and playing rock 'n' roll music. That will be great!'

KR was very good at clearing his past and at the same time he was clearing out old stuff in his home. Talk about releasing blockages on an energetic level and seeing the result in the physical world! And it shows in his joy and happiness over his American car and rock and roll.

MR

MR, 22, was the son of KR [*see above*]. He was living with his father but had good contact with his mother, who was now living with another man and her new children.

His life had not been easy. As far back as he could remember he had been worried to death about his father, especially when he had tried to commit suicide.

He had been bullied in school and had felt very vulnerable. He was overweight and had often been teased over his appearance. He found it difficult to get close to people, although he often fell in love with women. It could be anyone and any age!

He had used cannabis in the past but now only smoked tobacco. Sometimes he felt like smoking cannabis again, but there was a voice inside him telling him not to. He had been treated for psychosis twice, probably triggered by using cannabis. At least that was what the doctors said.

After being treated at a psychiatric clinic, he had been diagnosed with low-level schizophrenia and he was taking medication for it.

His memory was very poor, to the point where it was almost impossible for him to learn anything. (My opinion was that he knew a little about a lot of things and had simply been told – and believed, that he had a bad memory.)

He had no job. During the day he spent time with a group of other young people with psychological problems.

He and his father decided to share a set of SRTLFs and I encouraged them to clear their past with each other and then other members of the family and so on.

The next opportunity I had to talk to MR was three months later over the phone. His voice was very clear. He said:

'Over the last month I have felt much happier than I have ever done before! And you know what? I have stopped drinking diet soda! I had been drinking at least two litres a day for a very long time. Suddenly I realized, I don't know how, that the artificial sweetener aspartame was poison! I don't want to drink poison. So I changed from diet soda to ordinary soda, because I thought that sugar was better than poison. Then I remembered that I had chosen the diet drinks in the first place because of being overweight. Sugar makes me fat, so sugar is also a kind of poison. I didn't want to be poisoned, so now I'm drinking sparkling water instead. Much better for my health, you know!'

I told him that he had done a splendid job and gave him a tip about programming his tap water the same way that Masaru Emoto does [by writing positive words or affirmations on a piece of paper and pasting it onto a water container with the words facing in so that water inside can read it.] In combination with his frequency work, MR can reach his goal – to feel good and be healthier.

Before we ended the conversation he asked me if I could recommend books about Tesla. He was eager to go to the library. The world was opening up for him…

YT-I

YT-I, 42, was just married. She had three teenage children from two different relationships. She had always had a complicated relationship with her first husband, the father of her oldest son. The son himself had had various problems, both with his studies and socially, and been a computer game addict. He was currently studying in another town.

YT-I had a daughter and a son from her second marriage. Their father had been very controlling and patronizing. Her daughter wasn't happy about sharing her mother with her latest husband. She also had a lot of problems, both physically and mentally, and was being treated by a psychologist.

YT-I herself was under pressure, tired and suffered from migraines. Her problems with her children were casting a shadow over her happiness with her new husband.

She started working with the SRTLFs and the SPTCF.

Soon after YT-I's first session she had a terrible migraine. She held the SPTCF for a while and soon she felt better. She could go on with her work and put the SPTCF away. A little later the headache started to come back and she held the SPTCF again. The headache slowly subsided and she kept the SPTCF in her pocket for the rest of the day.

Suddenly one afternoon she felt very energized. She did something she hadn't done for a very long time: emptied all the kitchen cupboards and cleared out all the stuff she didn't use anymore. It felt so good.

Meanwhile her daughter was putting on a CD of the musical *Mamma Mia*. The music reminded YT-I of her own teenage days and she started to sing and dance. Her daughter followed her and they kept on until the cd ended! Wow, how long had it been since they had had so much fun together?!

Christmas was getting closer and her oldest son was expected to come home over the holidays. Close to his arrival her daughter broke down and told YT-I that she didn't want him to stay in the house. She revealed that she was afraid of him because of his many outbursts when they were younger. He had also been very dismissive of her.

The only thing YT-I could do was ask her first husband to let their son stay with him during the holiday. She thought he wouldn't do it, because he was always negative and never wanted to help; besides his relationship with their son was bad. But before she went to bed that night she put the SRTLFs on his name.

The day after, she plucked up the courage to phone him and briefly explain the situation.

Surprisingly, he said, 'Poor girl, it is not right that she should be afraid. Of course he can stay here.'

This was unexpected. He had never done anything to ease the situation with the children before. A huge burden was lifted from the family and Christmas went smoothly.

YT-I has realized that clearing her past will help her go in a new direction and is continuing the work.

N/CJ

CJ was the carer of a boy, N., 12, with severe autism. She had been working with him since he started school and spent six to eight hours daily with him five days a week. We were talking about his limitations and I became curious about how the SRTLFs would affect him. She agreed to introduce them to N. and his mother and see what they could do for his development.

The first time N. held the SRTLFs was when he had his daily massage. CJ gave him a massage for about 20–30 minutes every day because of spasms when he was tired. The first obvious change came instantly: he lay still and became very relaxed. No cramps and no anxiety were shown.

After a few weeks CJ realized that N. was generally more aware of his environment. Earlier he had been closed off and difficult to get in contact with.

His mother was of the same opinion:

'N. has been more and more focused. He can also keep focused on a special task for longer periods. His language has developed too. He can be more precise than before. He also shows his feelings now – he shows when he is sad and cries, for example. Previously he couldn't do that.

N. can't hold a pencil in his hand, so instead he uses a computer to learn writing and spelling. He can write more words than several months ago.

He is also much better at listening to what people say and above all he understands better. He is working with sounding new words, one word at a time. He can say more and more advanced words and it won't take long before he can read for real!

Exercises that were too difficult for him early in the autumn are now too easy for him. I'm always having to find more challenging ones! All this improvement just through holding the SRTLFs daily!'

His mother is so grateful and happy. She is convinced that the SRTLFs are supporting her son's entire system. The work with N. goes on…

The SRTLFs and Me

These are some of my personal experiences with the SRTLFs.

My Daughter and I

The relationship between my daughter Meher and me has always been a complex one. We can both truly say we love each other, but equally truly it may be said we have not always liked each other. In fact I say, only half in jest, that we have been on the verge of divorce many times. At times we have been quite out of synch in the way we have thought and acted. We are very different in temperament and it has often seemed we have different values too.

But when the chips were down and my life was a shambles, it was my daughter who helped me financially for several years, otherwise I would have lost my house. She also took out a loan of US$ 10,000 to buy the equipment to start me on my next adventure, even though she knew I had been super foolish in losing all my money. It was a huge act of love and trust on her part.

There was still a lot of ambivalence between us, but the good thing was that we never gave up on each other, in spite of all our misunderstandings and disappointments.

When the Luminator came into my life, we both went to the US to train with Patrick. When he imaged us together I could see in dramatic terms that our relationship was not what either of us wished it to be. We were very incoherent with each other. That was a real moment of truth. I have never forgotten those images.

When I was expecting my daughter, I wanted a son. I adored my husband and wanted to have a little one just like him. I can truly say that I loved my little girl once she was born, and my second child was a boy, but my daughter always felt hard done by, even though both my husband and I tried to be even-handed and did not have favourites. Her litany was always: 'It's not fair!'

Many years later I realized that when she was in my womb, she would have known that I wanted a boy and must have felt the pain and the feeling of being 'less than', and this imprinted message played out in real life where she always felt that somehow she was loved less than her brother.

I understood through my work with the Luminator that one could heal events in the distant past and the effect of that healing would be felt in the present. So I tried an experiment: I held the SRTLFs, did a feeling visualization of that little foetus when she was in my womb and sent her a thought-feeling transmission. I told her I loved her dearly and that she was very welcome. And I knew the job was done. The old imprint was neutralized.

I then waited for a sign to tell me that I had achieved my aim. I did not have long to wait. Within a minute or so the phone rang – it was my daughter. She said, 'Hi, Mum, I am out and about. Can I come and have a cup of tea with you?' Normally she does not ring me on her mobile casually; it just doesn't happen.

Since that experiment there has been much more tenderness and acceptance on both our sides and our relationship is on a different trajectory. And I am grateful.

My Mother

I have lived in London for the last 32 years and my brother left home to study and then settle in the US some 40 years ago. My dad, as I mentioned earlier, passed away at the age of 56 in 1976, and my mother has lived on her own from 1978 onwards. She was never emotionally manipulative and did not interfere in the lives of her children. She was a true sweet mother who would do anything for her children and grandchildren and never ask for anything in return.

In 2006 she became very ill with shingles and this was a watershed for her. Before that, though she was 82 years young, she was full of fun, very active and handled all her financial affairs and her life with no input from us. She looked 20 years younger than she was – all my life we had been mistaken for sisters. After the illness, everything changed. She lost her physical strength, withdrew into herself and would hardly speak .She completely lost interest in her financial affairs and we had to handle everything. It was distressing for us all.

After this watershed event, when I visited her and it was time for me to return to London, for the first time in her life she started to cry. I had never seen my ma cry and it really tore my heart. I held her and reassured her, but she could not stop weeping. I knew what would help: I put one particular ZPA frequency in her left hand and the weeping stopped immediately. She calmed down and was fine after that. The effect was dramatic and instant. We could speak after that and she was coherent.

Obviously my brother, my daughter and I visited her many times after that and the process and the frequencies worked every time. In 2009, when the SRTLFs were ready, we sent her the new frequencies and the young woman who looked after her had instructions to put them in her pockets every morning for 20 minutes. In the space of two months she became noticeably more coherent and in December 2009 she did not weep when I left

Mumbai for London. I cannot tell you how relieved and happy that made me feel.

Writer's Block, Remote Imaging and the SRTLFs

It was February 2011 and I was stuck and I knew it, but did not know exactly what to do to resolve it. The book I was writing was very important to me — a life task which I could not back away from, not that I wished to back away — but I had come to the realization that I was stuck and needed help. I had been sitting dutifully in front of the computer and though I knew what the book was about and had excellent material to go into it, the blank screen stared at me and the words wouldn't come. I realized that I had been feeling 'blah' and disconnected for a couple of weeks and joy and laughter had been noticeably absent. Not a fun place to be and not a good space from which to undertake a major project such as writing.

My dear friend and agent Marianne and I were chatting on the phone one day and out of the blue she said to me, 'Thrity, ask Meher to do an assessment for you.' She meant a VRIC imaging session. I hadn't told her about the writer's block I was experiencing, but she knew anyway.

For various reasons I knew I could not ask my daughter to do the assessment, but I went to bed very late and got up with an amazing idea. It happens frequently that I put myself through hell and then while I am asleep my super-conscious self works away at the logjam my personality and my emotions have created and gives me a very clear course of action as soon as I wake. The answer comes as a feeling and a knowing, and the moment I accept that course of action as the right one, I feel a sense of relief or my heart lifts. I have learned to totally trust this process and follow through without question or compromise — the results are always amazing.

So, when I woke, my course of action became clear. I realized that since 2005 I had experienced a lot of 'traumas' (I call them 'purifications' now), yet had not cleared them using the SRTLFs as

I told all my clients to do. I use the SRTLFs regularly, but strangely I had not done the clearing of these 'traumas'. How crazy is that?!

As I reflected, the main events came to mind: the death of my great associate Patrick Richards in 2008, which had been devastating for me, the dreadful illness which had struck down my mother in 2006, the fallout of which was still very much ongoing, the extremely traumatic events in mid-2005 (I won't go into the details) which resulted in the illness in early 2006 that nearly killed me (again, I won't go into the details, as it involves others and it would not be a useful exercise). In addition there was all the turbulence and turmoil when my book was published in 2008. When I looked back on what I had gone through, I found it extraordinary to think that I had not done the clearing earlier. However, what is done is done. I am not a great one for recrimination.

As I went over the events, quite dispassionately I realized that I could still feel the charge around them. Over the years I had done a lot of inner work to heal the hurts, so there was not a great deal of charge left, but obviously there was something remaining, or I would not be stuck.

I did not want my hurts to stand in the way of my life's work. All of us experience hurt, ridicule, betrayal, rejection and disappointment at some point. Often our greatest teachers are the people we love the most. I needed to simply look at what needed to be resolved at this deep level so my creativity could flow effortlessly through me. I decided to use myself as a guinea pig and to do some imaging for research purposes.

The experiment was simple. I imaged myself using the remote VRIC imaging method. Then I placed the photos of the various persons or groups next to my photo and re-imaged each one. This was done by placing their photos to the right and left sides of my photo, just as if they were standing to my right and to my left. This showed me clearly who was impacting me and on which side. Please understand clearly this was not an exercise in blame at any level. People you love can impact you greatly, I know that absolutely. I had been spot on when I had picked the persons to image myself with. Every single one had impacted me on either the left or the right side.

The next step was to do the clearing with the SRTLFs. I held the photo of each person or group with the SRTLFs and the Divine Mother photo and made a simple affirmation: 'I love and accept [name of the person] exactly as they are. I love and accept myself exactly as I am.' This took less than a minute each.

As soon as I had cleared myself with each person I re-imaged myself with their photo. My photo, which a few minutes before had been fuzzy and incoherent, became clear, sharp and coherent – the emotional charge was gone.

You will be surprised, or not so surprised to know that this simple process cleared all the energetic challenges which had been with me for several years in the space of a few minutes. I could feel the relief and the grace – I felt completely different in that short time. All the heaviness and the 'blah' had been replaced with lightness and wonder. I was back to being myself – the way I wanted to be.

Literally within minutes of completing the experiment, the ideas and the words were flowing. I completed almost 1,100 words that day, the procrastination had gone. Thank you, Marianne, thank you, universe, and thank you to the great teachers whose images I used that day and who let me know unequivocally that I co-create my own reality and that I have access to the power of grace to help me change whatever I wish in this simple, exquisite and extraordinary way.

And you can too – no imaging required! It really is as simple as that.

CHAPTER 14
Family Dynamics

'As the family goes, so goes the nation and so goes the whole world in which we live.'

Pope John Paul 11

O VER THE YEARS doing VRIC imaging we had observed a curious phenomenon. Initially for a few years we would image everyone with the photo of one person at a time. Then one day a young man brought the photo of his entire family and asked to be imaged with it. We had never done that before. The results were shocking – his VRIC image became totally incoherent. As I reflected on this, I realized that family dynamics can very often be the cause of dysfunction for many if not most people. After this we started imaging all clients with the photo of their whole family and have found that the vast majority become very incoherent. Families can cause incoherence. *(See Plate 7)*

Let us examine some of the dynamics involved.

Parents and children: There is a lot of pressure on parents to do the right thing by their children. People go to all sorts of absurd lengths to be a good if not perfect parent but find that despite everything they do, the results, as observed in the behaviour of the children and their own inter-action with them, leave much to be desired. The so-called generation gap becomes wider and both sides lose hope of reaching an understanding and enjoying a happy relationship.

Whole disciplines have been developed to take care of this problem. Parents and children may go through counselling, psychotherapy and psychoanalysis, but hundreds of hours of talk may come to nothing. This expert and that may be consulted, but real change may remain elusive.

So often parents are made to feel guilty – by the media, by the so-called experts, by the authorities, social services and the like. If only they did their job properly, they are told, their children would be well behaved and everybody would be happy and society would not face the problems it faces today. Single parents are singled out for a disproportionate amount of blame. So the sorry saga goes on.

The father came with his eight-year-old son. He told me he was a good boy, but that he had a slight problem with reading. He tried hard and was not the worst in the class, but could be a lot better. He was also quite bois-terous in a nice way. Was he hyperactive?

In my view the child appeared normal, not hyperactive, but I could see why, from the father's perspective, the boy would appear over-active. I looked at this tired man and this bright little boy and felt it was the father who needed help.

Some say the sins of the parents are visited on the children, but I would say it is the suffering of the parents that is imprinted on the children. I have seen this time and time again. When the parent becomes well and happy, the child improves in amazing ways. This is especially true for mothers – very good mothers, who do everything for their children with no thought of themselves, who run themselves into the ground and get sick and tired and in the end no one benefits, certainly not the children. It is important for mothers to take care of themselves. When they are well and happy, they will see their beloved children become well and happy too.

Aline phoned. Aline did not like making phone calls. And Aline had very strong likes and dislikes!

Aline had longed for a baby with her beloved husband. After great difficulty and great ease, she had fallen pregnant. She had wanted to be the perfect mother. She had gone to all the classes, learned to breathe correctly, done the yoga and still had a tough time, but it had all been worth it when she had held her baby in her arms – her very own little girl.

Now a distraught Aline was leaving a voicemail – panic and pain in her voice.

I was very fond of Aline. She was an endearing mixture of vulnerability, gutsiness and courage and a very talented artist. She trusted me enough to ring me when she was in trouble – and she wasn't big on trust.

I called her. 'What's up?'

She was in floods of tears.

'My milk seems to be drying up, my breasts are tender, the baby hurt my nipples, I am trying to expel the milk so I can keep on breastfeeding her, but her appetite is increasing and the flow seems to be decreasing. Oh, Thrity, I so wanted to feed her!'

More floods of tears.

Her little world had collapsed. The baby was crying all the time and her beloved husband was upset.

'So, you're a terrible mother who cannot even feed her baby?' I asked.

'Yes, exactly,' she said.

'And of course because you are this terrible mother everything is wrong and nothing will ever be right again. If you can't be this perfect mother then you are obviously an absolutely useless good for nothing mother who cannot do anything right. So you have every right to be unhappy and of course this will make Baby very happy.'

Aline stopped crying. The smile was back in the voice – the picture I had painted was so extreme and so absurd, she had to laugh.

'Do you want to be happy?' I asked. 'Do you want your baby to be happy? It is very easy to be unhappy and not so easy to be happy. But Baby is happy when Mum is happy. Try it. Don't be a perfect mother, be a happy mother. You wanted this baby so much – now you've got her, are you always going to find a reason to be unhappy? What effect will that have on the baby and what is the example you are setting – a "perfect"ly unhappy mother who always tried so hard and never made it?

'It is perfectly reasonable and laudable to want to breastfeed your baby, so try relaxing and visualizing your breasts overflowing with your love for her instead of drying up with your worry for her and see what happens.

Whatever happens, you have done the best you can and your baby will be fine when you are relaxed and happy.'

I knew Aline would always be an excellent mother. Aline, however, had to discover this for herself.

Lotta Naess: AS-K

AS-K, 48, was a highly accomplished woman. She was married, had three children and had a great career. Her father had taken his life when she was a few months old and she had a complicated relationship with her mother. She came to the session with a clear purpose: to strengthen her marriage.

Because she was working hard and the children were taking up a lot of time, she and her husband were drifting apart. He had suggested many times that they go away for a weekend together, but she felt terrible at the thought of leaving the kids at home with their grandparents. So she had turned her husband down many times – and that made her feel terrible too!

Two months after our first session, when she had held the SRTLFs for ten minutes, she was back again and the first thing she said was that she had booked a trip to London. She and her husband were going by themselves! They were going to buy Christmas presents and enjoy London at Christmas-time. And the best thing was that she felt fine about it.

She also felt that she had dropped something heavy. It was as if she had been walking around carrying a big stone.

In the New Year she also agreed to go skiing with three fellow workers at her office, all by herself – no children *and* no husband! She was bubbling with happiness!

She commented:

'It is very obvious that I have been released in some way… I think I must have been holding myself back. But now I know my family can do perfectly well without me – it's no big deal to them when I am away from home. It works very well even when my husband and I go away together. I feel as free as a bird.'

The Effects of Divorce *(see Plate 6)*

Today divorce has reached epic proportions. In the West apparently one in three marriages ends in divorce. In the East it is different, but divorce is becoming more common there as more women become educated and economically independent. Often it is no one's fault and two good people may not get along and relationships may end for many reasons. Putting aside the rights and wrongs of the case, whichever way one looks at it, one thing is certain: there is a lot of unhappiness for the couple involved. This is of course communicated to the children, who sense things are not right between the two most important people in the world to them. They can be traumatized by this unhappiness, however much the parents seek to protect them. Their world shakes and stability is gone. Am I loved? Will I be OK? Did I do something wrong?

Can anything be done to help mitigate this insecurity and unhappiness on all sides? There is one radical solution that has emerged as a result of 15 years of research using the zero-point alignment frequencies (the SRTLFs from 2009 onwards) combined with coaching.

WS

This boy was 10 years old when he came for a VRIC session. He was troubled, but bright, articulate, truthful and insightful about himself and his feelings – in my view quite an exceptional young person. His parents had separated when he was quite young and his father had a new partner who was now expecting her first child. WS had become insecure, unhappy and difficult to handle. He told me he 'felt scrunched inside' when he was with his father and his partner.

It took just two little 'magic' creams (zero-point alignment frequencies) in his pockets for him to adjust to this difficult situation. The only thing I told him was: 'Love is not limited. Your parents will love you as much as ever. People just love the best way they can – and that isn't always the way we would like.'

This wise little one completely got it. And he hasn't looked back since.

As an aside, when his little sister was born a few months later, an event he had previously been dreading, he became a wonderful and loving big brother and in a few months his little sister loved him right back. She would light up whenever he was around – he was her favourite person.

He says:

'I was sad that my mum and dad broke up at a very early age. Thrity took some photos of me with my parents and then she gave me some creams to put in my pockets for a few weeks after that. Well, basically it sorted out all my problems.

I was very unhappy – I was sad, angry and jealous – and then all of a sudden after I went to see Thrity, I just felt this click, and knew that everything would be fine again and that Mum and Dad breaking up wasn't that bad a thing, it was just meant to happen. And with my sister I now feel absolutely fine. What happened was pretty unbelievable, but it was magic.

Life became peaceful after that. Now I am a lot more relaxed and happy. It literally changed my life.'

AL (See plate 5)

AL had initiated her divorce and it hadn't been particularly pleasant. The post-divorce relationship was understandably cold and communication between her and her ex was the absolute minimum. They would meet to pick up and drop off their daughters at weekends and holidays but there was very little conversation at these meetings and in fact AL's ex did not seem to even want to look at her.

AL dealt with this as best she could, as she wanted the best for her daughters and knew they needed their dad in their lives. She made sure that she did not talk badly about him to the girls. But life as a single mother with two young daughters was not easy. She knew she was in trouble. So she came to see me for a VRIC assessment.

When I imaged her with her daughters, she was OK. Next I took another image with her and her daughters with one difference: I asked her to hold a photo of her ex-husband. The results were shocking to her, but pretty much what I expected: her image was badly fragmented and incoherent. But even more telling was the effect on her daughters. Though they were not holding their dad's image, they fragmented badly. So AL could see why she and her daughters were in difficulty. The unresolved, unspoken emotional charge around the challenging and painful events of the divorce had not been healed.

AL told me she had done her inner work of forgiveness, and I believed her, as I had known her a long time and she had always been truthful. However, the imaging showed that there was some way to go.

By this time I had the prototype SRTLFs and so I had her hold the two frequencies along with the photo of her ex-husband, had her two girls stand beside her and took another VRIC image. To her relief and amazement her image, which a minute before had been completely fragmented, was sharp, clear and coherent. Her daughters' images were clear as well. AL's response was, 'Wow, this is magic!'

The trauma and tragedy of that painful event and the hurt and the havoc it had created had all dissolved in a millisecond, just by holding two miraculous little pieces of glass encoded with the light-energy-information of grace and love.

The story does not end there. I instructed AL that she was to use the SRTLFs every day, but as importantly she was to place them on the photograph of her ex-husband every day, as he needed healing as much as she and her daughters did. Obviously she could not tell him to hold them as they were not on real speaking terms. But the VRIC images had clearly demonstrated that everyone heals or no one heals. AL was a bit dubious as to whether this would have any effect, but she trusted me enough to follow my suggestions.

A couple of months later I phoned her to ask her permission to use her VRIC images for the Supercoherence DVD and she gave me her permission. I was also curious to see whether anything had changed either in her relationship with her children or her relationship with her ex-husband.

She reported that a couple of weeks after starting using the SRTLFs, she and her daughters met her ex-husband in town. What happened caught her by surprise. For the first time since the divorce, he looked directly at her and said, 'I still miss you every day.' The stone wall of hurt had come down, to be replaced by the strength to be vulnerable. No, it does not mean that they fell into each other's arms and got back together again, but some internal barrier was dissolved and what was always underneath could show its brave, shy and shining face to the one who had 'hurt' him so badly. And a huge invisible lethal burden of suffering was lifted from that whole fractured family.

AL writes:

'When I first came to see you, I was wholly captivated by physical issues and wasn't ready to look at any underlying emotional ones. Using the system was not dissimilar to turning a key that, in my case, unlocked deeply repressed feelings. With such an energetic shift occurring there was no chance of a return to the old way of thinking and feeling.

What did this mean for my marriage? As a result of being a lucky recipient of the system [Luminator and VRIC imaging] I had two children and, as a consequence, had moved out of London with my husband to live in Devon, but it was becoming increasingly clear that I was being untruthful to myself, and therefore anyone near to me, by staying with my husband. My elder daughter in particular was like an emotional barometer reflecting the over-charged atmosphere between us and responding with equally over-charged behaviour.

After the inevitable separation I worked hard at finding it in myself to move on and forgive my ex-husband for all the hurt that I felt he had inflicted. I really thought I had achieved this and was surprised at how hard handovers with the children and the subsequent fall-out continued to be. I still had latent anger and it became clear that I hadn't managed to forgive him, despite all my good intentions and soul-searching. I could see this was continuously difficult for the children so I decided to take the girls and myself to Thrity to see if we couldn't shift this emotional stone wall. It was essential to the girls and their father that I let go of the unforgiving part of myself that I couldn't contact by myself.

Thrity suggested I put two Supercoherence frequencies [SRTLFs], on a photograph of my ex-husband, one on the right and one on the left. [AL was also asked to use the SRTLFs herself.] This is where the process is so extraordinary: this seemingly small act tapped into the unhappy part of myself that I was still holding on to and dissolved it. With this came a subtle energetic shift that was seismic. I could feel on a cellular level, without having to overthink it, that I had let go of something that was holding us all back. On some level it was clear that my ex-husband knew it too and in turn he found he could talk to me again.

The ramifications of something so nebulous are hard to describe in words, but it has had a freeing quality that is noticeable in all our lives. When you learn to forgive, or are enabled to forgive, it doesn't stop with the first person. The Supercoherence process has allowed me to look kindly not only on my ex-husband but also on other people, and I feel I can let go of past suffering.

As a result of not holding on so religiously to suffering, all sorts of unexpected things have happened that perhaps couldn't have happened if I hadn't used this process, and it hasn't stopped with me. My children are finding a new confidence and regaining the peace within themselves that was badly shattered after the divorce.

Lately I have put the SRTLFs on a photograph of my elder daughter, who is unhappy at her new school, with the Supercoherence I Am

Female frequency and the written statement: 'I deserve and accept the very best in life. I love and approve of myself just the way I am.' Both of us were feeling utterly overwhelmed by the demands of her school and we were busy expressing it with anger and shouting and were unlikely to find a resolution. But, like magic, just putting the frequencies on a photograph has helped us both to take a decision that has benefited her and opened up a stream of possibilities that we are all excited by. Anything feels possible now.'

Grace always is and love never dies.

As I write this case study, I realize that it is 1st March – my wedding anniversary. I have been divorced since 1989. I initiated the divorce, just as AL did. Remembering this has brought back many memories, but the residual feeling is gratitude for the good times that we had together, and the pain and sadness have dissipated. My ex-husband lives in Mumbai for part of the year and in London for a few months each year with our daughter. I phoned him this morning; he is always happy to hear my voice. I asked him whether he knew what the date was. He laughed as he realized that he hadn't remembered that it was our wedding anniversary. There was no embarrassment, only ease and the comfort of knowing we have known each other for several decades and the friendship and tenderness between us are still very much there.

On reflection, perhaps we are better friends now than we were when we were married. In fact since he got the SRTLFs he has said 'I love you' to me more than he ever said it in the many years we were married. I am grateful that he is in my life. And no, it does not mean that I am going to remarry or that we will live together again.

A Soul's Journey – Healing the Feminine Line

I have known J. for well over a decade. She initially came as a client and stayed to become a friend. She has used the SRTLFs since late 2009.

J. is very pretty – tall and slim with soft green eyes that would melt anyone who looked into them. Gifted with an extraordinary eye for colour and an artistic temperament, but 'dyslexic' by her own count, she has a sweet and gentle disposition, is not given to confrontation and is definitely not a warrior. But when I first knew her she could be secretive. She would often tell you what she thought you wanted to hear. When she first came to see me it was clear that she did not like her mother much, but adored her dad. At the time I did not know that she had run away from home and cut all contact with her parents.

She had been adopted when she was six weeks old. Her biological mother had had an affair with a married man and she was the unexpected and unwelcome result. Years later her adoptive mother told her that as a baby, she did not smile for her first year. J. said, 'I never felt that I belonged.'

Her childhood was difficult. Her adoptive parents loved her, but her mother was extremely strict and J. did not have much freedom. At 11 years old she was sent to a boarding school run by nuns where life was equally restrictive. 'The food was diabolical – the best supper was cold chips and fish fingers.' (This explains why she has always been indifferent to food and never really cooked.) Baths were allowed twice a week. Freedom and fun were unknown.

Her parents had also adopted a boy, and this brother was treated very differently from J:

'He was allowed to do everything – he could go away for a week with his friends, he could do anything he wanted, and yet I couldn't do anything. I wasn't allowed any friends, I wasn't allowed to go anywhere, I wasn't allowed to do anything. I wasn't allowed to go to people's houses, people weren't allowed to play with me, I couldn't have sleepovers... When I went to boarding school, if I went to a friend's for a weekend, my mother would be on the phone questioning me about I had done. In the school holidays I wasn't allowed to see anyone. I had to go to work with her in the car. She seemed to want to control every aspect of my life and in the end I just couldn't take it anymore. I was about 17 then and had not long come back from boarding school. At least I had a little more freedom there. At home it seemed as though everybody was turning against me, trying to keep me in my place, which was, effectively, locked in a room. So I ran away.'

For several years J. had many adventures, went abroad, did beauty therapy and then settled into an ordinary but stable job at a major department store. At one point, around 19, she tried to commit suicide by taking an overdose, which, fortunately for her, did not do the job. I asked her why she wanted to kill herself. She told me that she had felt trapped and that there seemed to be no way forward.

The sad thing was that in these years of no contact with her family, her beloved father died and J. did not find out until two months after he had gone.

When I met J. she was in her late thirties, had a stable job and was in a relationship that had lasted six years. She described it as abusive. However, he paid all the bills and she kept all the money that she earned. She never did any cooking or housework and did not really know how to run a house. She felt she was 'trucking along' and had no particular ambitions for her life.

But life had other plans for her. She decided she wanted to clear her past family traumas and came to see me. At that time we did not have the SRTLFs, but the process was the same in that we used frequencies to neutralize the pain in her important past relationships and create coherence in her energy field and in her life. We used VRIC imaging to know which frequencies would do the job.

By this time J. had not been in contact with her parents for well over 15 years. Shortly after the clearing was done with her mother, though, by some strange 'coincidence' her mother found out where she worked and came to find her. J. got the shock of her life when she walked into the store. So the relationship was re-established – though there was some justifiable mistrust on both sides.

Then J's relationship with her partner came apart as he started having an affair with a woman much older than J. This was a bitter pill for J. to swallow. After a lot of turmoil, her partner moved out and J. had to contend with running her own life. She muddled through somehow and managed to pay her rent and bills. But the thing was that now she was in charge of her life properly for the first time in many years, if ever. It was an uncomfortable step, but a step in the right direction. She was no longer just 'trucking along'.

After that her work life took off and she started being recognized for her talents. Her personal life was another matter – she went into another relationship, and another, and another, and then at the age of 43 found herself pregnant. Suddenly all bets were off. Her fragile relationship with her mother became chaotic again:

'Mum went up the wall. She had been a health visitor for 40 years and had looked after children and babies and when I had my baby obviously I did not know what to do with her, but Mum did, and so it was "Oh, you will never make a proper mother! Oh, you can't possibly handle this!" And everything went wrong with my partner and there was pressure from his parents – it was a nightmare on wheels. But I came through it and I got everything sorted out and got a nice little flat. My little girl was lovely, but Mum kept on saying I wasn't fit to be a mother and maybe she should take the baby off me.'

It took a couple of years for J's mother to acknowledge that despite all her misgivings, J. was turning into a very capable and caring mother. J. confided that her mother never praised her, no matter what she achieved. She had to be a perfect mother and perfect housekeeper and nothing she seemed to do was quite good enough.

J. had been working regularly with the SRTLFs ever since 2009. Recently, however, she came to see me. She walked in through the door and the first thing she said was, 'Thrity, your frequencies are amazing.' Then she came out with an utterly extraordinary story:

'My mother said she was coming down for half term and I was dreading it, as I was sure I was going to be doing everything wrong for her again. But this time it was different. When I collected her from the railway station she was like a little old lady sitting there and I said, 'Come on, Mum,' and she lit up. And the first night she was at the flat with me she got talking about all kinds of different things. Obviously she wanted to talk – we were up till 1.30 in the morning! – and she finally told me that she had been sexually abused between the ages of 14 and 16 by a member of the family and that is why she had been so protective of me all my life. Everything kind of fell into place then and my mother was like the 14-year-old she was never allowed to be and all the control, the hardness, everything turned into giggles and it was so beautiful to see.'

Hearing this, I was touched beyond words. After 72 years this woman had told her dreadful secret to her daughter. Some huge emotional inner knot had dissolved. The 'controller' could decide to be vulnerable.

J. continued:

'She had never told another living soul. There were bits of it that she didn't tell me either and I had to piece it all together. The person who abused her gave her £400, which was enough to buy a big house with three-quarters of an acre of garden. And knowing my mum and how she was completely mad about babies and how she couldn't have any of her own, I feel that obviously she had an abortion that went wrong and left her unable to have children, which is why I got a lot of grief when I got my own girl, because it was so painful for her.

Knowing this has made my life better, it has made my daughter's life better and it has made my mother happier. The frequencies have allowed us to understand each other. And once you understand where someone is coming from then everything makes sense. So for 47 years I have been nailed to the floor and suddenly what has happened? It has all dissolved.

I have never seen my mother so happy and love is just pouring out of me for her now because I understand all the hurt she must have been through. It doesn't matter that she was so regimental with me anymore, because it wasn't due to something I had done, it was something that had happened to her, and she was just trying to protect me and love me... When she explained, it was as though a huge weight had been lifted off both of us. Even though it was a terrible thing, we had smiles on our faces because it explained everything. Before, I couldn't understand why my mother didn't love me and now I knew she did.

I always loved my dad, because he was gentle and soft and sweet and kind. But he had his problems too. He was an alcoholic. He was a weak man, but she could never have coped with a strong man, because it would have broken down her barriers. She needed someone she had to take care of and who would comply with her wishes, which made them perfectly suited. But he was a nightmare. She had to take the cheque book away from him, as he just drank away all the money. She was controlling, but capable and hard-working and loving without any of us realizing it. She made it very difficult for us to love her as well – in fact I think she made it impossible for anybody to love her. Perhaps deep down she didn't feel worthy of being loved – and now she does. It has taken her till 86, but it is a beautiful thing to see.'

And in the context of a soul's journey, of course, it is no time at all. The cycle of healing will be completed in its own time and one does not know how long this will be, but in my opinion the SRTLFs shorten the cycle. They can dissolve suffering like this with this ease and sweetness and no effort.

J. concurred:'There were no tears, no crying, no hugging, no having to say "I forgive you", just a beautiful feeling of forgiveness floating over, forgiveness and love – in fact more love than forgiveness, because there was nothing to forgive because people are just human and it doesn't matter what happens, you just have to try and deal with everything with love.'

J. can't stop smiling. I am delighted.

When I first heard that J. was pregnant I thought she was being very foolish to have a child at that late age. Babies are hard work and how was she going to manage a career and a child with no proper support from a partner who lived many hours' drive away? Today, after four years, I understand that for J. to heal her life and make sense of her soul's journey, nothing else would have done the job. No successful career, no amount of money would have sufficed to fill that hole. The hurt, the rejection and the resentment could only be healed by loving and giving to a child who was her own. This child would be totally loved, she would never be given away, she would receive the best in time and attention and freedom and fun that was possible.

I have to say that J. is an exemplary mother. She is soft and sweet with her little daughter. I have never seen or heard her raise her voice, let alone raise a hand to her. She is always kind, yet gentle and firm at the same time, and the little one is fearless, confident, very bright and well behaved. J. does over-compensate and runs herself into the ground so the little girl is denied nothing, but she is no longer just 'trucking along' – her life is committed, passionate and deeply meaningful.

Though there was huge chaos for a couple of years after J. had her daughter, she has built a sweet life for herself and her little girl and has healed her own life in the process. She gives unstintingly and will do anything and everything for this girl – everything that she would have liked to have had done for her and that she missed when she was a child. She has very little money, but says that she is the happiest she has ever been in this lifetime and probably many lifetimes – with this little soul companion who came to teach her how to be truly happy.

Now the whole female line has been healed and the future for J's mother, J. and her little girl looks bright and free from the guilt, blame, shame and pain of the past. Only J. used the SRTLFs, but the healing and the consequent happiness went up the line to her mother and down the line to her child.

Just as suffering muddies the past and the future, in that the suffering of the parents is passed down to the children, so coherence clears the past and makes the future bright for all. And it only takes one person to shift from the cycle of incoherence to coherence. It is important and interesting to note that it took years for the cycle of healing to complete – 47 in J's case, 72 in her mother's case – so one does not know how long a cycle may take to complete; it does when it does. But please know that it *always* does and in my opinion the SRTLFs shorten the cycle. Your soul is always on your case. Until both J. and her mother could lay down their invisible lethal burdens of suffering the cycle could not complete and the circle could not close. At any time before these momentous healing events unfolded, J. could not have known or even considered the possibility that her mother loved her as much as she did or how much love there was locked inside herself for the frail, 'rigid', 'oppressive', 'controlling' human who was her beloved mother.

CHAPTER 15
Clearing the Conception Pre-birth and Birth Imprint

'The deepest imprinting for the personality
of the human develops in the womb'

Dr. Brent Babcock

MILLIONS OF US have either had a traumatic time in the womb or during the birth process or both. Or maybe our life in the womb and our birth process was without problems, but we picked up some of our parents' anxieties during that time. What kind of invisible load are we carrying now from that?

Ultrasound, intrauterine photography and hypnotherapy show us that the baby is a conscious sentient being which thinks feels and responds in intelligent ways previously thought impossible. In the Supercoherence system we have always known that conception, pre-birth and birth are major life events for us humans and leave deep emotional imprints in the field. This is now confirmed by many experiments and studies done elsewhere. As early as conception, whether the child was conceived in love or as the result of force, whether the mother's pregnancy was happy, unhappy, or traumatic can mean the difference between a happy life or a dysfunctional one for the child. Re-birthing, NET (Neuro Emotional Technique), hypnotherapy and some Light/colour systems are some of the ways that are used to help with the healing of these invisible wounds to the psyche and the soul. These techniques are effective and powerful, however in my view there is another simpler, easier, quicker and even more powerful way to neutralise the effect of these imprints using the SRTLFs.

As part of clearing the imprint of our past, we can clear the conception, pre-birth and birth imprints with the SRTLFs. I wish to thank Sandra Fiquet for the gift of these processes to the Supercoherence system.

Clearing the Conception Imprint

- Write a note which says: 'Myself at the moment of my conception.'
- Hold the note with the Divine Mother photograph in the left and then in the right hand for ten minutes each side whilst holding the SRTLFs (green in the right hand and pink in the left hand).
- Add photos of your mother and father to the note along with the Divine Mother photo and the SRTLFs and hold for ten minutes each side.

Clearing your Pre-birth Imprint

- Write a note which says: 'Myself when in my mother's womb.'
- Hold the note with the Divine Mother photograph in the left and then in the right hand for ten minutes each side whilst also holding the SRTLFs (green in the right hand and pink in the left hand).
- Then add your mother's photograph.
- Then swap your mother's photograph for your father's photograph, still holding the note, the SRTLFs and the Divine Mother.
- Hold both parents' photographs with the note, Divine Mother and SRTLFs.

If you do not have photographs you can simply write the name of the person/parent on a note and use it to do the clearing. (*See plate 9*)

If you do not know who your parents were, you may write my 'my biological father in this lifetime' or 'my biological mother in this lifetime' on notes in place of the photos.

Clearing your Birth Imprint

- Write a note which says: 'Myself during my birth.'
- Hold the note with the Divine Mother photograph in the left and then the right hand for ten minutes each side whilst also holding the SRTLFs (green in the right hand and pink in the left hand).
- Then add your mother's photograph and hold it with the note for ten minutes in the left and right hands, one at a time.

You may or may not feel anything during these processes, but they will clear the emotional charge around past events and relationships that are still present in your energy field and in your unconscious.

The effects of this can be wide-ranging, as shown by the following case history from Supercoherence practitioner Sandra Fiquet:

My partner and I had been invited to a wedding. It had been arranged that the ladies of the close family would be given an orchid to wear and the other ladies would be given a carnation. On the way there, my partner received a phone call from the groom saying that they had run out of orchids and would I mind wearing a carnation instead? I really didn't care. It was just another wedding, another flower, whatever... I said, 'Sure, no problem.'

Then my partner said to me, 'That's your pattern again.' And he was right.

As far as I can remember, the 'pattern' started when I was going to pre-school, at the age of four or five. During the breaks, we were let out to play outside. There were lots of outside toys to play with like large balls, scooters and tricycles, but somehow by the time I got outside, all the best toys would already have been taken by the other kids and all that would be left for me were the boring buckets and spades in the sandpit.

When I went to an afternoon fancy dress party and biscuits and honey cakes were passed around on plates, when the plate came to me, there were only crumbs on it.

As life went on, those 'small incidents' carried on. When going to a restaurant, it often happened that once I had ordered something, the waiter would come back to say they had just run out of it. Shops would often have just sold the item I wanted to someone else. It didn't bother me that much (except perhaps the honey cakes); I always thought, 'Oh well, never mind.'

But this 'orchid event' really made me think. In my mind's eye, I saw myself as a vibrating tuning fork sending little waves out into the universe. During the wedding and over the following couple of days, I asked myself over and over again, 'What is it that I'm vibrating and sending out for this pattern to come back to me?' I was really intrigued.

I had done a lot of work on myself – personal development and clearing – but there was obviously something else there.

Then a thought came up: 'What about when you were in the womb?'

And yes, stuff had happened to me then. It had first come up several years before when I had been doing a coloured light session using my SRSII (Jacob Lieberman's Spectral Receptivity System). When looking at the colours from the dark red through to the orange, I could have sworn there was someone behind me with their hands around my neck trying to strangle me. Of course there was nobody there, but a part of me was struggling to breathe and it was a bit scary. As the coloured light moved on to the yellows and so on, the feeling disappeared.

A few days later I was telling my mother about my weird experience and she told me that when she was six months pregnant with me, my father had attacked her in a fit of rage for some unfounded reason and had put his hands around her neck. Soon after, she was told she would have to spend the rest of her pregnancy resting in hospital otherwise she might lose me.

Then several years later I had a coloured light session in Thrity's large Monocrom Dome. It wasn't my first session – I always loved going in there. But this time, when the dark red appeared, a part of me just wanted to run out of the door, and again I wasn't breathing normally. Luckily, another part of me reasoned that I was only in the dome and that I should stick with it. Whatever was coming up had to be cleared. So I hung in there and purposefully went back several times to that dark red until eventually I felt reasonably calm with it.

I thought the coloured light work had cleared whatever had happened, and I'm sure a lot had cleared. But I thought, 'Why not do some clearing with the SRTLFs as well?'

I was thinking that although pre-birth, my life in the womb was still part of my current life. It was a bit like preparing oneself behind the curtain before appearing on the stage of our world.

I wrote the note: 'Myself when in my mother's womb.' I held the note with the Divine Mother photograph on the left then the right for ten minutes each side whilst also holding the RTLFs. I had very tingling hands.

Then I added my mother's photograph.

Then I swapped my mother's photograph for my father's photograph, still holding the note, the SRTLFs and the Divine Mother.

Then I held both my parents' photographs with the note, Divine Mother and SRTLFs.

And it was during the last configuration (using both parents' photographs) on the left that a quiet tiny little voice came up in my head saying, 'I don't count and I don't matter.' And it kept repeating, 'I don't count and I don't matter.'

I wonder how I felt in the womb during my parents' fight? Obviously a part of me had wanted to leave and 'run away', but maybe also (or because?) I didn't count and I didn't matter?

That was when I realized that's what I had been unconsciously broadcasting to the universe with my 'out of tune tuning fork'! That was why there wasn't any stuff left for me a lot of the time – because a part of me believed I didn't count and I didn't matter! A part of me I had been totally unaware of had, invisibly to me, been shaping my reality.

After this particular clearing, I didn't feel like doing anymore for a little while as I wanted things to settle. As a side note, my period started two weeks earlier than normal after that.

A few weeks later, I did a follow-up clearing with a note saying: 'I do count and I do matter.' Again, I held it for ten minutes each side, but I didn't use either of my parents' photographs this time.

Interestingly, whilst holding the note, I suddenly became quite tearful and I kept tasting salty water, as if I was choking on it. It felt as if I was drowning, so much so that I was coughing quite a lot and was struggling to breathe whilst holding the note. But I still stuck with it – it had to clear.

At the end of the session, for good measure, I said out loud for each side: 'I do count and I jolly well do matter!'

A few weeks later, a photograph kept popping up in my head – the photograph that had been taken on the day I was born. In it, my head was pear-shaped, as forceps had been used. I remembered my mother telling me many times that she was terrified that my head would stay that shape despite the doctor's reassurance that it would not. Thinking about the photograph, I realized I might well have gone through some kind of trauma during the birth process itself.

I saw the birth process as a transition, like crossing a bridge from one world to another, whilst still being part of my life. So why not do a clearing for that particular moment?

So I wrote the note: 'Myself during my birth.' I held it with the Divine Mother photograph on the left then the right for ten minutes each side whilst also holding the SRTLFs. I experienced lots of yawning when holding it on both left and right.

Then I added my mother's photograph. For some reason, I didn't use my father's photograph or both my parents' photographs, although I had them to hand – probably because I thought the birth process was between me and my mother only. I didn't analyse it at the time, I just went with the flow. Maybe I will do the clearing with those configurations later on at some point to make it complete.

Anyway, again I experienced lots of yawning when holding the note, Divine Mother and my mother's photograph on the left and right and the words 'chronic anxiety' repeatedly came into my head when holding on the right.

I thought, 'What chronic anxiety?'

Then morning anxiety came to mind. For what seemed to be forever, when waking up in the morning I'd had a feeling of anxiety gripping my gut. And yes, sometimes we all worry about something, but that didn't justify the intensity of the anxiety I'd had every single morning ever since I could remember. It felt almost visceral. Mostly, I hurried to get up to focus on doing something – anything – as it disappeared soon after that.

So, as a next step I decided to write the note: 'I am chronic anxiety free, chronic worry free, I am calm and at peace within' and held it for ten minutes on each side with the Divine Mother photograph and the SRTLFs.

On both sides, but a bit more on left, I felt something melting and dissipating inside immediately. I suddenly felt very light, as if I was floating. I then felt so extremely relaxed that everything, the house and the whole world, could have collapsed around me and it wouldn't have bothered me at all! That was amazing and it was lovely to feel that way.

As a side note, I had a nosebleed on and off during the whole of the following day. This has happened before, after doing energy work. My period also started a week and a half earlier than normal after that.

That visceral morning anxiety disappeared completely and hasn't reappeared since. I now wake up feeling neutral, rather than starting the day with an invisible heavy weight, which is really nice.

To think I had been carrying that weight, unaware, since I was born is unbelievable.'

Imagine how it would be if both parents used the SRTLFs during the pregnancy and kept their systems coherent – what a beautiful starting gift it would be from the parents to their beloved child. Also how the future trajectory of humanity could be changed if the photo of each newborn baby could be placed with the SRTLFs and the Divine Mother image. Coherence, clarity and super function with no emotional imprinting from the very beginning of life becomes possible - we would usher in the golden age of the universal human – the future of humanity would be bright.

CHAPTER 16

Clearing the Ancestral Line Imprint

"Our history begins before we are born. We
represent the hereditary influence of our race
and our ancestors virtually live in us"

– James Nasmyth

TODAY MOST OF us know that we inherit certain physical traits and characteristics through the genes of our parents. However I would like you to consider the possibility that all their emotional experiences are also encoded at different levels of your being. You not only carry your past in your cellular memory and energy field, you carry the emotional history and conditioning of all your ancestors as well. This hidden invisible information also has an important part in shaping your perception and therefore your reality and your destiny.

As Sandra Fiquet recalls, 'About three weeks after doing the womb/birth clearing, on 28 August 2011 I was watching a BBC programme called 'The Nine Months That Made You'. It was a programme in the *Horizon* series about 'how the time in the womb could affect your health and personality'. Because of my previous clearing, I wanted to know what it had to say, but as it happens, it didn't go the way I thought it might and focused on nutrition. But it included film clips of the Second World War, when people were undernourished and hungry due to food rationing, and when those clips came on, I started to cry. Those images had a distant familiarity, as if an old memory was coming back. I thought that my reaction was a bit weird, but just put it down to being emotional that day for some unknown reason.

Then on 18 September, I felt compelled to do some clearing with the note 'I feel safe and I am safe.' The reason I wanted to do this clearing was because I had noticed the underlying pattern of a sense of a lack of safety. This had started in the womb [*see above*] and had carried on in later life.

During this 'I feel safe and I am safe' clearing, tears came out of nowhere when I was holding the note and the Divine Mother on the left. I had no idea why I was crying – the tears just came. Then memories came back of not feeling truly safe with either of my parents.

However, the night after that, I had the first of what turned into several Second World War-related nightmares. In it, I was in a German prison camp and I had worked out a plan to escape. The chance of succeeding was very small, but I went for it. As I was crawling under some barbed wire and three-quarters of the way out, a soldier spotted me and shot me in the back of the legs. Then he walked up and looked into my face.

In another dream, German soldiers had decided to requisition our house to use as a meeting-place. They forced us out at gunpoint and we only had time to pack the bare minimum to take with us. We had to leave practically all of our stuff behind.

In yet another dream, I woke up on a pile of clothed bodies and suddenly realized they were all dead. Then I remembered that I had slept on top of a pile of corpses to hide from the soldiers so that I could escape later on.

Those dreams were less than pleasant and the feel of them lingered throughout each following day.

Because of all those war-related dreams and my reaction to the war malnutrition film clips, I decided to do some clearing with a note. I felt really silly doing it, but I thought there must be something there otherwise I wouldn't be having those reactions and nightmares.

The note I worked with was: 'Myself during the war.' I really didn't expect anything to happen at all. But oddly enough, both my hands tingled a lot when I held the note, and this happened for both sides.

At the end of the session, a small part of me felt strangely lighter, as if something had lifted.

And the nightmares stopped.

A week later, I was chatting to my mother on the phone and without explaining to her why I wanted to know, I asked her how the Second World War had impacted her parents and her grandparents. Her response astounded me. She said her father (so my grandfather, whom I had seen only occasionally when I was little) had been made a prisoner of war when he was about 18 and had been imprisoned in a labour camp in Germany and had tried to escape.

And her grandfather (my great-grandfather, whom I remember seeing just a few times when I was little) had been a builder. During the war, the Germans had tried to force him to build buildings and roads for them, but he had refused. So the Germans had taken away his ration books and he had been unable to get food for his family and they had been extremely hungry.

I then asked my father about the war and his parents. I told him about the nightmares I had had and asked if any of those corresponded to any family war stories. He said that his uncle (on his mother's side) had been in a German labour camp and had managed to escape. He had hidden during the day and walked and crossed rivers at night. And my grandparents had left their house to go to a safer place and had taken their silverware with them. They had left the house of their own accord, so it wasn't exactly like my dream, but the bottom line was that they had left their house, taking just a few items with them.

In view of all of this, it looked as though I had been carrying war-related memory imprints from previous generations. In fact, I could now see that some of my previous behavioural patterns could have related to that, such as not wanting to waste things, and feeling guilty and avoiding eating something nice when I was on my own because I felt it should always be shared. I had thought that those patterns might be the result of a lack of self-worth and had done the clearing for that, but they had remained until I did this ancestral clearing.

When my mother was little, her mother sent her to a strict Catholic boarding school. Her sister and two brothers were allowed to stay at home, but my grandmother wanted my mother to stay at the boarding school even at weekends and holidays. The reason is still unknown. My mother told me so often what a terrible time this had been for her, that sometimes I almost felt I had gone through it myself, and it felt like a heavy burden every time she told me about it. For whatever reason, something inside pushed me to do some clearing with it. Again, I felt silly doing it, but following my recent experience of ancestral memory clearing, I went ahead with it.

I wrote the note, 'Myself, when I was at the Catholic boarding school,' even though this was one of my mother's traumatic times, way before I was born. I actually wrote it in French, as there seemed to be much more charge in French than in English.

Nothing particular happened during the actual clearing, but the next day I had quite a few flashbacks of when I was little. Then over the next two to three days I also had some strange images of when my parents met for the first time, along with their associated feelings. I could see my father walking down from his parents' house to the dance hall one evening. He was glad to get away from the house, as he kept being told off and told he was good for nothing by his dad, and going out would allow him to show off, which would make him feel better. And I saw my mother going from her strict environment to the same dance hall on the same evening. She was also glad to be out. Her breathing was lighter from her sense of freedom and she was full of hope. I saw them meeting up, with my father spinning her yarns that he was a pilot. (My mother had told me this, but I had forgotten about it.) As he was telling those lies in order to make himself big, he was feeling much better about himself and for once he felt in control of his life. My mother wasn't sure what to think, but she liked him. He was a breath of fresh air after her very harsh mother and the strict religious boarding school. And so I saw those two sad and lost humans connecting on that particular evening, both with heavy emotional loads and both desperate to get away from their hurt and sadness. But their loads were so heavy that they were helpless to prevent them from controlling their lives. I could see each of them bent under the weight of a very heavy sack across their shoulders. I could feel the extreme sadness in each of them and somehow a sense of the futility of life came up from my father. There were those two beings at the start of their life journey together, and I could feel a (or their?) deep sense of waste, loss and sadness.

I was really depressed and tearful during the next two days. I also felt really tired over those two days, as well as on the third day. This clearing really knocked the stuffing out of me.

As a side note, a few days after the clearing my period unexpectedly started a week and a half early and was painful for an unusual length of time.

But a couple of weeks later, I felt I had been 'cleansed'. It's a funny word to use but it's exactly what it felt like. It was a bit like when the landscape and the air look all shiny and clean after the rain. I felt just like that.

So I wonder who else could be affected by ancestral memories?

If someone knows that their parents or grand-parents or even great-grand-parents went through some traumatic events, I think it would be worthwhile for them to do the clearing with the note 'Myself during [traumatic event]', as if they had gone through it themselves.

Ancestral Memory Clearing

I had been working on my computer for most of the day with the SRTLFs on my keyboard (I have noticed I am more focused and efficient that way). Suddenly the internet connection was lost. I tried everything, to no avail. And all the stuff I had to do was reliant on accessing the internet. What a nuisance! I held the SRTLFs in my hands for a short while to calm down.

But no sooner was I holding them that the thought came up of clearing all the ancestral memories and conditioning passed down to me by my parents. I made a note to add it to my 'Clearing List', but the idea had a real sense of urgency, which was unusual. As I was thinking about it, still holding the SRTLFs in my hands, a huge shiver went through my whole being and my hair stood on end. Something was going on. So I thought, 'Well, I cannot do any work at the moment, so I might as well use my time for something useful.'

I wrote the note: 'Myself with all the memories, ancestral memories, conditioning and ancestral conditioning passed on to me by my mother.'

Note: I chose *not* to use the photograph of my mother. It also felt important to do this clearing with my eyes closed, as I didn't want to be distracted by my present surroundings.

While I was holding the SRTLFs, the note and the Divine Mother photograph on the left, flashes came up of white-walled corridors with several nuns walking along. I had a sense of being in a very strict environment and the place felt quite cold.

Then images came up of being inside a medieval castle in a large room with large hanging greyish-blue drapes on the high stone walls. Then more images came up of the castle, but of the outside.

Then I had flashbacks of a dream I had had a while back in which I was a baby in medieval times lying on a fortified wall.

When making the statement 'I love and I accept myself exactly as I am' out loud several times at the end of holding the SRTLFs, I felt a long shiver run through my whole body.

When I was holding the SRTLFs, the note and the Divine Mother photograph on the right, I got flashes of medieval archers shooting arrows with their large bows from the top of a high wall (the images were similar to the dream I had had).

Then images of an old steamer ship came up. The ship was sailing from right to left. It had four chimneys in a straight line. Strangely, this image was in black and white.

Again, when making the statement 'I love and I accept myself exactly as I am' out loud several times, I felt a long shiver run through my whole body.

Then I wrote the note: 'Myself with all the memories, ancestral memories, conditioning and ancestral conditioning passed on to me from my father.'

Note: I chose *not* to use the photograph of my father. It also felt important to do this clearing with my eyes closed, as I didn't want to be distracted by my present surroundings.

When holding the SRTLFs, the note and the Divine Mother photograph on the left, I found a strong sense of poverty came up. There was a strong sense of lack on all levels, but mainly on the material level, with thoughts of lack of food, lack of shelter, lack of warmth, constant strife and struggle, feeling cold and always being in survival mode. Images came up of snow and a flimsy wooden house with the roof in disrepair.

The whole of my left side felt very heavy, as if under the weight of a huge boulder, so much so that my breathing became very shallow because of the weight.

Then, when making the statement 'I love and I accept myself exactly as I am' out loud, I saw in my mind's eye loads of dark grey particles flying away vertically from my system, looking a bit like a swarm. I repeated the statement two or three more times and each time I saw more grey particles flying away until there were none left.

When holding the SRTLFs, the note and the Divine Mother photograph on the right, I saw many images of weapons, of bombs flying around and of war. Again, a feeling of deep struggle came up.

Then a phrase popped into my mind two or three times: 'I have to prove myself, I have to prove myself.' It faded after a short while and was replaced with 'I don't have to prove myself, I don't have to prove myself to anybody.' Again that came to me two or three times and then gently faded away, at which point, I saw in my mind's eye lots of black particles flying away very fast vertically from my system in one go.

From that point onwards, I felt something melting inside me and felt as if I was sinking into a giant deep warm cushion. It was orangey-red and extremely soft. I felt lovely and warm throughout my whole body. Then images of a tropical beach came up and I was sitting there enjoying the warm late-afternoon sun. The images of being deep in the warm cushion and on the beach alternated, and with each change I became more relaxed, almost floating.

I made the statement 'I love and I accept myself exactly as I am' out loud several times and I felt so happy I felt like giggling.

I felt much lighter after this session, which surprised me, as I hadn't felt down before. But something had definitely shifted. Another invisible load had gone.

As soon as I finished the clearing, I turned back to my computer keyboard and tried the internet connection again and it was working fine, as if nothing had happened! That was really weird. It was as if 'something' had cut off my access to the internet in order to force me to do the clearing right there and then, as if it was so urgent that it couldn't wait!

I felt this clearing went much deeper than the previous one, as this time I didn't restrict it to any specific known traumatic events but included all memories and all forms of conditioning.'

This is perhaps the most important and powerful process for using the SRTLFs to break the cycle of human suffering.

CHAPTER 17

Death and the Multi-dimensional Universe

"The soul comes from without into the human body, as into a temporary abode, and it goes out of it anew it passes into other habitations, for the soul is immortal."

– Ralph Waldo Emerson

THE VEIL BETWEEN the dimensions is thinning, it seems, and communications from the 'other side' are coming through more easily than ever before.

Healing across the dimensions is also possible, and easy, with the use of the SRTLFs.

SRTLFs and the Other Side

This case study comes from Sandra Fiquet:

'Father is Now Proud of Me'

BH, 54, was often told by her father, before he died, that the work she was doing was idiotic and that she was good for nothing. Her mother, on hearing this, would just keep quiet. BH asked me how she could neutralize this using the SRTLFs.

I gave her a protocol to follow, holding her mother's photograph, then her father's photograph, then both together, with the Divine Mother photograph and the note 'Myself, each time my parents told me that my work was idiotic and that I was good for nothing.' I specified that she should carry it out without the TV on, or any music, and without any other distractions.

We spoke on the phone a couple of days afterwards. She said she had felt her arms were very heavy at the end of the session and she had felt so very relaxed that she could have gone straight to bed. She had also been physically quite bloated for the past several months, and the day after doing the clearing that had totally disappeared.

Then a couple of days after that she e-mailed me about something extraordinary that had happened to her the day before:

'In the afternoon, I went with P. to a personal development event and during the second half there was a medium through whom I had had a message from my father about six months before.

Because I'd already had contact with him, I didn't expect anything. But all of a sudden, before the medium even started to officially address the audience, he said, 'I see here, near this lady [and he was pointing at me], a flock of ducks flying back. I have a message for this lady from a man who used to hunt and who died when outside, close to nature. His birthday is in September.'

I knew it was my father, as I remember he took me duck hunting with him when I was a child, in a hide in wetlands. Furthermore, his birthday was on 9 September.

The medium told me that my father was encouraging me to do what I was doing and that he was proud of me because I was evolving. He said he could see that now, as he had evolved himself and he was beautiful in his soul with the angels.

Is it the work with the stones [SRTLFs] that I did, thanks to you, at the start of the week which made him want to get in contact with me? Because this corresponds exactly to the work done with the stones.'

After her amazing e-mail, I gave her a call and she also said that her father had apologized to her through the medium and said that she should continue the work she was doing.

Her father had died of a heart attack several years before whilst pruning roses.

Suicide

I read recently that someone commits suicide in the UK every 85 minutes. The large majority are young men, who see no future and have lost all hope.

A young friend in Ireland is terribly distressed at the moment, as someone she knows, a young man who was a brilliant student from a good professional family, has hanged himself. For parents there can be nothing more terrible than to lose a child in this way. Why did they not know about their beloved child's unhappiness and how can they ever forgive themselves? Their lives and the lives of the other members of the family can be destroyed in the aftermath of such a tragedy.

My own son told me many years after the event that he wanted to commit suicide at the age of 17 because of the physical abuse he suffered at a school in the UK. At the time we did not know what was going on or we would have addressed the issue head on. I am glad and relieved that he managed to somehow stay the course and did not do anything drastic. I know how devastated and shocked I would have been had he decided to take his life.

Lotta Naess

A year and a half ago, my eldest son's best friend, just 19 years of age, went into the forest and hanged himself. My son was devastated. Why didn't his friend ask for his help? So many questions – with no answers. The whole family was upset. I immediately put a pair of SRTLFs on the boy's photo, as a blessing and to heal the pain.

A week later I had an e-mail from the boy's e-mail address. Before this I had never received an e-mail from him – after all, he was my son's friend.

The e-mail contained a lot of garbled numbers and letters which made no sense, but the subject line was clear. It said: 'Long time no see.' That was all. My son and I were astounded by this communication.

A week later I received another e-mail from the boy's account. Again it contained garbled letters and numbers and again there was one clear line which simply said, 'I am fine.'

I never received an e-mail from that account again.

Lotta Naess: U-MF

I met U-MF when she was in deep sorrow. She was 76 and during the past year had lost eight of her friends. When her best friend died of cancer, it seemed that she could not stop crying.

U-MF's husband was not very nice to her. Probably he could not stand seeing her so upset all the time, but instead of comforting her he just shouted at her to stop crying. That made it all worse. Her daughter-in-law, a client of mine, called me and wanted to give her mother-in-law a set of SRTLFs.

Since U-MF had a lot of problems with her hips and found it difficult to move around easily, I paid her a visit at home. And she listened with all her senses. We got along very well and she agreed to do some work with the SRTLFs.

Three weeks later I went to visit her again. She welcomed me in and we had not got further than the hallway when she turned around and spontaneously said: 'Am I mad? Because my best friend Kiki, who died recently, is here with me every day and we talk to each other. Could that be possible when using the SRTLFs?'

'You are not mad,' I said.

We sat down and had a long conversation about life and death.

She also told me that she had stopped crying so much. 'Sometimes it comes over me that I have almost none of my friends left and I cry a little, but then it is all fine again,' she said.

U-MF is much happier now. Life is a bit easier and she feels calm.

The Magic and Miracle of my Mother's Death

It is 11 November 2011 – 11.11.11 – and something strange, unexpected and wonderful is happening: something heavy has been lifted from me and I feel light and happy. Should I feel like this less than a month and half after the 'death' of my darling mother?

The strange truth is that I cannot feel the sadness that overwhelmed me in the first days and weeks, only a lightness. This is in striking contrast to when I lost my father. I was inconsolable then, and for a year afterwards the pain of that event would strike me out of the blue and I would be flooded with tears, which I would hide from my mother. So what is different this time around?

The main difference is that thanks to the SRTLFs, my inner eyes and ears are open to seeing and hearing the workings of the 'other side'. I do not look for 'signs', but do not deny or dismiss them either, as I would have done before. I know the reality of the multi-dimensional universe, but have not experienced it in action in a personal way in this context. But I am about to be educated.

The first miracle was that I was able to be present for my mother's death even though I live in London and she was in Mumbai. When my father died I was in Mumbai, just an hour's drive away, but could not be there with him in time and never got to say goodbye. This time I was several hours' flight away on a different continent, but I was able to be there for my ma, as was my brother, who lives in the US, and my daughter, her eldest granddaughter, to whom she was very close. And I know she would have wished us to be there.

My daughter and I reached Mumbai on the afternoon of 1st October and she left on 2nd October in the morning – peacefully, with no distress of any kind. She just gave up her breath, went to sleep and that was that. She made it easy for us in her leaving, just as she had done all her life long. This experience taught me in real terms that dying was nothing to be afraid of.

We have special prayers and ceremonies for four days after a death occurs. Two priests came and here was a strange thing: one of them had the same name as my father and the second one had the same name as my mother's beloved brother, who had died many years before. Unusual? Coincidence? To me it was clear that this was a message telling me in a very literal, in your face way, that her husband and her brother were there to help her on her onward journey. She was being looked after and cared for and I did not have to worry or fret.

That was just the beginning – there was more to come.

In India we celebrate two birthdays, one by the English calendar and the other by the Parsi calendar. In my mum's family they celebrate the Parsi birthday. My Parsi birthday happened to fall while I was there, just a few days after my ma's passing. I was in no mood to celebrate as I was still locked in the sorrow of my mother's death, but there was a nice dinner for the family and my darling cousin, my departed uncle's daughter, was invited. She is, incidentally, a Supercoherence practitioner and uses the SRTLFs daily.

As soon as she came in, she said to me, smiling, 'I've got a message for you.' She meant from Mum.

In her younger days my mother used to sing a lot. Usually she sang English and American pop songs of that era. The house would be filled with her singing, and I still remember the happy feeling that pervaded the home. Her sisters also sang a lot; they were a musical family. After my ma's passing I found her songbook, in which she had written down the words of all her favourite songs.

Anyway, my cousin has an hour's drive each way to work. She spends that hour listening to music. On her way to work on the day of my Parsi birthday, out of the blue a song came on the radio that she instantly recognized as one of my mother's favourites. Normally that radio station plays music of the seventies and eighties, but this one was from an older period, so it was unusual. The timing was not lost on my cousin – my ma was singing for me on my birthday and was telling my cousin to give me the message. The way the message was delivered was impeccable, as the only person in the world who knew the song's significance and the day of my birthday was my cousin. And she was going to see me that evening. It could not have been more perfect.

To top it all, to make sure that my cousin got the message, my ma repeated it in the evening. On her way home my cousin listens to a 'random' selection of songs which she has on her usb. To her delight and amazement, that evening another's of my mum's favourite songs, 'Everybody's Somebody's Fool' by Connie Francis, came through. My darling mother was communicating through the dimensions and telling me not to be unhappy. It was the best birthday gift ever.

The most amazing event was yet to unfold.

My mother owned an apartment in Mumbai which she had bought over 30 years before. The original deed of sale and other papers were in a file in a safe. After her death we took the file to the lawyer, as the ownership had to be transferred to my brother and me.

However, there was a shock waiting for us. The lawyer discovered that an important paper was missing. If we did not succeed in finding that document, we would have to go through a lengthy legal process which would cost us thousands of pounds.

We had no idea of where to look for this paper – after all, it was 30 years old and it was not in the designated file. We resigned ourselves to going through the legal process; there was no other option.

It was time for me to go back to my home in London. It was my last day and my brother and I were doing some final clearing of papers and other stuff, as the apartment would have to be locked up. In our tradition it is the custom to give gifts of cash to mark a happy occasion. These gifts are put in envelopes with the greeting written in red ink, never in black or blue ink. Red is a celebratory colour in that tradition. These envelopes are often kept as mementoes of different occasions, after removing the cash of course. So there was a pile of white envelopes there with happy messages. I gave them to my brother to have a final look through before throwing them away.

A minute later, there was huge excitement. My brother, who is an engineer and not given to flights of the imagination, was beside himself. In that pile of empty gift envelopes there was another envelope, a gift of a different kind. It was unopened. It was date-stamped 30 years back and contained the missing documents – a parting gift from my mother to her beloved children. For us it was an unmistakable miracle and a direct communication from our sweet mother.

So you can understand why I feel no sadness so soon after her 'death'.

I have come to understand that physical death, which holds such terror for us humans, is neither a defeat nor a disaster but simply a transition to another very real dimension. It is known that energy cannot be destroyed; it only changes its expression. If matter is energy, as Einstein proved over 100 years back, then it stands to reason that as we are fundamentally energy beings, we cannot really 'die', only change our expression. And yet all of us have 'died' many times before and will do so again and again until…

Until and unless we can look death in the face and stare it down, we can never live fully and well. In fact we are so afraid of dying that we forget to live and hide our light under the bushel of our fears. It is the big elephant in the room which everyone pretends isn't there – because if we are to truly acknowledge the inevitability of our death, nothing would make sense and be worth doing – or would it? It depends on your point of view.

In the eloquent words of Steve Jobs:

'Your time [on Earth] is limited, so don't waste it living someone else's life. Don't be trapped by dogma – which is living with the results of other people's thinking. Don't let the noise of other's opinions drown out your own inner voice. And most important, have the courage to follow your heart and intuition. They somehow already know what you truly want to become. Everything else is secondary. Remembering that you are going to die is the best way I know to avoid the trap of thinking you have something to lose. You are already naked. There is no reason not to follow your heart.'[14]

Many years ago I used to work with someone who said he had a 'serious disease'. He would keep saying he was 'terminal' and would always expect preferential treatment as a result of his 'condition'. One day I got tired of this manipulation and told him, 'We are "terminal" from the day we are born.' And that is the truth of it. None of us knows when we are going to die, but it is a sure bet that it is going to happen.

So, while I love my life and intend to live it fully with passion, purpose and fun and enjoyment, I know with absolute certainty that I and everyone I love will die to their bodies at some point, sooner or later as their soul decides. But death does not hold the terror for me that it did before I entered the multi-dimensional miracle zone of the Luminator and the SRTLFs.

My poet friend Sylvia Eagle had this poem come through two years to the day after her daughter died. She said she did not feel that the words were her daughter's, they just came upon her that morning as she was half awake. She had to scramble to get them down on paper before they escaped back to where they had come from:

'Don't call me dead,
I am transcended.
One of my live in realities is ended, and I am somewhere new, it seems,
Where now I am awake to how all of our intertwined
realities are lived from dreams.
Don't call this dead –
I am alive, but not as I was there.
But everything is in me present.
I am so near. I feel, I see, I think, I hear and all my memory is clear.
Don't call me dead –
I am alive and so are you.
For now there is some form of glass between
us through which I cannot pass,
But love still can and will now pass between us,
Sometimes in little dreams, it seems.
Some dreams don't need for us to be asleep,
Nor is this strange.
I now have more, but different range.
Don't call me dead –
We live to learn and I am learning now.
We live to love and keep on learning how.
Don't call this dead,
I am as alive as you.
And this and all I have said is true.'

CHAPTER 18

The Supercoherence I AM Universal Frequency

'Beyond our ideas of right-doing and wrong-doing, there is a field. I'll meet you there. When the soul lies down in that grass, the world is too full to talk about. Ideas, language, even the phrase "each other" don't make sense anymore.'

Jelal-ud-din Rumi

The Frequency of Oneness – The Next Evolutionary Step

THIS NEW FREQUENCY only emerged in 2011. We had been having such wonderful results for the past two years with the SRTLFs, then the Supercoherence IAM Male and Female and the Supercoherence Panic to Calm frequency, that I did not think that there would be any more Supercoherence frequencies. But I was mistaken. I was in for a surprise.

Three Supercoherence practitioners whose opinions I trust and value told me that sometimes they were wearing the IAM Male and I AM Female frequencies *together*, along with the SRTLFs, and were getting good results. So I took notice.

Then something happened which really brought home to me why this fusion was not only useful but totally imperative.

From 1998 until late 2010 I did not look at the news and did not watch television. However, one day in 2010 I decided that I would watch the news on the internet as I wanted to experience what most people experienced in their everyday reality. My question was, would I lose the sense of well-being and clarity that I had acquired as a direct result of my starvation diet of no news? Would my belief systems hold under the onslaught of bad news that I knew would come at me once I decided to open the door that I had closed for so many years?

I have to say that the initial experience was not pleasant – in fact it was overwhelming. I wanted to run away and close the door on all the bad things that were happening. I found my creativity dried up and my sense of self got slightly lost as I found myself engulfed by the immeasurable chaos and suffering that seemed to be out there in the world.

I also frequently visited a website called TED.com, which hosts some interesting talks. But the one common theme, which coincidentally was on both the news and on TED, that touched me personally and brought me to near despair was the trafficking in young children – where young ones were sold or enticed into slavery and prostitution. Who were these 'monsters' who could do this to another human soul?

What if these monsters could be made to see themselves as souls – would this open their hearts and their eyes and make them choose a different course of action? What if they could *only* see themselves that way and no other way? Could we wipe out this ugly tragic cycle of pain and exploitation?

I think so. The Supercoherence IAM Universal frequency (SIAMUF) came into being as a result of this experience.

Every Supercoherence frequency broadcasts a very specific silent message. This message is transmitted in light-energy-information code and is read and responded to by your energy field and by everyone else's field as well. Though it is silent, it is exact, specific and powerful. Once you decide to wear the frequency, know that you will perceive everything and everyone through the filter of the encoded message. You cannot override it or change it and will be subject to it. Everyone who comes in contact with you physically or energetically will receive this message and sense the difference in you and will respond differently than usual.

The Supercoherence IAM Universal frequency contains the fusion of the male and female frequencies plus a third secret frequency to enhance the two. This means that the two opposing polarities have been fused and become one and cannot be separated. When you fuse two frequencies, the new frequency is neither one nor the other but a third, which is different from both the original constituent frequencies and broadcasts a different message. This allows the emergence of the whole integrated soulful human and replaces the old conditioning and unconscious programming at the central point of being from where perception is shaped.

The silent message of the Supercoherence I AM Universal frequency is 'I AM U':

'I am a soul and a universal human.

I recognize that you are a soul and a universal human.'

Before you are male or female, you are a soul and a human.

Before you are black, white, brown, yellow or green, you are a soul and a human.

Before you are European, African, Asian, American, French, English, Indian, Pakistani, Chinese, Japanese or whichever 'nationality', you are a soul and a human.

Before you are Hindu, Muslim, Jew, Buddhist, Christian, atheist, Zoroastrian or whatever 'religion', you are a soul and a human.

Before you are a slave, a servant, master or boss, rich or poor, educated or not, you are a soul and a human.

All the above categorizations divide us and prevent us from seeing who is in front of us. We have forgotten that which unites us and can mostly only see that which divides us. Our conditioning and programming run very deep and have been there for a long time. The cultural traditions that have been handed down through the generations make it difficult, if not impossible, to truly neutralize this conditioning, even if we wish to. This unconscious blindness is the cause of wars and hatred, discrimination and the hideous suffering that we inflict upon ourselves and one another.

This frequency, however, reminds us that we can never be less than the greatest king, queen, guru, rock star or millionaire, or whoever we see as greater than we are, nor can we be higher than anyone, no matter who we are. There is nothing higher than recognizing ourselves as a great soul on a journey, learning to love and be loved. Once that happens, we automatically recognize this in the 'other', whoever they are, and can honour them as we honour ourselves.

Of course, as with any new Supercoherence frequency, we have been testing it out with various people using VRIC imaging. The Supercoherence IAMU frequency has had to be calibrated with the Luminator to make sure that it created coherence, as it needed to be verified. We tested it initially with old clients who already had the SRTLFs or the SIAM Male and Female frequencies and then also with a few people who had no experience of any of the Supercoherence frequencies and no knowledge of the programme. The results of the imaging confirmed that this new frequency worked with everyone across the board.

The following case study illustrates in real terms what happens as a result of using the Supercoherence IAM U frequency. The lady is a highly evolved human who has done her inner work for many decades.

She writes,

"Dear Thrity, it was good to talk to you on Tuesday, but you must have felt that I was rather disturbed. It has all turned out well and as the story has much to do with your frequencies. I am going to tell it to you.

About 6 years ago I started to have high blood pressure and excessive heartbeat. I went to my homeopathic doctor and he gave me my constitutional remedy which helped very well. For 5 years I was free from symptoms. At the beginning of this year I discovered the (Supercoherence) frequencies and I started to work with them. I did all the work to clear my past with the SRTLFs and I wore the IAMU daily. By late spring the symptoms came back. I didn't know what to think. Didn't I work on myself since 30 years? Haven't I done all that work? And still I am critical, not trusting, anxious and and and. On top of it all came that now I was frightened. Am I ill? How bad is it? And so on. I wore the PTCF

(Panic to Calm frequency), but with no effect. I went back to my doctor and he gave me the same remedy but in a higher potency. In the same week you gave me your (2nd) book and from all these cases you describe I got some idea what has happened to me. All that old stuff popping up, old feelings, hurts that I had thought I had processed long ago. But it hurt my self esteem very much, I felt unworthy, incapable, a fraud. But what could I do about it? I wore all the frequencies daily. Yesterday I had a dream, which impressed me much: someone showed me a house. There was a very beautiful room, furnished with the most beautiful things, all in white and full of light. But the light was flickering and went on and off. I thought: how can anyone live in that beautiful room with that light flickering all the time. I didn't know, what this dream meant. Today I got a delivery of books I had ordered. And what is to you "Talking with Angels", to me are the books of Thoth. I got his newest book "The Crystal-Chakra". I opened it and read two sentences and everything fell into place! The frequencies have made me coherent, so all the things that were not in accordance with me stood clearly out. Everybody has these less perfect sides. But instead of letting them go into the light by forgiving myself, I started to feel badly about them. I criticised myself, felt angry and got desperate. I lost faith in myself and in everything I had learned up to now. But you cannot live in a place, where the light goes on and off! Love and light has to be "on" always , in every situation. I wrote the whole story down into my journal and you know what happened? The symptoms disappeared instantly! The pressure in my body stopped and I realized how much I have put myself under pressure by the idea to have to be perfect!!!!

Isn't this an amazing story? I am very happy about it and I realize that you never stop learning even after 75 years of life."

The SIAMUF is not about strengthening the 'you' or the 'I', but about dissolving the difference between the 'you' and the 'I' so that we understand that I am you and you are I and we are one — and that we are both universal humans. It tells us that we no longer need to protect or to be protected but can live our lives from the heart-full, mindful space of innocence and vulnerability.

As Rumi says:

'Your task is not to seek for love, but merely to seek and find all the barriers within yourself that you have built against it.'

With this frequency, the barriers have been dissolved and the new universal human has been born.

CHAPTER 19
Love

'Without love nothing can be
Not light-awareness, not silence and peace,
Not shining force and joy.
The shining ray – joy! Brings glowing;
Peace and silence fulfill.
Awareness enlightens.
But only love unites.

Love is above everything
And love is in everything.'

Talking with Angels

THE SUPERCOHERENCE SYSTEM is all about a return to love – but what is the true nature of love? It may not be what we think. When we speak of love in this system I have to tell you that it is not sweetie-sweetie or romantic or sentimental. It is hard for us to know the magnitude, the depth, the all-encompassing, all-pervading and uncompromising nature of the love that is the true nature of the universe. Ever since the disconnection from zero, human love has been frail and conditional and bears very little resemblance to the love that is possible. We talk of unconditional love, but have no clue of how to access it for ourselves or extend it to anyone else. The closest we come to it on the Earth plane is the love that the mother extends to her child – that is, when she is not suffering herself.

Human 'love' has many expressions, not all of them benign. Literature, history and life show us that we hurt and kill others for 'love' of country or religion. We have done this for millennia and continue to do this today. On a personal level, 'lovers' can kill out of jealousy and young girls be killed by their brothers and fathers in so-called 'honour' killings.

I have come to the conclusion that we do not know what love is and are addicted to suffering. We take the most precious gifts that the universe extends to us and we spoil them through our lack of understanding and awareness.

This was brought home to me in a dramatic way by two powerful but different experiences I had in Jerusalem in 1996. There are some experiences that touch you, move you and remain with you for a lifetime. I remember these as vividly as if they had happened yesterday.

Old Jerusalem

I had been invited to speak at a conference in Tel Aviv. This was the second time I had been to Israel and I was determined to visit Old Jerusalem. I wanted to experience what it felt like to walk down those ancient streets which had witnessed so many extraordinary events. I wanted to visit the Wailing Wall, the Al Aqsa Mosque and the Church of the Holy Sepulchre. So I went there by bus. I did not take a guide or a friend but went on my own, as I wanted to experience the feelings and not have to listen to someone telling me the 'facts'.

At one point I came upon a museum featuring the history of Jerusalem. I walked in and had a good look. It brought home to me yet again that the history of Jerusalem had been bloody. The Romans, the Greeks, the Christians, the Jews and of course the Muslims had all shed blood and created havoc and suffering in the 'Holy Land'.

I walked down the Via Dolorosa, the narrow cobbled street down which Christ was supposed to have walked bearing the cross. I stood by the Wailing Wall, where Jews have stood and prayed for thousands of years, and went and sat by the great Al Aqsa Mosque. I finally ended up at the Church of the Holy Sepulchre.

As I sat in the courtyard of that ancient place, I was bemused. What did it all mean? All this bloodshed, pain and suffering, hatred and ferocity, temples being torn down, people massacred, all in the name of God. How could one begin to understand such violence being perpetrated in the name of the divine? How could people be so blind and ignorant? I desperately wanted to understand.

The answer, when it came, was a surprising one: it was love – always love. Yes, it was brutal, yes, it was misguided, yet it was only ever love of the great truth as they saw it. This insight offered me an understanding that I have never forgotten: that it is always love that is the great force that has created human suffering – simply because we have not understood the simple truth that 'God' is everything and everyone and everywhere. Several hundred years later we do not seem to have learned much and still continue to create havoc in the name of the One who is the All.

It is time to do something different.

The Strength of Love

It was a demonstration using kinesiology, also called muscle testing – right-brain stuff which accesses the wisdom of the body and bypasses the linear left brain. The demonstrator picked a woman from the audience and brought her to the front of the room. She was the guinea pig. We were the audience of about 50 people.

The first step was to test her baseline strength. This was done by the woman holding her arm fully stretched at shoulder level. The practitioner then instructed her to remain strong and pushed down on the arm. She tested strong.

Then the practitioner instructed us to project hate at her. So 50 persons were now projecting hate at this lone woman. We were not touching her or saying anything – it was all silent and invisible. He tested her again and her arm tested weak – which meant that her body-mind recognized the feelings that were being projected at it and could not handle it and collapsed.

Then he asked us to continue projecting hate at this lone woman and asked her to project love back at us. He tested her again. While a minute back she could not hold her arm up, now she tested strong. The hate of 50 people had been neutralized by the power of love. So love makes the body strong – the cells and the muscles love it when you love.

It was a dramatic illustration of how love conquers hate.

Supercoherence: The Physics of Love

When I discovered the power of the zero-point alignment I was sure I had found the Holy Grail of human potential. If we could neutralize deep hidden trauma as fast, simply, easily and consistently as we did, we had reached the ultimate goal. But we had not. Something vital was missing. And I did not know it. So what was the missing element – the most important one of all?

It was love.

I realized this in 2008 when the image of the Divine Mother was added to the configuration and the miracle that lay hidden revealed itself: the human system became coherent – or, rather, supercoherent – when it was aligned (using the SRTLFs) with universal unconditional love as symbolized by the super high frequency of the Divine Mother.

I call supercoherence the physics of love – where the laws of love and light, of coherence and order, come together and show us in real terms our true nature. I have to say that when I first thought of the name *Supercoherence: The 7th Sense* for my first book, I did not fully understand what supercoherence was. I knew only that it was coherence plus something more, much more. It took me eight years to discover what that something more was. Then the Divine Mother came into the picture and showed me the real meaning of the word.

For me, the inescapable conclusion was that the universe at its most fundamental and all-encompassing level of expression is love. Love is the great intelligence.

When you use the Supercoherence Return to Love and IAMU frequencies, through an act of grace you are reconnected to that place within you where this love with no boundaries, barriers or barricades, this unconditional love beyond reason or compromise, is waiting for you. It has always been there, only you did not know it and therefore could not taste its pure sweetness. Now you can.

CHAPTER 20
The Nearly Impossible Project

'There are those who look at things the way they are, and ask why... I dream of things that never were, and ask why not?'

Robert Kennedy

Voiding Karma

THIS HAS BEEN a contentious issue over the years. When I say that the zero-point alignment actually voids karma, people get really indignant about it and want to know how it is possible – after all, there is the law of cause and effect and does crime simply go unpunished and shouldn't one pay the penalty for one's misdeeds, if not in this life, then in the next incarnation? And what about evil?

I know karma exists as long as you are out of zero. But the divine does not have karma – it is all-accepting, all-understanding and all-loving. Beyond the law of cause and effect, there is another realm where the law of cause and effect is nullified and replaced with grace. And as the angels confirm, "Grace is above the law."- *Talking with Angels.*

Love is the ground state of the universe and the universal human, which the SRTLFs clearly show. Every event and action seen through the eyes of that understanding shows us that karma is simply our misperception, our distorted understanding of events that we class as suffering. In reality they are simply the cosmic intelligence asking us to heal and to realize that which we always are.

If I understand the universal intelligence to be benign and loving and not angry or vengeful, then where does karma fit into it?

I think it is time that we realized that we do not need 'karma cleansing' – there never was any karma, simply the cycle of suffering because of our lack of understanding of who we really were.

Love clears karma instantly, and our source code, as revealed by VRIC imaging, using the SRTLFs and the photo of the Divine Mother, is pure all-encompassing love, acceptance, intelligence and super-function. In the face of it, every trauma and emotional charge is neutralized, karma is void and the cycle of suffering which has been the unfortunate heritage of humanity for millennia is at an end.

What is Evil? How to Break the Cycle

'DO NOT CHANGE THE BAD – STRENGTHEN THE GOOD.

Thus the good will absorb the bad which is all around it.' *Talking with Angels*

And yet where are we today? Looking around us, it seems that the cycle of suffering is alive and well on Earth today. Only recently in the UK, for example, there was a case of a young man kidnapping, raping and killing a young schoolgirl. It turned out that he had killed several young women. He is now in prison for life and yet unfortunately there are several other cases where this same tragic scenario has been played out. Then there was the recent horrific case where a young man in Norway went on a rampage and shot and killed 69 teenagers with total ruthlessness and plunged a whole nation into grief. And shows no remorse for what he has done. Then there is human trafficking, where young girls are enticed with promises of jobs and then forced into a life of prostitution and murdered if they don't comply with their captor's wishes. Young men are sold into slavery and forced to work for no pay and minimal food in degrading conditions. Yes, unbelievable as it sounds, slavery exists today.

On a larger scale, wars rage in so many parts of the world, and killing, destroying, raping and pillaging are all justified in the name of one cause or another. And we have equipped ourselves with weapons of mass destruction which have the potential of wiping out the entire human race and wreaking havoc on all the living creatures which share the world with us.

Yes, despite all our great 'advances' in science and technology, we are no less savage than when we were living in caves.

How can we break this cycle which it seems has plagued us forever? The task seems impossible and our only option seems to be to reconcile ourselves to more of the same for as long as we exist on this Earth. Yet carrying on the way we are ensures our destruction, the very destruction that none of us want.

So what are our options? Is there another way? What can we do to change our destiny?

This was a question that bothered me a lot. On the one hand there was the normal reaction of revulsion, repugnance and sadness that all of us have when faced with the fact that humans can inflict extreme pain on other beings. When a little baby is murdered, when a woman is raped in front of her children, or the daughter raped in front of the mother, or the father tortured and killed in war, the instinctive visceral response is to annihilate the criminal, the enemy and the terrorist. The anger that wells up says they should be punished in exact measure to their crime – the eye for an eye, tooth for a tooth approach. And then maybe we can all be safe – until the next time. If the criminal is under lock and key and is punished severely enough, then the needs of justice and an orderly society are served. After all, crime deserves punishment, wrongs need to be avenged and revenge, retribution and retaliation can all be justified in the appropriate circumstances… can't they? But we have been following this method of punishment and more punishment for many eons and everyone knows that there are severe consequences if we commit a 'crime', so why has crime not disappeared or lessened over the thousands of years that humans have been on Earth?

My personal crisis of understanding was brought up when I decided to read the news after a gap of 12-plus years, as recounted earlier. The news fed to us by the media, which gorges on bad news, is not happy-making or productive in any way. It also implicitly tells us that apart from what they say is happening, there is nothing else of any real consequence taking place in the world. I could soon see that I was taking on their viewpoint and was losing sight of the big picture that I knew to be true – in fact far truer than their distorted, loaded and limited view.

How to integrate these two glaringly different realities – the one portrayed by the media and the one of possibility created by the Supercoherence process and the SRTLFs? How to dissolve this Mount Everest of insane entangled energy of rage and pain and shame, grief and blame and transform it into the sanity of peace and love?

To begin with, after a few days I curtailed the amount of news I watched to a few minutes a day and kept a close watch on my thinking and feelings after the exercise. I did not stop completely, as I wanted to see and feel the cumulative impact it had on people, bearing in mind that most watch the news on a daily basis – or even an hourly basis if addicted to it.

The understanding that I have come to after processing this information is that we are seeing the symptoms without understanding the underlying processes that created the disease. We are seeing the rotten fruit without understanding that the roots of the tree run very deep and in fact the very seed from which those roots came needs to be healed. In other terms, the vast dysfunction and suffering that we see in the outer world are the unconscious forces of our collective unresolved suffering seeking healing and resolution.

The resolution of this process, which seems impossible at the physical level, lies in the elegant parallel universe, the universe that I have been exploring since 1995 with the Luminator and VRIC imaging and later with the Supercoherence frequencies. Over the years we have seen clients come in with long lists of symptoms and experience incredible results by simply restoring coherence. We have found that every one of these clients has been disconnected from zero. But coherence has been the master parameter and the master reset button which has neutralized the dysfunction and restored function. We have *never* addressed the symptoms directly, simply cleared the field by creating coherence. All of the amazing results at the physical level have been achieved by changing the information at the unseen quantum level, using only light-energy-information tools.

As a result of these experiences, I have come to understood that this mountain of accumulated suffering is not anyone's fault, shocking as that seems. Or, to put in another way, it is everyone's fault. Because of the disconnection from zero it has been inevitable and in fact could not have been avoided. The doors of human perception which shape our reality have been distorted for millennia, for whatever reason, and we are seeing the accumulated results. But now the cruel joke that we have had the misfortune to participate in has been unmasked.

If restoring supercoherence and the reconnection to zero work at the micro level for each client, as far as I am concerned they will work at the macro level for humanity.

The question now is how do we do this? What is the way forward? What is the next step?

I realize that what I am proposing may sound totally absurd, ridiculous and even nonsensical, but I must beg your indulgence while I put some of my crazy speculation in front of you and see if it makes sense.

Here are some points for your consideration:

- You know the extreme power that is held in the subtle realms and the zero point field and now that power can be accessed by you and me.
- You have seen what the SRTLFs are capable of in the case studies you have read.
- We have access to zero, the master reset button, for the mainstream of humanity and can neutralize suffering and trauma at the speed of light for anyone and everyone.
- We can go backwards in time and clear all imprints of suffering.
- Our source code, as revealed by the SRTLFs and the Divine Mother image, is the intelligence of love in its purest form and it is now possible for anyone to access it for the asking, including 'criminals', 'victims' and everyone in between.
- Grace is always present and available for us all in real practical terms.
- The possibility of clear, coherent perception for the many, leading to coherent thought and intent and creating coherent action, could tip the balance and put us on a supercoherent trajectory of love and function.

Knowing these new realities, do you think, or feel, it is possible to unleash a chain reaction of love on this planet? Dare we consider that we – you and I – can usher in the new golden age of the loving universal human?

I think this is both possible and probable. It has to start with you and me and each one of us being ready, willing and able to let go of our suffering.

My heart soared when I read what the angel said when it was asked about evil and wars: 'Evil does not exist, there is only force, that has not yet been transformed' Now we have the tools for that transformation.

If this makes sense to you, will you help yourself and your fellow humans to find the love that is waiting for us all?

The universe and your soul await.

AN OFFER AND AN INVITATION

WOULD YOU LIKE to discover your "nearly impossible project"?

You are important to you. A life of significance, meaning, passion, purpose and simple happiness is our birthright and our responsibility. Is your life all you wish it to be?

Finding your life's purpose and the reason for your soul's journey is your greatest project.

Have you truly engaged with your life or is it mundane and mediocre?

By reading this book you have completed an important yet small part of the journey. I thank you for that. However as one journey ends another begins – are you ready to take the next step in the adventure that is your life? It is my hope and wish that you wish to engage with the magic of supercoherence for yourself.

As you will have noticed this book is not primarily about theory (though there is some) it is about the new miracle power tools, and the only way to know what they can do for you, is to experience them. Will you take that leap into the unknown?

It does not matter who you are, wherever you are in your life, whatever traumas and troubles you have been or are going through, there are many more possibilities for healing, happiness and function than you can imagine. I invite you to step through the portal of miracles.

I wrote this book for you and I am happy if it helped you in any way.

I would love to hear from you – what you think, how you feel, what difference the book made for you. I value your feedback.

These are the immediate steps you can take to start opening to the magic :

Please leave your questions and comments for me at

http://supercoherenceReturnToLoveBook.com

I will send you an invitation to a free teleconference where I will be happy to answer any questions and keep you informed of new developments. The Supercoherence system is always evolving so new frequency tools and techniques of using the Supercoherence system's tools are always being discovered. So please keep in touch,

One Last Thing…

If you believe your friends would get something valuable out of this book, I would be honoured if you'd post your thoughts on Facebook, Twitter and/ or Google+.

If you feel strongly that this book made a valuable contribution to your life, I'd be immensely grateful if you posted a review on Amazon.

All the very best to you.

Thrity

THIS IS A short list of books that have helped me in my exploration for this present book. I have also included my first book as it will give you a much deeper understanding of the roots from which this extraordinary system came. There was a much longer list in the first book "Supercoherence The 7th Sense". I did not wish to repeat that list in this book. If you wish to see that list please go to www.supercoherence7thsense.com/booklist and check it out. Neither of these lists are "complete" but they helped me understand my work better and put it in some context.

Recommended Books

Supercoherence – The 7th Sense – Thrity Engineer

Life Force the Scientific Basis – Claude Swanson

Tuning the Diamond – Susan Joy Rennison

The Genie in Your Genes – Dawson Church

Science and the Akashic Field – Ervin Laszlo

Zero Limits – Joe Vitale

Kryon - The End Times – Lee Caroll

The Physics of Miracles – Richard Bartlett

Transurfing Reality – Vadim Zeland (4books)

Source – Joseph Jaworsky

The Science Delusion – Rupert Sheldrake

Wholeness and the Implicate Order - David Bohm

Stroke of Insight – Jill Bolte Taylor

The Honeymoon Effect – Bruce Lipton

My Twin Vanished – Did yours? - Dr. Brent Babcock

The Mind of Your Newborn Baby – David Chamberlain

Windows to the Womb – David Chamberlain

How to Use the SRTLFs

'Your life is the instrument with which you experiment with truth.'

Thich Nhat Hanh

Getting Started

THE PINK (DROP) and green (round) Supercoherence Return to Love frequencies form a pair and must be used at the same time. They are side sensitive, which means that they need to be held or carried in the correct hand or pocket. The pink SRTLF is to be held or carried on the left side and the green SRTLF is to be held or carried on the right side. Under special circumstances this can change.

As an **everyday practice** you can hold or carry the SRTLFs (green on the right, pink on the left) every morning for 20 minutes. In the evening, at the end of the day, use them reversed (pink on the right, green on the left) for about ten minutes. You may increase the time gradually over a period of weeks.

There are huge benefits in following this simple effortless practice. When your energy system accesses zero in this way, stress is not allowed to build up. This is one way to keep well, as your system has a chance to repair itself every day.

Using the SRTLFs daily also allows us to use our life-force energy efficiently, as our energy system learns to remain coherent and operate close to zero, the point of optimal function. Because it is coherent, we are more aware and will feel our discomfort more quickly and therefore be able to address it before it starts to build up to unmanageable proportions.

Clearing the Imprint of the Past

You can use the SRTLFs to clear the imprint of the past. The process is powerful and works for everyone. We strongly recommend that you do it once your system has adjusted to the SRTLFs. This can take a few weeks from when you first start using them on a daily basis

Clearing your Family Relationships

Take out your family photos. It is important to have separate ones of your father and mother, of your brothers and sisters and of yourself as a baby. You should also have one of your parents together. It is good if you also have a single photo of your whole family when you were a child or a teenager. This is a good starting-point.

If you do not have your parents' photographs, you may write their full names on a piece of a paper and use them instead. If you do not know who your parents were, please write "my biological father/mother this lifetime" on the note.

Please do this process even if a parent or other family member has passed on.

Even though you may have other relationships which may be challenging right now, it is better to clear the family timeline as far back as possible. You can clear your energetic relationship with anyone using this process, but do the family first.

All steps should be done on both sides – the right side/hand and the left side/hand

We have found through testing with VRIC imaging that holding the Divine Mother photograph along with the SRTLFs softens, strengthens and enhances the effectiveness of this process.

- Hold the green SRTLF in your right hand and the pink SRTLF in your left hand.
- Take each photo of your family members in turn and hold it,

along with the photo of the Divine Mother and the SRTLFs, for five to ten minutes on either side.

- The third step is keeping the SRTLFs in the relevant hands hold the Divine Mother image and the photo/note of the person/s with whom you are clearing, with both hands together for a few minutes.

- The final step at the end of each clearing: holding the SRTLFs and the Divine Mother image and the photo of the person you are clearing with say "I love and accept myself exactly as I am and I love and accept (the name of the person you are clearing with) exactly as they are".

- Repeat this process with the photos of everyone in your family. Do the same with the photo of the whole family.

Clearing Other Relationships

If there is someone with whom you have had a particularly difficult relationship, make a special effort to get their photo.

Hold it first in one hand for five to ten minutes and then in the other hand for five to ten minutes. Then do the same with both hands together.

You may choose to work with someone you have or have had issues with or people you love and want to connect with or send loving energy, thoughts or attention to. It does not matter whether the person is physically close by or not, or even if they have passed on, the process still works. It will give you freedom from the past pain and this will be of immense benefit to you and give you renewed energy and hope.

You can enhance the results by your conscious participation in the following ways:

Affirmations

Whilst holding the pink SRTLF in your left hand and the green SRTLF in your right hand, you can make any affirmation that you choose. It is best to say it verbally, not just think it and repeat it a few times.
Some suggestions:

- 'I feel calm/strong/centred/joyful/hopeful, etc.'
- The statement we have tested the most and found extremely effective is: 'I love and accept myself exactly as I am.'
- Also, 'I love and accept [the person you are having the challenge with] exactly as s/he is.' (If you can't bring yourself to say 'love', simply say 'accept' and hold the frequencies until the feeling changes, as it will.)
- Another important affirmation to be used especially when things are going 'wrong' (courtesy of James Wong) is to simply say your name followed by "All is well"
- You may also use any other affirmation that is right for you at the time,
- Just make sure you are holding the SRTLFs.

Calming Emotional Distress

Hold the SRTLFs in your hands (rather than just carrying them) and make a statement, for example, 'I feel calm/relaxed/centred' or 'Even though I feel fearful/anxious/upset, etc., I still totally and completely accept myself.'

In difficult or stressful circumstances, you may choose to try reversing the SRTLFs (i.e. hold the green one in the left hand and the pink one in the right hand) until you feel calmer and more stable. After that, please put them back in the usual configuration, i.e. pink on the left and green on the right.

In case of extreme distress or emotional crisis, use only the green SRTLF in the left hand until you feel more settled.

Suggested Ways of Using the SRTLFs

Here are some additional suggestions of how to use the SRTLFs. There are many more.

- Clearing the past.
- Clearing the family line.
- Clearing the conception, pre-birth and birth imprint
- Clearing places.
- Making coherent decisions.

- Working with challenging situations.
- Working with pets.
- Working with plants...

Explore, experiment, experience – use your body as the laboratory and your life as the experiment. Use your awareness and trust what it tells you. Use your inspiration – you are limited only by your imagination!

My Desert Island Book: Talking with Angels

MANY OF THE quotes in this book have come from *Talking with Angels* by Gitta Mallasz. I have been a voracious and eclectic reader since I was very young and I have obviously read many books in that time – probably a few thousand. But if I had to live on a desert island and could take only one book, this would be that book.

The book came into my life several years back, in the late nineties. I am not sure exactly when, but it was definitely after the Luminator arrived in 1995. Since then it has been the book I go to when I am in trouble and it is the only one I have by my bed constantly.

In general I do not read angel books – in fact this is the only one I have read to date. I am also not fond of channelled books and this is a channelled book. So the cosmic joker has certainly been having a laugh at my expense there! So much for my prejudices.

What initially hooked me was a review which had some quotes from the 'Angels'. At the time the miracle that is the Luminator had come into my life and I had started to understand the reality of the magical energy universe. These angels, who had no names, talked of light-matter and light-awareness, and for me this resonated with the new understanding of the human as *photo sapiens*, or a being of light, which was the central and key understanding revealed by the Luminator. The other idea that enchanted me was that the way forward was the new. And the Luminator was *new*. So

I bought the book because of the quotes. And I am grateful that I let go of my prejudice, as if I had not, I would have missed out on the great gifts that were on offer.

Quite simply this book contains the most modern yet timeless and pristine teachings that I have ever encountered. They are not sweetie-sweetie and are intense and severe at times. But they touch my soul and make me understand my life and my work better. And show a clear and impeccable way forward when I get stuck...

NOTES AND REFERENCES

Introduction

Steve Jobs, Apple advert, 1997

Chapter 2

1. Quoted in Susan Joy Rennison, *Tuning the Diamond: Electromagnetism and Spiritual Evolution*, Joyfire Publishing, second edition, 2006
2. Mae-Wan Ho, http://www.i-sis.org.uk/quantumJazzBiology.php
3. http://www.kyrene.org/staff/sreed/amsitech/activities/fiboptic/fiboptic. htm
4. Shift Happens, Karl Fisch and Dr. Scott Mcleod - YouTube

Chapter 3

1. http://en.wikipedia.org/wiki/Temperature
2. David Bohm, Wholeness and the Implicate Order, Routledge, 2002
3. Gitta Mallasz, *Talking with Angels*, Daimon Verlag, 1988
4. Gitta Mallasz, *Talking with Angels*, Daimon Verlag, 1988
5. Gitta Mallasz, *Talking with Angels*, Daimon Verlag, 1988

Chapter 4

1. http://xnet.kp.org/permanentejournal/winter02/goldtolead.pdf
2. http://xnet.kp.org/permanentejournal/winter04/childhood.pdf

Chapter 9

1. scratchcomputing.com/articles/whatis_source.html

Chapter 11

1. en.wikiquote.org/wiki/John_Carew_Eccles

Chapter 16

1. Steve Jobs, http://thinkexist.com/quotation/your-time-is-limited-so-don-t-waste-it-living/406623.html